At a time when many believers are deb[...] piety vs. social activism, John Barber redefines the entire discussion to say that God's exciting plan for His Church includes both. Throughout my 55 years as a believer, I have always emphasized seeking both personal intimacy with God and working to preserve the culture. But perhaps you struggle with how to rectify these important mandates. If ever a book had the potential to revolutionize your view of the Christian's role in the world, this is it.

Bill Bright
Campus Crusade for Christ

Here is a book which ties together the two great commands of God: the Cultural Mandate and the Great Commission. The author does this, not in complex theological postulates, but in the most personal, autobiographical, and anecdotal style. In the process, he introduces the reader to a variety of insights into the moral, political, and social conditions of our time. A practical guidebook for Christians of all persuasions.

Dr D. James Kennedy
Coral Ridge Presbyterian Church

I have often complained about recent Christian critiques of culture, that they are often based more on sociology and history, than on Scripture. The result is disappointment and frustration. Many Christians have forsaken social activism, since history seems at first glance to be moving against us. John Barber's book does precisely what is needed. He advocates a clear program for Christian cultural activism, based on the biblical program of the Kingdom of God. He shows that we need to emphasize both the Cultural Mandate (filling and subduing the earth) and the Great Commission (making and teaching disciples of Jesus). And he shows that although we sometimes endure defeat, God's plan cannot fail. Barber also brings to the task great gifts of clear writing and illustration. I hope that many read this book and act on its program.

John Frame, Professor of Systematic Theology,
Reformed Theological Seminary

John Barber has written a very practical and balanced apologetic for Christians to fulfil their Cultural Mandate and the Great Commission responsibilities in a post-modern cultural context. What makes the work so helpful though is that unlike so many others, his is an unswervingly biblical apologetic. Instead of falling back on sociological or historical analyses, he has relied almost entirely upon Scripture. As a result, *Earth Restored* is not only refreshingly free of the rancour we've come to associate with the partisan screeds in the contemporary culture-wars, it is also remarkably forthright in addressing the most plaguing problems of our day with insight, principle, and grace.

George Grant
author, Director of the King's Meadow Study Center

EARTH RESTORED

To Bonnie, my better two-thirds

EARTH RESTORED

CALLING THE CHURCH TO A NEW CHRISTIAN ACTIVISM

JOHN BARBER

Christian Focus Publications

John Barber has served as an itinerant evangelist, church planter, host of a nationally syndicated radio program, and writer for Dr. Bill Bright. He holds degrees from Westminster Theological Seminary and Yale Divinity School. John is ordained in the Presbyterian Church in America. He currently lives in the Orlando, Florida area with his wife and two children.

© John Barber 2002

ISBN 1-1-85792-720-6

Published in 2002
by
Christian Focus Publications, Ltd.
Geanies House, Fearn, Tain,
Ross-shire, IV20 1TW, UK

TXu 1-003-015

www.christianfocus.com

Printed and bound by
Guernsey Press, Guernsey

Cover Design by Alister McInnes

CONTENTS

INTRODUCTION

In 1999, two things happened that caught my attention. First, in March a Paul Weyrich article for the *Washington Post* called cultural conservatives to abandon attempts to reclaim the culture. Paul Weyrich, president of the Free Congress Foundation and a leading figure among grass-roots conservatives since the late 70s, was also instrumental in helping to launch the 'Reagan revolution'. In fact, it was Weyrich who coined the phrase, 'moral majority'. One can thus appreciate the magnitude of the tremor that rippled through the conservative world when this field general of the culture-war called the troops to declare their 'cultural independence'.

Second, Cal Thomas, a nationally syndicated columnist and journalist, and Ed Dobson, an evangelical pastor in Michigan, wrote *Blinded by Might,* which is the book equivalent to Weyrich's letter. In the early 80s, both Thomas and Dobson were key figures alongside Jerry Falwell in the work of the Moral Majority. Eventually, Thomas and Dobson became disheartened with the Religious Right and its lack of progress in reversing America's moral decline. They have now joined ranks with Weyrich in calling Christians to end any effort to reform the culture, but instead to limit our work to prayers, evangelism, and personal discipleship, in the belief that this strategy will prove more effective in changing the culture from the 'inside out'.

As I pondered Weyrich, Thomas, and Dobson's well-meaning counsel, it occurred to me that, although some of their points have merit, in the final analysis their cure is worse than the disease. It is true that conservatives have not witnessed the pace of cultural reform they once hoped to see when the Moral Majority was formed in 1979. And perhaps a few evangelical leaders got too politically involved and were corrupted by the same lust for power that drives the Washington 'sleaze-machine'. However, as I meditated upon the matter, I thought, 'Is God calling the Church to solve these problems by going underground?' It took me only but a second to conclude, 'No'.

Upon further deliberation, it struck me that the source of Weyrich, Thomas, and Dobson's new-found pietism was neither that conservative Christians had failed to reclaim the culture, nor was it that politics was corrupting the evangelical church. Rather, it was that these men had lacked the theological foundation to help them persevere through a series of failed expectations. They were unlike the 'tree planted by the water, that extends its roots by a stream and will not fear when the heat comes; but its leaves will be green, and it will not be anxious in a year of drought nor cease to yield fruit' (Jeremiah 17:8).

It was then that I saw the great need among evangelicals for a solid theological position in the culture-war. Thus, I sat down to write an apologetic for the role of the Church in the culture. For years, gifted authors have produced many books and articles, seeking to encourage believers to assume a transforming role in the public square. How would my contribution be different?

I have always felt that most works written in defense of Christian, social activism have fallen somewhat short. The source of my belief is that most authors typically lean too heavily upon America's 'Christian heritage' and/or a wide array of sociological studies for support, instead of Scripture. I firmly believe that America's roots are thoroughly Christian and that any reasonable person should be able to see that many of this nation's major institutions, including the media, public education, and government have launched an all-out assault upon the Judeo/Christian ethic.

Nevertheless, believers must be extremely careful not to place too much emphasis upon history and reason as the underpinning for their social activism. This is because history and reason are as much the product of opinion, as fact. And opinion is like the nose on your face – everyone has one. Clearly, American history can provide important examples of how great figures from the past wrestled with the relationship of faith to what is best for society, and shocking statistics of America's slide toward Sodom can quickly get the blood boiling and stir people to action. But what if America had no Christian heritage? What if the Founders had been heathens? What if recent trends in society were friendly to Christians? Upon what basis would the Church legitimize its social activism? Unquestionably, conclusions drawn from historical evidence and empirical studies are important for shaping our appreciation of the value of an active faith in the culture. But nothing must take the place of God's inspired Word as the *foundation* for the believer's role in the public square.

Problematically, many evangelicals are reluctant to build a theory of social activism upon the Bible's teaching. The cause of this unwillingness is not due to any deficiency found within Scripture, but rather is the result of growing resistance within Evangelicalism to a theological position called 'theonomy' or 'reconstructionism'. Defining theonomy is difficult, mostly because a large number of distortions and misconceptions of the teaching do exist and, what is more, leading theonomists represent a diversity of thought. However, the one point all theonomists can agree on, and which has many people up in arms, teaches that the Church is called to 'reconstruct' society according to the pattern of biblical law, especially Old Testament law. The fear is that this program, if implemented, would *force* all people, Christian or not, to abide by biblical directives. (Note: anyone that works to apply Christian principles to government and society at large *will* unavoidably find themselves in agreement with at least some of the underlying principles of theonomy).

The emphasis on biblical law as a means to advance a visible expression of the kingdom of God in the world is to the discredit of theonomy. On the other hand, theonomy's strength is that it offers a systematic theology in support of Christian activism – something that is sadly lacking from most activists of the Religious Right. Despite this strength, it is the theonomist's misuse of theology that has had the unfortunate result of scaring away scores of evangelicals from seeking to build their cultural activity upon *any* theology. Many authors that do use the Bible to support some form of Christian activism are therefore hesitant to offer their readers much more than a series of isolated proof texts on the subject for fear they may appear as heretics.

In their effort to distance themselves from reconstructionism, many defenders of Christian activism have adopted an opposite and equally heretical position on God's law – antinomianism. This is the belief that under the dispensation of the gospel, the believer is under *no* explicit obligation to Old Testament law. The word 'antinomian' comes from the root word, *antinomy*, which refers to antagonism between competing principles – in this case the law and the gospel. Without offering a full critique of antinomianism, suffice it to say that Christian activists that ascribe to this view of the law have played right into the hands of the 'spirit of lawlessness' they claim to be fighting.

This brings me to *part* of the contribution I wish to offer to the debate over the believer's proper role in the culture. I seek to motivate Christians to be active in present-day culture, and to build that activity upon a firmer biblical foundation than what has been laid in the past, while steering clear of extremism. In other words, I want us to seek after the 'whole counsel of God' and to do so in the confidence that the Holy Spirit will guide us into all truth. Once we begin down this path, we have taken on a distinctively theological task.

My views do not rely upon the courage of Christian patriots of yesteryear or upon the need for a godly presence in electoral politics, although we shall briefly examine these factors. Rather, my thesis is entirely dependent upon the Bible's teaching on the kingdom of God and its implications for the culture. For those readers that possess understanding into the history of theology, my method is to take the 'redemptive historical' approach to theology and apply it to the various subjects that I address.

What is my thesis? It is that God's purpose is to *restore* the earth to His glory, and to use His Church, in obedience to the Cultural Mandate and the Great Commission, to achieve His goal. Thus, spirituality is to touch and inform *all* of life, not just personal morality. Because God is working to restore 'all things' the Church must also be working to restore every human institution, including the fine arts, the media, education, politics, journalism, law, and more.

Due to the uniqueness of my perspective, I would be wrong to lead the reader to think that this book is nothing more than a defense of *traditional* Christian activism. Rather, I want to go *further*. My belief is that most Christians who are working to reach the world for Christ do not understand that, with the coming of God's kingdom, a new order with the power to redeem *all* of life has also come. For them, being 'salt' and 'light' has been limited to restoring family values and civil virtue, when really God's ambassador is called to represent an even greater plan – *cosmic redemption*.

Therefore, in addition to offering a defense of Christian, social activism against the biblical bankruptcy of religious pietism, to which Weyrich, Thomas, and Dobson now aspire, this book is also critical of the conventional philosophy, methods, and goals of Christian activism. I wish to use my apologetic to introduce a call for a *new Christian activism*. This is a type of activism that is centered in, and which advocates, the meaning of the kingdom of God for society, rather than the restricted benefits of one political agenda over another.

What is the fundamental problem? It is that both pietists and activists are biblically lopsided. Normally, Christian, social activists are committed to the Cultural Mandate, while typically Christian pietists are dedicated to the Great Commission. Activists stress change at the institutional level, while pietists contend that real change in society is only possible to the extent that human hearts are changed. A new Christian activism will seek to restore planet earth by combining *both* the activists' stress upon cultural restoration *and* the pietists' emphasis upon evangelism and discipleship.

In Chapter 1, I begin to lay the foundation for my thesis with a discussion on the most common element within God's kingdom – the sovereignty of God. Throughout the remainder of Chapters 1 and 2, I offer five principles of a biblical worldview, which build upon the foundation of God's sovereign control over His world. These principles, or 'building blocks', further support the notion that God is dead set on restoring all of life to His glory and that an obedient believer is one that also has his sights set on this goal.

The reader will see that my principles of a biblical worldview are different to many others'. This is because most teaching on the subject of biblical worldview is *comparative*. By this I mean that most authors that seek to inspire a biblical worldview in others do so by comparing, for instance, the Bible's view on sex to the world's outlook on sex. Or they compare the Christian view of authority to the Marxist or post-modern view of authority. In essence, the comparative approach to biblical worldview is as much the child of sociology, as theology. In contrast, my principles of a biblical worldview are purely theological in nature.

In Chapter 3, I examine the fallacy of the Sacred/Secular distinction, and in Chapters 4 and 5, discuss God's plan to restore planet earth, which includes His twin mandates: the Cultural Mandate and the Great Commission. Chapters 6 and 7 offer a critique of both Christian activism and pietism in light of the failure of both camps to restore planet earth to the glory of God. Chapter 8 addresses realistic expectations in the culture-war and is what I consider to be the theological 'epicenter' of the book.

Because a new Christian activism seeks to combine the best of both pietism and activism, Chapters 9 through 14 examine six key areas (representing pietism and activism) the Church must address as part of its uniform plan to restore planet earth. Chapter 15 concludes with a call to be vigilant in light of the fact that each of us shall someday stand before the Lord to account for our obedience to His call to disciple the nations.

Although this book issues a call for a new Christian activism, there is really nothing 'new' about it. Rather, its beginning dates to the time when God created the first couple and told them to 'fill the earth and subdue it'. It is the average believer's lack of familiarity with the comprehensiveness of God's summons that makes it *appear* new.

Finally, I have endeavored to make this work more than an exercise in abstraction by sprinkling in many personal stories. The book is as much a biography of my spiritual journey, and subsequent growth in the subject of Christianity and culture, as it is a teaching device. My hope is that it will help to open your heart and mind to God's call to ministry in a new light.

One

GOD IS IN CONTROL

Many years ago my mother told me that when I was a small child, I would hold tight to the wooden bars of my crib and sing the song, 'He's Got the Whole World in His Hands' at the top of my lungs. Since I had not even learned to walk, much less talk, I'm sure that what my mother meant to say was that I goo-gooed that famous song so many of us learned as children in Sunday School. In fact, I made this point to my mother, but 'No' she said, 'you sang it all the way through'. I thought better of arguing with her. She seemed so proud.

To this day I find her story incredible. But one thing is certain. God does indeed have the whole world in His hands. Make no doubt about it. God is in control. God is sovereign.

When speaking about God's control over all things, theologians often refer to the sovereignty of God. God's sovereignty reminds us that He maintains a supreme position of authority and rule over man and the rest of creation. It is from His position of absolute control over all of life that God has the ultimate bird's-eye view of the world.

Many people, however, believe that theologians place far too much emphasis on God's sovereignty. 'Sovereignty, sovereignty, sovereignty' a friend once said to me. 'All you theological types ever talk about is sovereignty! What about the love of God?' Also, I remember a discussion I had as a student many years ago with a professor at the Yale Divinity School. While the two of us were standing in front of my mailbox, he thought to tell me that, 'the love of God is higher than his sovereignty'. I responded by reminding him that God is not a totem pole. He just walked away.

Certainly the love of God should not be played down at the expense of His other attributes. But what both my friend and the professor failed to understand was that before we speak about God's love, we should first speak about God. This is what the sovereignty of God allows us to do. A. W. Pink put it best when he wrote, 'The sovereignty of God. What do we mean by this expression? We mean the supremacy of God, the kingship of God, the god-hood of God. To say that God is sovereign is to declare that God is God.'[1]

While many people would agree with Pink's simple, yet profound, definition of God's sovereignty, they live as though the world was run according to chance or luck. They view the world like a Las Vegas casino. Yes, the owner runs the place, but he has no say in the outcome of the game (or at least he shouldn't). Rather, winning or losing depends solely on the roll of the dice. But this is not the way God relates to the world He has created. Because God is God, He not only has a voice in the outcome of the game, but also is carefully working His will in and through all things unto their appointed end. A simple way to remember this is to memorize the following point: *the world and all that it contains is subject to the eternal purpose and plan of God.*

But what is the eternal purpose and plan of God? I'll get to God's plan in Chapter 4, but now I will focus on God's *purpose* for the world. *God's purpose for the world is to restore everything that was lost at the fall – both in man and in the rest of creation – to its proper role of worshipping and glorifying Him.*

The great reformer, John Calvin, emphasized the extent to which God is committed to restoring all of life, when he noted, 'Christ is. . .the restorer of mankind.'[2] The idea that God wants to *restore* His creation may come as a tremendous shock. Since Hal Lindsay's popular book, *The Late Great Planet Earth*, 'gloom and doom' books, videos, and movies have literally saturated the Christian marketplace with the result that not only do most believers expect the planet to continue to deteriorate, but also will be disappointed if it does not. However, the Bible's view of the world, including the consummation of history, presents a place where God rules and reigns, having defeated all His enemies at the cross of Jesus Christ (cf. Psalm 2). From Calvary, until the final tick of history, the Bible presents the work of the Church in the world as nothing more than a 'mop up' operation (cf. Matthew 28:18-20). At times things will appear as though Satan is getting the upper hand, but even then the Bible tells us God is at work using everything at His disposal to achieve His eternal purpose of making all things kneel at His feet (cf. Romans 8:28-30; I Corinthians 15:28). The Church is clearly on the winning side of history!

What I have just shared is an essential part of what is called a biblical worldview. What is a biblical worldview? *A biblical worldview is seeing the world as God sees it. It is thinking God's thoughts after Him in ALL areas of life.* While many people think that God's Word only applies to areas like prayer, personal evangelism, and inward holiness, a biblical worldview assumes that the Bible also speaks to education, art, business, politics, technology, and more. Furthermore, a biblical worldview helps us see that God is sovereignly at work in every area of culture and society, restoring all of it to its proper role of worshipping and glorifying Him. Nevertheless, you may not believe that you hold a biblical worldview. Because it is impossible to grasp the remainder of this book without a biblical worldview, I want to use the rest of this chapter, and Chapter 2, to help you develop one. For some this may be review.

God Is

The first building block of a biblical worldview is God's self-existence. Have you ever had the pleasure of taking a long trip with your kids when they were really little? Remember all the things you had to take – the portable sleeper, the walker, their toys, diapers, bottle liners – just to name a few? And of course you had to take enough food along to feed an army. On one trip I thought I was going to need a separate truck just to carry all of my kid's stuff.

God is nothing like this, of course. Perhaps the most astounding attribute of God is what theologians call His aseity. It means that God is self-existent. He needs absolutely nothing outside of Himself to exist. God never has to pack. He has no needs. Rather, it is man and the rest of creation that needs God in order to exist. Bill Bright writes that, 'All creation relies upon God for existence and the maintenance of life. God has no need for anything and is not vulnerable in any way'.[3] Simply put, God is.

What's In a Name?

It is God's self-existence that is expressed by one of the names we find for Him in the Old Testament, 'I AM.' Although some Bible versions translate 'I AM' as Jehovah, the best translation from the Hebrew is YHWH, or Yahweh. This name first revealed to Moses was holy. It meant to the Israelites that God was the eternal, self-existent, Supreme Being. He had no beginning or end. If God never revealed another thing about Himself, the sheer fact that He was Yahweh, was reason alone to worship Him.

Why have I introduced the name of God? I stated above that a biblical worldview is 'seeing the world as God sees it'. Following this, there are few things that help us to see the world as God sees it better than God's name – His self-revelation. Let me explain.

If I were to ask for your opinion about the use of public funding for indecent art, how would you respond? I'll bet you would begin by saying, 'Well, I think...' Now stop right there. You see what most people really mean by, 'I think', is 'I feel'. The fact is most people make decisions emotionally. From decisions about which wallpaper looks best, to the killing of the unborn, our emotions supply the major catalyst for the positions we take in life.

Nonetheless, many people place a distinction between making good or bad choices based upon the presence or absence of emotion in the decision-making process. 'Don't make your decisions based on emotion,' people say, 'you'll be sorry.' But isn't it true that even when we make good choices our emotions are involved?

Jonathan Edwards, the great intellectual light of the 18th century, wrote a lengthy essay entitled, *The Freedom of the Will.* In it Edwards argues that our actions are based upon our strongest inclination at a given point. Certainly there are things we are compelled to do like die and pay taxes. But even so, we do them against our strongest inclinations to live and to spend the cash on things like season tickets to the Orlando Magic. However, where there is no constraint and our inclinations are free, we will follow them every time. And it is also true that our inclinations are complex. They are made up of facts, reason, and emotion. Once we have reasoned through the facts, it's our emotional state at the time that almost always casts the deciding vote. As long as the Holy Spirit governs our emotions, we have confidence that our choices and actions will be wise. It is when our sinful, human nature takes control of our emotions, that our decisions get us into trouble.

Take Old Testament Israel for example. The book of Exodus is replete with examples of Israel's faithlessness after God time and time again proved He could be trusted. In Chapter 17, we see that God has led Israel out of Egypt, has turned the bitter water sweet at Marah, and has provided manna and quail in the desert for all the people to eat. But what happens when the Israelites camp at Rephidim and there is no water? Wham! They hit the panic button. 'Give us water that we may drink' they cried. So what happened? Sin. The Israelites weighed the self-revelation of God to Moses that He was 'I AM' against their instinct to survive, and decided that their adrenal glands knew better.

The fleshly tendency on the part of the Hebrews to disobey God partly explains why the name Yahweh was paramount throughout Israel's wanderings in the wilderness. God's divine name acted as a constant reminder to His people not to allow earthbound considerations to dictate their decision-making. It was His name which, more than any other thing, provided the Israelites the basis for an *objective* look at life, themselves, and the issues confronting them.

Today the challenge remains the same. Referring to Israel's wanderings in the wilderness, Paul writes, 'Now these things happened as examples for us, that we should not crave evil things, as they also craved.' We are all prone to forget God and His viewpoint and revert to our own perception of reality when trouble strikes. Then sin is crouching at the door. But the lives of Moses and Joshua reveal that success in manoeuvering through the maze of life's challenges is guaranteed when one keeps one's eyes trained on God and sees the world from His perspective.

God is One

The second building block in constructing a biblical worldview is God's unity and simplicity. The *Westminster Confession of Faith* says that God is 'without...parts'.[4] Many years before the confession was drafted, the Old Testament revealed this very fact. 'Hear, O Israel! The Lord is our God, the Lord is One' (Deuteronomy 6:4). This statement is known as the *shema.* It was absolutely central to Israel's confession and worship of God.

The importance of the *shema* to Israel tells us something. It reveals that although it was not the gospel, the *shema* was good news nonetheless. Notice how Deuteronomy 6:4 begins with a proclamation, 'Hear, O Israel!' The opening pronouncement reminds us of the great 18th century, open-air preacher George Whitefield. The evangelist, who may have been the most popular figure in America during his time, was known to preach in the city of Philadelphia to throngs estimated as high as thirty thousand people. But even as great as was George Whitfield, no evangelist ever commanded the attention of people the way Moses did when he called the nation of Israel to worship. Why was the *shema* good news to Israel?

It distinguished the Lord from the gods of the surrounding nations in the minds of the ancient Hebrews. Unlike the God of Israel, the false gods were not 'One'. They had parts. And they had parts because they failed the first test of being God. They were not self-existent. They were a part of the creation itself. In fact the false gods didn't exist at all. They were really nothing more than an extension of the people's concern for fertile crops.

How do these facts help us develop a biblical worldview? If God is One, then we should expect to see continuity – a oneness – in the creation. Paul tells us in Romans 1:20, 'For since the beginning of the world His invisible attributes, His eternal power, and divine nature, have been clearly seen, being understood through what has been made, so that they are without excuse.'

Paul is clear that the creation testifies to God's existence and holds all men responsible for their sinfulness. Additionally, the creation testifies to God's 'divine nature'. This is a clear reference to the Old Testament idea of the self-existent God, who is One. Take a look at

God's creation and what do you see? You see the atom, cellular structures, and DNA – just a few of the brilliantly complex, yet orderly witnesses in God's courtroom to the fact that 'the Lord is One'.

Salvation on the Installment Plan

But if God is One, why is it the viewpoint of numerous Christians that in salvation, God exists in parts? A friend once shared with me that he accepted Jesus as his Saviour as a child. But it wasn't until he was a young adult that he received Jesus 'as Lord'. Now in my friend's perception of his born-again experience, he may have accepted Jesus in two installments. However, the Bible clearly says, 'the Lord is One'.

I am well aware that the reference to Jesus as 'Lord and Saviour' is more a reflection of people's failure to comprehend His Lordship from the start. But I can't help wondering if this duality between Lord and Saviour in the minds of many believers is not symptomatic of a much larger problem. Do Christians truly understand the 'divine nature' of God?

Understanding How Big God Is

A compartmentalized view of God can lead to nothing less than a compartmentalized view of His creation and the role the Church is to play in the world. Perhaps this is why many in the Church view private piety and social activism as competing ideas. Or why the Church in America has failed to reconcile the fact that the earth is destined to burn up, with its mandate to impact every culture for Christ. And it may shed light on why many believers are failing to connect their personal faith to their lives in the business world. There is, of course, a solution to these failures. Repentance. The Church must internalize the full meaning of the unity and simplicity of God, change its thinking, and act accordingly.

I recall when I was a boy playing in a field with my buddies. We were crawling on a big rock, when suddenly one of us noticed the tail of a snake sticking out from under the rock. We jumped off and began to look for the snake from different positions around the huge rock. Instantly one of my friends yelled, 'It's over here!' But then my other friend exclaimed, 'No, the snake's over on this side.' Amazed I replied, 'Hey, the snake's over here too!' One of the boys then said, 'Wow, there must be three snakes!'

We stopped to analyze the situation when suddenly the truth hit us. There were not three snakes. There was only one. The snake was so big that its body could be seen at three different sides of the huge rock. It didn't take but a split second for the three of us to 'repent' of our foolish desire to catch this snake. This was no ordinary snake. Our respect for the creature outweighed any thought that we could capture it.

Likewise we must understand how big God is. His unity and simplicity alone dictate to us the conditions of worship. God's divine nature also informs the *scope* of our faith. *Faith should pervade every area of life because God's unity keeps the world He has created together as a platform for faith.*

Nonetheless, most believers possess a 'fragmented' faith. They believe a little bit about this and a little bit about that, but do not possess a biblical picture of how all the various pieces of life fit together. This is because most believers have failed to decipher the implications of the oneness of God for everything in the world. This failure partly explains why the Church is neglecting its job of restoring every area of life unto the glory of God. A person that does not have a picture of a completed puzzle in front of him to help put together a 1000-piece puzzle-set will be lost when it comes to constructing the puzzle. Although the world is full of many and diverse pieces, God's oneness is like the picture of the completed puzzle on the front of the puzzle-box. It is the key to seeing all of life as a unity, which in turn, helps us to restore it perfectly.

God is a Jealous God

That God is a jealous God is the third building block in developing a biblical worldview. God charged Moses to both deliver and teach the law. Deuteronomy 6 details commands God expected the Israelites to obey as they entered the land of Canaan to conquer it. Let's look at a few verses. 'You shall not follow other gods, any of the gods of the peoples who surround you, for the Lord your God in the midst of you is a jealous God; otherwise the anger of the Lord your God will be kindled against you, and He will wipe you off the face of the earth. You shall not put the Lord your God to the test, as you tested Him at Massah. You should diligently keep the commands of the Lord your God, and His testimonies and His statutes which He has commanded you' (Deuteronomy 6:14-17).

Notice the Bible doesn't say that God will *become* jealous if Israel follows other gods. It says He *is* jealous. Jealousy is intrinsic to the unchanging nature of God. For God to be God, He must be jealous at all times. Jealousy defines Him. In fact Moses says that God is so jealous that His very name is Jealous: 'For you shall not worship any other god, for the Lord, whose name is Jealous, is a jealous God' (Exodus 34:14). I'll bet you've never seen a bumper sticker that says, 'God is Jealous'.

Go to the Rock

Why is God so jealous? Does He have an insecurity complex? No. However, Moses gives us a clue. In Deuteronomy 6:14, Moses reminds the Israelites about the disaster at 'Massah'. This is the name Moses gave to the place where the Israelites grumbled against God when they found themselves without any water to drink. Remember the story? Israel tested God, yet in His mercy God provided water from the rock at Horeb for the people to drink.

In referring to this rock, Paul makes a rather astonishing observation: 'and they all drank the same spiritual drink, for they were drinking from a spiritual rock which followed them; and the rock was Christ' (I Corinthians 10:4). The Old Testament abounds with rich symbolism and allegory. Often the Bible interpreter has to do some digging to uncover the treasure of allegory in Scripture. Not here. Paul is crystal clear that the rock the Israelites drank from, was a type of Jesus Christ. In fact, most Bible scholars point to God's instruction to Moses to strike the rock with his staff, to say that this is a type of the crucifixion of Christ. Just as Moses struck the rock and water poured from it, so Christ was pierced with a spear and blood and water poured from His side.

But there is more. God did not choose a rock to represent Christ at random. There are some interesting facts about rock. Although there are many rocks in the world, there are only three types of rock: igneous, metamorphic, and sedimentary. All rocks fall into one of these three categories.

Igneous rock is formed when fire and hot solutions such as lava cool. This process points to God where the Bible says, 'for our God is a consuming fire' (Hebrews 12:29). Metamorphic rock is formed through the alteration of pre-existing rock by such agents as pressure and heat, which literally change the rock from within. This feature is characteristic of the work of the Son of God, who enters into our lives and transforms us from within (cf. Romans 8:28-30). Finally, sedimentary rock is formed as a result of the smoothing and chipping of wind and water upon pre-existing rock, whose particles then come together to form new rock. This action is analogous to the work of the Holy Spirit who smoothes and chips away at sin and forms us into new creatures in Christ (cf. Romans 8:1-11).

God, through the use of rock, is not only pointing us to Jesus, but to the biblical doctrine of the Trinity. The significance of the analogy increases even more when we understand the importance of rock. It was a surprise to me when I first discovered that all material things have rock as their common source. Whether it's your furniture, the stove, the clothes on your back, or your car, all these things share rock as their source.

What's the point? You've been patient, so here it is. Just as rock is the common source for everything in the material world, so God is the common source for all of life. God is the ultimate source for every need the world could ever have. To say that God is a rock, is just another way to say that He supplies *everything* in the world with its life and meaning.

This explains why God is so jealous. In an age of increasing compartmentalization, we are inclined to think in terms of 'personal' religion and that God won't mind if He's not invited to be the Lord of everything in our lives. But the Bible says that God is jealous over Himself (cf. Ezekiel 39:25), meaning that He hates it when we fail to involve and worship Him in the midst of *all* of life's challenges. God plans to be included in our work, our play, culture, politics, and society.

To think that there is another source for answers to questions that arise in these areas is an invitation for idolatry.

God is All-Powerful

The fourth building block in constructing a biblical worldview is that God is all-powerful. You say, 'Oh I agree with that! But Satan has power too. Never underestimate the power of the devil!' But I do underestimate the power of the devil, and you should too. When we say that God is all-powerful, the 'all' part means the devil has *no* power, at least none he can call his own. Let me explain using this illustration. Wiggle your index finger. Go ahead, wiggle it. There you go. Now wiggle your nose. I know you're wondering, 'Why is this nut asking me to wiggle my nose?' Trust me. Just wiggle your nose. That was a little more difficult, wasn't it? Now wiggle your stomach muscles. No, not your abdominal muscles – your internal stomach muscles. Stumped, aren't you?

All right, I'll let you off the hook. You can't wiggle your internal stomach muscles. That's because your stomach muscles are 'involuntary muscles'. Unlike voluntary muscles, you need some other means to move your involuntary muscles. You can't control this type of muscle. Fortunately your brain tells the involuntary muscles what to do without you even thinking about it.

What do involuntary muscles do? Involuntary muscles are in your stomach contracting and relaxing to allow food to pass into your small intestine. You can go about your business while digesting your food, and your involuntary muscles do all the work. You don't have any say in the matter. Involuntary muscles are everywhere inside of you helping many other internal organs do their work. You don't have to do a thing. Just let the involuntary muscles do their job.

The Bible tells us that we are 'fearfully and wonderfully made' (Psalm 139:14). It also tells us the remarkable way in which our bodies function is a witness to the eternal power of God (cf. Romans 1:20). As I contemplate the amazing relationship in the human body between the brain and the involuntary muscles, I see a picture of a bigger world. Just as the brain controls all of our involuntary muscles, so

God controls His creation. God is the one who facilitates everything in creation. His omnipotent power is absolute.

Our involuntary muscles remind me of another created being – Satan. The devil appears in the Bible very early. He beguiled Eve, and soon thereafter the first couple are eating from the forbidden fruit. Sin enters the world. Ever since, a battle has raged in the world over the souls of men. But the Bible is also very clear that Satan is not all-powerful. Like all created beings, Satan is completely dependent upon God to do anything. None of Satan's power is his own. He is incapable of exerting independent control. All of his power comes from God. Like the involuntary muscle, Satan can only accomplish what God allows.

In commenting on God's almighty reign over the devil, R.C. Sproul says, 'It is important to note that not only did the devil have to get permission to torment Job, he didn't even have the power to do so unless God granted him that power'.[5] He further states, 'God is sustaining the devil every second he exists. If the Father wished that the devil were no longer to exist, it wouldn't take any strain on him to accomplish that task. He would not even have to speak, "Let there not be a devil". Rather, all He would need to do is stop speaking, "Let there be a devil".[6]

To listen to many preachers today, one would think that Satan has a power equal to God's. It's like God is the 'Jedi Knight' and Satan is 'Darth Vader' commanding the rebel fleet. However, both the Old and New Testaments contradict this fable. The psalmist writes, 'The Lord has established His throne in the heavens; and His sovereignty rules over all' (Psalm 103:19). And Jesus said, 'All authority has been given to Me in heaven and on earth' (Matthew 28:18). R.C. Sproul writes, 'There is no question anywhere in the Bible of whether God is mightier than the devil.'[7]

Two Kingdoms?
If Satan has no power or authority independent of God's, then why does Jesus say that Satan has His own kingdom? In correcting the Pharisees who claimed that He was casting out demons by the power of Satan, Jesus said, 'And if Satan casts out Satan, he is divided against

himself; how then shall his kingdom stand?' (Matthew 12:29). And why does Paul write, 'For He delivered us from the domain of darkness, and transferred us to the kingdom of His beloved Son' (Colossians 1:13)?

Clearly Satan has a kingdom. The next question is, 'What does Satan have that Jesus could call a kingdom?' Let's use the process of elimination to answer this question. First there is the earth. The earth is full of evil. Perhaps Satan owns the earth? No. Moses, who was God's own mouthpiece to the nation of Israel said to Pharaoh, '...that you may know that the earth is the Lord's' (Exodus 9:29). So the earth is out.

The government is certainly rotten. Is government a part of Satan's kingdom? No. Although human government resulted as a matter of necessity in order to curtail the effect of sin in the world, Moses tells us that God instituted government. After the flood receded God gave this law to Noah, 'Whoever sheds man's blood, by man his blood shall be shed; for in the image of God, he made man' (Genesis 9:6). Capital punishment was the first law of the land. So government is out.

How about those who govern? Certainly those pork-barrel politicians are in Satan's camp! Not really. At least not in their capacity as legislators. Paul says, 'Let every person be in subjection to the governing authorities. For there is no authority except from God, and those which exist are established by God' (Romans 13:1). Scratch the politicians.

How about an easy one? The world. The world is unquestionably a part of the devil's kingdom, right? This is true, however the Greek word for world (*kosmos*) does not always have a negative meaning. There is the positive sense of John 3:16 which reveals that 'God so loved the world'. Someone might argue that God can still love those who are in Satan's kingdom with a view toward deliverance, and indeed he would be right. But this point only weakens any claim that Satan has a kingdom equal to God's.

Now you're getting wound up. 'It's MTV' you say! 'Music television must be a part of Satan's kingdom!' Well, yes… and no. Culture is an interesting study. Beginning in the first chapter of Genesis, God lays down a mandate to man to 'dress the garden' (cf. Genesis 1:28-30).

Man is the pinnacle of creation. As God's 'vice-regent' he is charged with subduing the created order. This subjection of the rest of creation would, in turn, produce a culture that reflected God's sovereign rule. Thus the idea of culture is not of the devil.

Then there is the ability to create, which is necessary to the flourishing of a culture. In that God is the Creator, the ability to create music and the other fine arts comes from Him. But *what* is created may be a different story. When art reflects a world without Christ – a world of disorder and chaos – then that art becomes a vehicle for the kingdom of darkness.

Kingdom With a Small 'k'

This brings us to what *is* a part of Satan's kingdom. Earlier I mentioned the Greek word, *kosmos*. It means 'order' or 'arrangement'. In its negative use the world is an organized system that is under Satan's control. It includes everything that is evil. Hence, John concludes, 'the whole world lies in the power of the evil one' (I John 5:19). Two closely related words are *kosmikos*, meaning 'worldly' or 'pertaining to this earth', and *kosmoskrator*, which refers to the strong lusts and desires that the Bible forbids (cf. Titus 2:12). So it seems that not the world, but worldliness – the world system – is a part of Satan's kingdom.

The Bible also teaches that demons and the world of the occult are a part of the devil's kingdom. In Ephesians 6, although Paul does not mention Satan or his kingdom, the Christian's struggle is against those 'world forces of darkness' that have played an essential role in his domain since the heavenly revolt (cf. Isaiah 14). And the Bible also is clear that hell is a part of the devil's kingdom (cf. Revelation 9:11).

Paul makes perhaps the clearest pronouncement that the unbeliever is also under the rule of Satan until the time that Christ delivers him. In his stirring defense before Agrippa, Paul declares that Christ sent him 'to open their eyes so that they may turn from darkness to light and from the domain of Satan to God...' (Acts 26:18). John agrees stating, 'the one who practices sin is of the devil...' (I John 3:8).

We see from the above examination of Scripture that perhaps the devil has been given more credit than he deserves. His kingdom of death is limited to the worldly preoccupation with the 'lust of the flesh, and the lust of the eyes and the boastful pride of life' (I John 1:16). The world system that traffics in lust also is in Satan's domain. His kingdom is administered by a fallen host of evil spirits. And his most prized possession is the lot of men he has had in his grasp since the introduction of sin into the world. Worldliness, death, devils, hell, and unrepentant sinners – that's what he's got.

King Over All

On the other hand, Jesus Christ rules far above every name that is named (cf. Philippians 2:9-11). Not only is the devil subject to God, but everything he has is being taken away. 2 Samuel 23:6 predicts that God will wipe away Satan's kingdom. Jesus' first words in His public ministry declared that He had come to contest Satan's kingdom, 'Repent, for the kingdom of heaven is at hand' (Matthew 4:17). Jesus saw His power to heal and to forgive as a means to lay waste the devil's fortress (cf. Matthew 12:25-30). What the consistent message of the coming of the kingdom of God tells us is that even the little bit that Satan has, or will have, will be taken away only to become God's in the end. And that which God does not choose to keep, will be burned up (cf. Matthew 7:23).

It is an undeniable fact that God's absolute power over His creation opens up endless possibilities for the Church to be active in the world. To deny this by saying the world and its cultures are owned lock, stock, and barrel by the devil is a cop-out. God reigns. God rules. And God expects nothing less than for His Church to reign and rule with Him. That the sovereign God is all-powerful over all of life compels His followers to bring 'every thought captive' to Christ. Until we do, our job remains incomplete.

Now let us examine the fifth and final building block of a biblical worldview: the gospel of Jesus Christ.

Two

THE GOSPEL OF THE KINGDOM

Some time ago I had the rather unpleasant experience of attending the funeral of a baby boy. He was the son of a close friend with whom I had spent some time evangelizing the inner city of Philadelphia. At this time I was hosting a syndicated radio program called *America in Focus*. The program looked at contemporary public policy and other cultural issues through the lens of the Bible. It was during those years that much of my thinking on Christianity and culture was formed.

Several of the people at the funeral were acquaintances who knew about my radio program and some of them looked at it rather warily. Their attitude was that my ministry had abandoned the gospel for a less important 'social' gospel. In fact, as I was leaving the sanctuary, I walked past a couple of old acquaintances as they were discussing something. As I passed, one of them said to the other, 'The only hope today is in the gospel.' It was clear that my friend was directing his 'salvo' to me. I didn't say anything. I just kept walking. But I thought to myself, 'Did I abandon the gospel when I began to apply it to the culture?' I was quite disturbed at his remark.

About the same time, I was asked to appear as a guest on another issues-oriented radio program, this one based out of Chicago. The interview was quite stimulating. Afterwards, the host and I talked for a bit. He told me about a time when he approached a man looking for support for his radio show. The man replied, 'I only support the work of the gospel.' Clearly my friend was hurt as well.

Obviously we radio commentators had a different understanding of the meaning of the gospel. And yet we, along with the friends who disagreed with us, were all saved. The differences that separated us had nothing to do with the core of the gospel, but rather with its scope and implications for the world. No, I don't think I abandoned the gospel when I went on the radio to talk about cultural issues. So let me share some things I believe the Bible teaches about the gospel and how it relates to redeeming all of life.

The Purpose of the Good News

You'll recall in Chapter I that I shared four building blocks of a biblical worldview. I'll continue with the fifth building block: the gospel of Jesus Christ is concerned with the restoration of the whole of life. To prove this let's begin with the question: Who's the gospel for?

One doesn't need to be a Christian for long to discover there are many approaches in the Church for evangelizing the lost – the *Romans Road* and the *4 Spiritual Laws* – just to mention a couple. These are excellent tools for giving a person a basic understanding of the gospel. In fact, perhaps you are one who came to Christ as a result of someone lovingly telling you about Christ using one of these methods. The problem is there is far more to the gospel than what the average evangelistic encounter generally has time to cover.

As a result of these popularized versions of the gospel, it has become widely accepted that the far-reaching purpose of the gospel of Jesus Christ is to save me. It's all about my sin and how much God loved me and gave up His only Son to die upon a cross – for me. Now certainly, people need to apprehend the gospel or to make it personal. But here's the question: is the gospel only about little, old me, or is it about something bigger?

It's about something much bigger. Jesus made the clearest pronouncement that His work was for the glory of God: 'I glorified Thee on earth, having accomplished the work which Thou hast given me to do' (John 17:4). Jesus also said that the fruit of the gospel in the Christian life has as its purpose the glory of God: 'By this is My Father glorified, that you bear much fruit, and so prove to be My disciples' (John 15:8).

There is not a single verse in the Bible that says our joy in the Christian life is the gospel's ultimate concern. You can't even find a verse saying our salvation is the end-all of God's plan. However, the Bible is replete with verse after verse pointing to God's own glory as the whole reason behind the work of Christ. In the end, the gospel is not for our glory – even for our salvation. It's for the glory of God.

God's Goal Is Cosmic Redemption

Someone might say, 'The fact that the gospel is meant to glorify God, doesn't mean that the scope of the gospel includes all areas of life.' On the contrary, that's exactly what it means. The Bible teaches that not only is the gospel designed to glorify God, but also everything that is in the world is here for the specific purpose of glorifying the Creator. Paul writes, 'For from Him and through Him and to Him are all things' (Romans 11:36). Elsewhere Paul writes, 'For by Him all things were created, both in the heavens and on earth, visible and invisible, whether thrones or dominions or rulers or authorities – all things have been created by Him and for Him' (Colossians 1:16). And John declares, 'Thou art worthy, O Lord, to receive glory and honor and power: for thou hast created all things, and for thy pleasure they are and were created'(Revelation 4:11, KJV).

However, since Adam's transgression the world has been full of people, trends, ideas, and institutions that stand in rebellious opposition to God. This is where the gospel comes in. Paul writes, 'For it was the Father's good pleasure for all the fullness to dwell in Him, and through Him to reconcile all things to Himself, having made peace through the blood of His cross; through Him, I say, whether things on earth or things in heaven' (Colossians 1:19-20).

Note that Paul doesn't say that God reconciled only sinners to Himself at the cross, but rather He reconciled 'all things' to Himself (See also Ephesians 1:22). New Testament scholar N. T. Wright observes, 'He [Paul] is emphasizing the universal scope of God's reconciling purposes; nothing less than a total new creation is envisaged.'[1] Through the remarkable event of the crucifixion all things were delivered over to Christ. It is as Paul says in 2 Corinthians 5:19, 'God was reconciling the world to Himself.' The blood of Jesus Christ supplies the foundation for nothing less than cosmic redemption!

The scope of redemption applied is identical to the scope of redemption accomplished. In His post-resurrection appearance to His disciples, Jesus claimed 'all authority over heaven and earth' (Matthew 28:18). It was in this comprehensive authority that Christ sent His followers into the world to affect His victory in human hearts and at every level of society and culture. The end product of Christ's atoning work, according to Paul, is nothing less than the tangible submission of all things to the feet of Jesus Christ (cf. I Corinthians 15:25). N. T. Wright continues, 'What, then is the scope of this new creation? Because humanity plays the key role in the ordering of God's world, human reconciliation will lead to the restoration of creation, just as human sin led to creation's fall...God will eventually remake the world and its power structures so that they will reflect His glory instead of human arrogance...God plans for an eventual complete harmony, new heavens and new earth. All evil is to be destroyed through the cosmic results of the resurrection.'[2]

Does the universal scope of the gospel mean that everyone is saved? No. In the wisdom of God, He made man in His image with the power to rebel against Him. Paul does not attempt to harmonize the universal scope of the gospel with men's rejection of Christ. Rather, he merely emphasizes the truth of the inclusive nature of Christ's work and its application to the eventual restoration of 'all things'.

If God's goal is to restore 'all things', then this must be the Church's goal as well. Saving souls and practicing personal piety is important, but not enough. Rather, we must also work toward reclaiming every human institution, including politics, the fine arts, science, economics, media, and more. Because Christ's work of redemption extends to all things, 'whether thrones, or dominions or rulers or authorities', to Him all things must be presented.

No Escaping God's Purpose to Restore All Things

There is another way to look at this truth. In Scripture, the glory of God and the salvation of God are inseparable. This is very important. By linking His glory to His salvation, God has insured that every place the gospel of salvation goes forth into the world, men will encounter His glory. And everywhere that God's glory shines forth in the world, men will be faced with the testimony of God's saving power. In Psalm 96:2-3, the salvation of God is on a par with His glory, and vice versa. The result is that the whole earth is full of God's glory (cf. Isaiah 6:3), while the ends of the earth have seen the salvation of God (cf. Psalm 98:3). Elsewhere, to even speak the gospel is synonymous in Scripture with the telling of God's glory: 'Tell of His glory among the nations, His wonderful deeds among all the peoples' (I Chronicles 16:24). And God's revelation of the gospel in the stars is identical to the revelation of His glory (cf. Psalm 8).

The all-embracing significance of both the glory and the salvation of God in the world reveal that God is dead set on restoring all of life. To illustrate, let me tell you about this cute little thing my dog does. I have a Scottie named Andy. When Andy is about to lie down, he frequently performs this little dance first. He'll walk over to the spot, but instead of just lying down, he turns around in circles for about ten seconds or so. Then when he's good and ready – plop – down he goes. I've often wondered what in the world he was doing. Then one day it hit me that Andy was mapping out his spot before he actually committed to it.

When God wed the gospel of salvation to His glory and then filled the whole earth with both, He told us right then that He was 'mapping out His spot'. He wants man, He wants the creation, and He wants everything for His glory. Isaiah declares, 'For the earth will be full of the knowledge of the Lord as the waters cover the sea' (Isaiah 11:9). The time is coming when God will have all of creation – not just in principle – but also in practice. It may not be today. It may not be tomorrow. But the day is coming when planet earth will be restored!

The Simple Gospel Couldn't Have Been Simpler

Jesus Christ was very much aware of God's intention to restore all of life, and get all the glory as well. He also knew that the human heart was fully capable of resisting God's objective because it is deceitfully sick. When Jesus first began His public ministry, He purposely made God's agenda so simple and to the point that no one could miss it: 'Repent, for the kingdom of heaven is at hand' (Matthew 4:17). Jesus didn't present a plan of salvation. He confronted men with the fact that a new kingdom had come and that its work wouldn't be finished until all things were made new (Matthew 13:31-32). The people of Jesus' day didn't need to think long to understand what a kingdom meant. Everything that walked, crawled, or stumbled belonged to God. And that's the way it would stay.

But Jesus also knew how hard it would be for us to 'get the picture', so He performed miracles to drive His point home. His miracles sent a message loud and clear that with the coming of the kingdom of God, Satan and the kingdom of this world were smashed to smithereens. The earth was under new management. The blind received sight, the lame were made to walk, the lepers were cleansed, the deaf could hear, and even the dead were raised. Was anything missing?

But Jesus still wasn't finished. Just to make sure that everybody knew what they were getting into – that they were going to help Him win the world for the glory of God – Jesus laid out requirements so stringent for becoming His follower, they would have made the saltiest of Navy recruiters blush. The first order of business was to forsake the world. Jesus said that if any man wanted to become His follower, he could deny everything the world could offer him, take up his cross – and follow Him (cf. Luke 9:23).

Once, a man who heard about Jesus wanted to become one of His disciples. He said to Jesus, 'I will follow You wherever You go.' Jesus replied, 'The foxes have holes, and the birds of the air have nests, but the Son of Man has nowhere to lay His own head' (Luke 9:57-58). This is another one of those 'hard sayings' of Jesus authors talk about. And I'm sure that this man was absolutely stunned at Christ's response. But the Bible doesn't make a distinction between the 'hard' and the 'soft' sayings of Jesus. Everything Jesus said was hard for the human ear to hear because Jesus never spoke at the level of what people wanted to hear. Rather, He spoke at the level of what people needed to hear.

Jesus perceived that this man's interest in following Him was self-centered. Either he had a problem with materialism, or his knowledge that Jesus was a popular figure prompted him to want some of the glory for himself. But Jesus basically said to the man, 'So you want to follow Me? Do you have any idea what you're asking? It gets so bad out here that often I don't even have a place to lay my own head at night. And you want to come and follow Me?'

Jesus taught that not even the people we love are to be permitted to get in the way of making the kingdom of God first in our lives. Jesus was so committed to this notion He wouldn't permit a young would-be follower to stop at home to let his family know he was leaving to become a disciple (Luke 9:60). He even told a man to abandon his dead, Jewish father without a burial, but instead, to go everywhere and proclaim the gospel of the kingdom (Luke 9:62). In all, Christ's teaching lays down one of the most important principles of discipleship: there is absolutely nothing in it for us, but all is for the glory of God.

The Root of the Problem
The current mood within the Church – the American church in particular – has swung away from directing its worship and service to the glory of God and the restoration of all of life. Rather the emphasis is on finding Scripture keys to personal prosperity, clues for producing 'overcoming faith', and tips on dealing with stress. In many churches the altar for repentance has been replaced with a couch for analysis. Christian media is full of coaches, therapists, and facilitators, but there are few prophets in the line of John the Baptist declaring, 'Repent, for the Kingdom of heaven is at hand.'

Because far too many people have come to Christ as their helper, and not as their Lord, the Church continues to struggle with the Bible's presentation of the gospel as a kingdom that has the power to redeem all of life. The distinctive call to lose one's life in service of the kingdom of God has today been lost amidst the clamor for therapeutic sermons that are relevant and meaningful. This has largely been a problem attributable to the lack of solid church-based evangelism in our day. But churches that fail to correct the problem are no less guilty. The result is that churches are full of people who are in it for the blessings, and not for the glory of God. This is the root of the problem.

The Real 'Gift' in the Gift of Salvation

How can we change? The Church needs to renew its understanding of God's grace. Each time I contemplate Jesus' preaching of the kingdom of God, and the fact that God wants to use me to help restore all of life to His glory, it's not long before I'm feeling insecure. 'How can I do all this?' 'Do I count the cost of discipleship each day in my life?' 'Do I live for nothing less than the glory of God?' The second I begin to ask myself these questions I am instantly gripped by my sense of failure. My fleshly tendency is to resolve to do better. But trying hard to follow Jesus is a dead end. It's only when we understand the significance of 'unmerited favour' and the grace of God to us in Christ, that we can be effective servants of God.

In a powerful book called, *Grace Walk*, Steve McVey describes the evolutionary spiral downward he experienced through trying hard in the Christian life: 'I lived many years of my Christian life trapped in what I call the motivation-condemnation-rededication cycle. From the earliest years of my Christian life, I had a mental picture of what I thought I should be. In this picture there was always a wide gap between where I ought to be and where I was. Sometimes when I was especially motivated, I would feel the gap had narrowed a bit. When I was winning people to Christ or spending a lot of time praying and studying the Bible, I felt that I might actually one day be able to bridge the gap and be a victorious Christian.'[3]

Sound familiar? Throughout the book, the author continues to bring us back to the basics of what it means to walk in grace. As Paul said, 'For by grace you have been saved through faith; and that not of yourselves, it is the gift of God' (Ephesians 2:8). The concept of salvation by grace is unbelievably important in our walk. And yet, I'm going to ask you to rethink your position on salvation by grace. Now don't get nervous. I simply want you to begin to think about grace from another point of view. I want you to do this because I know how hard it is to reposition my own thoughts to the fact that the gospel has the glory of God as its ultimate goal. Like everyone, I'm forever thinking that it's for me.

So instead of thinking that salvation is a gift to you, I want you to dwell upon how you are a gift to God. When God sent Jesus Christ to die for our sins, the Bible says that He purchased us with a price – the blood of His only begotten Son (cf. Ephesians 1:14). Did you hear that? God purchased us! This means that believers are a gift God purchased for Himself! Yes it is true that Christ now belongs to us. But it is equally true that we now belong to Christ. It is correct that we possess the gift of salvation through faith. However, it is also true that God possesses us by virtue of having redeemed us from sin and death through the precious blood of Christ.

What's the point? Think about it. Each time you draw a mental picture of salvation by grace, you imagine that you are receiving something. But that brings us back to good, old me. But the end of salvation is for the glory of God. So here's the point. Salvation is not just God's gift to us. The gift God gives to us in salvation is that He has made us a gift to Himself! Here is the real 'gift' in the gift of salvation.

The message of God's love for lost sinners is simple and powerful. God came into the world and became a man just like us (cf. Luke 2:8-14). He lived the perfect life all of us were supposed to live, but did not (cf. 1 Peter 2:22). He died upon a cross to pay the full penalty for our sins (cf. Colossians 1:19-20). He rose from the dead three days later and then, after appearing to many people, ascended up into heaven (cf. Matthew 28). And today God calls all men to come and place their full trust upon Christ to receive forgiveness of their sins and the gift of eternal life (Ephesians 2:8-10). But let's be careful not to end the story here. Let's never forget: it is through the person and work of Christ that God makes us gifts unto Himself whereby He receives all the honor, praise, and glory (cf. Acts 20:28; 1 Corinthians 6:20; 2 Peter 2:1). We dare not let the message of salvation end on a man-centered note. It must always end on a God-centered note – the one that gives all the glory to Him!

Counting All Things Loss

When our perspective is right, and we are living our lives for the glory of God, it is nothing less than amazing what God can do in and through us. Let me tell you about a young man named Chuck. I met Chuck in the late 80s. Chuck was a young man whom Christ delivered from drugs. His life had been going nowhere until a young church planter came to Holyoke, Massachusetts, near where Chuck lived, to start an Orthodox Presbyterian Church. It wasn't long before their paths crossed and the pastor of the new mission lovingly told Chuck about Jesus. Chuck responded by asking Christ to come into his life. Everything changed.

Through an interesting series of events, I met the pastor of the Holyoke mission, and it wasn't long before he invited me to come and spend some time with his church. He asked me to work with the church for about six weeks. My mission was to help develop some ways for the church to reach the community through evangelism.

I remember the day I arrived. The pastor was eager for me to meet Chuck. We drove over to the restaurant where Chuck was working as a cook. We met and became friends quickly. It was obvious to me that God was doing a quick work in Chuck. You could see the love of Christ all over him, and how Chuck wanted to get busy reaching the community with the same love of Christ that had so dramatically changed his life.

Before coming to Holyoke, I had spent many hours in the streets of New England doing open-air evangelism. I explained to Chuck the type of ministry I had been involved in and that we might duplicate it in Holyoke. He was fascinated and eager to help. That I was planning to preach in the streets of Holyoke didn't faze Chuck at all. And the fact that Chuck wasn't turned off at the prospect of street preaching really excited me. I truly felt I had a fledgling evangelist on my hands.

One day, Chuck and I headed off for downtown Holyoke with our microphone and loudspeaker in hand. Now let me explain for those readers who hate street preachers that I wasn't the loud obnoxious type you may have heard about. My brand of street preaching was a bit more engaging. I tried to present a little talk on some subject that I believed would be of interest to the passers-by, and then I would try to engage a few people in discussion. The approach proved to be rather effective.

But back to the story. I asked Chuck if he would like to speak, to simply share his testimony. To my surprise, he agreed. It was very clear that Chuck was quite nervous about speaking in public (it didn't get any more public than this). We found a nice sidewalk, set up our battery operated loudspeaker, I handed the microphone to Chuck, and said, 'OK Chuck, it's all yours.' I stood back waiting to hear something from Chuck, but all I heard was the wind whistling through the microphone. I stood there and stood there – waiting. There was nothing.

I said, 'Chuck, are you OK?' Chuck responded, 'Just give me a minute.' So I waited and waited – but there was nothing from Chuck. Finally I said, 'Chuck what's the problem?' Chuck just looked over at me and said, 'I can't do it.' It seemed Chuck had an incredible case of stage fright. As I looked at him with a feeling of great sympathy, I simply said, 'Chuck, just think for a minute about what Jesus did for you.' Chuck looked at the ground trying to gain his composure. I said, 'Chuck, I want you to think through exactly what Christ did to free you from drugs and give you the gift of eternal life. Just dwell on Him.'

Chuck did. As I watched, the expression on his face began to change. It was like a power was beginning to course through his body. I could tell that Chuck was literally transforming on that street corner right in front of my eyes from a man afraid to speak out for Jesus, to a powerhouse for God. Then it happened.

Slowly, Chuck put the microphone up to his mouth and began to speak about Jesus. He talked for a couple of minutes about his former life on drugs and how Christ had set him free. He shared how people could know the same Jesus he knew if they would simply confess their sins and place their trust upon Him. Then Chuck put the microphone down to his side, looked over at me, and said, 'How was that?' You can imagine how I felt. I tried to hide my emotion, and so with a bit of a catch in my throat I said, 'I liked it a lot.' But here's the question: 'What happened to Chuck?'

Paul, in writing about the transformation Christ wrought in him says, 'But whatever things were gain to me, those things I have counted as loss for the sake of Christ. More than that, I count all things to be loss in view of the surpassing value of knowing Christ Jesus my Lord, for whom I have suffered the loss of all things, and count them but rubbish in order that I may gain Christ' (Philippians 3:7-8).

Whenever I read this passage of Scripture, I am reminded of my old friend Chuck and all of the other 'Chucks' in the world that Christ delivered from self-defeating lives to serve Him. Moreover, I am reminded about the power of Christ that enabled Chuck to declare the Lord on that street corner in Holyoke, Massachusetts. But the fact is you really are no different than Chuck. It is the power of the resurrected Christ that can also enable you to become part of God's incredible plan of global restoration. No, God is not calling you to single-handedly transform the world. But He is calling you to play your role. Deny yourself. Focus on what grace has done. You no longer belong to yourself, but to Him who purchased you with a price. Soon you, and everything your life touches, will be turned toward the glory of God.

Three

DEBUNKING THE SACRED/SECULAR DISTINCTION

If you have ever had the opportunity to study the great cathedrals of Europe, you know that the Church of the late Middle Ages understood how to embody its worldview in art and architecture. You also know that never has man built a space more completely devoted to the notion of worldview, than the great Gothic cathedral at Chartres, France. Built in the late 12th century, the cathedral at Chartres is the very embodiment of the message that Christ is Lord of both the sacred and the secular.

Prior to the construction of the cathedral at Chartres, the Roman Empire was the most influential political power in Europe. The political history of the High Middle Ages is a story of the struggle of kings to assert their rights as supreme feudal lords and to turn the Church into a servant of the state, which would allow the kings to control large political entities. This led to the state controlling appointments to church offices and buying and selling them. Thus was born the feudal church.

As the Roman Empire amassed greater power, resulting in greater intrusion into religious matters, opposition to the state eventually grew within the Church. Total papal sovereignty over the Church was begun by Gregory VII, who regarded himself as the 'Vicar of Christ', the sole spokesman for God. With the excommunication of Henry IV by Gregory, papal claim to universal sovereignty went unchallenged. By the 12th century, Pope Innocent III could sweep away all the limitations implied by the old oppressive order.

Gregory VII declared the Church to be the 'Kingdom of God' on earth, which is carrying out God's will – the redemption of mankind. Gregory gave the movement its more militant tone with his belief that the Church must become a visible community with its own head, its own law, its own resources, and its own liberty. And here is the crux of Gregory's position: that the state, the king in particular, was ordained to protect the Church, enabling it to carry out its mandate.

It was the message that Christ is Lord of all, including the king, that was articulated in the architectural genius of the great cathedral at Chartes. As the cathedral is understood to be a picture of the kingdom of heaven on earth, it reflects beauty, harmony of proportion, and perfection of form. The west facade, one of the most glorious of all the Gothic structures, is harmonized through decoration and proportion in order to give it an upward, reaching effect – reaching toward the purity of paradise itself. The ribbed vault helped architects fashion marvelously tall structures whose weight flowed to earth, yet whose lines and proportions reached toward heaven. This concept grips the mind and the emotions and lifts the worshipper to the realization that Christ is Lord of both heaven and earth.

The south side of the cathedral displays Old Testament figures whose message is to proclaim that the rulers of France are not independent of God, but in fact stand in the line of the great kings and prophets from before the time of Christ. The worldview of the cathedral is summed up through a figure of Christ appearing as Judge and Lord of the universe above the doorway with an assembly of twenty-four elders in the archivolts. Here the message is once again made clear that the ideal society consists in a harmony of spiritual and secular injunction, where Christ is the head of both.

Although the High Middle Ages continued to experience religious and political upheaval, the cathedral at Chartres remains an enduring testimony to the belief that life in all its parts can not be experienced nor even understood apart from the rule of Christ. This is certainly a far cry from the current mood in the Church that embodies much of its worldview in 'multi-purpose' rooms. There is no doubt that the cost alone of construction for a building similar to the cathedral at Chartres would prohibit most church building committees from considering the plan. However, I wonder if the overriding reason we don't have more 'Chartres' in our day is because we have such a lack of biblical worldview?

An Unhealthy Distinction
What is the problem? One problem is that, unlike those who planned the cathedral at Chartres, the Church of today generally does not understand the implications of the sovereignty of God over *all* of life. The assumption is that God makes a dramatic distinction between the sacred and the secular spheres of life in His work in the world. God is only interested in 'religious' things. Thus, the work of the Church should be restricted to evangelism, discipleship, and prayer. Everything else is getting involved in 'worldly affairs'. This applies to politics, the fine arts, and entertainment – to anything that is understood to lie within the realm of the secular.

The sacred/secular distinction is not so much a law codified by the Church. Nor does every believer accept it. It's an attitude – an attitude restricted mostly to the piety wing of the Church (although not exclusively restricted to it). So we don't have the *Sacred/Secular Church Manifesto* to examine. But we do have books by numerous Christian authors to muse over. And above all, we can examine this attitude in the life of the Church. It is when we look at these things we find this unhealthy position: *any explicit connection between the Lordship of Christ and the secular sphere is to be rejected.*

Upon Closer Examination
If we were to dissect the sacred/secular distinction, I believe we would find that those who ascribe to it assume the secular sphere to *have separate authority, rules of operation, and destiny* – quite distinct from the sacred. In fact, why don't we do just that. Let's dissect this

fish, beginning with the first assumption *that the sacred and the secular operate under entirely different authorities, or powers.*

Cal Thomas writes in the controversial book, *Blinded by Might: Can the Religious Right Save America?* 'It sometimes appears that nothing important can be done without a place at the political table and a piece of the political action. The reality is quite different – because we have a different definition of power, or should have.'[1] Here Cal Thomas distinguishes 'political' power from a 'different definition of power,' which according to him is a 'power that comes from making disciples, helping the poor, visiting the sick, rearing a child, and comforting the dying.'

But as we saw in Chapter I, there is but one power in the universe (cf. Daniel 2:37; Matthew 28:18-20). It was this power David drew upon in his *secular* capacity as King to help the son of Jonathan – Mephibosheth – who was crippled in both his feet: 'And David said to him, "Do not fear, for I will surely show kindness to you for the sake of your father Jonathan, and will restore to you all the land of your grandfather Saul; and you shall eat at my table regularly" (2 Samuel 9:7). How do I know David didn't draw upon *political* power to help poor Mephibosheth? He says in Psalm 79:11, 'Let the groaning of the prisoner come before Thee; According to the greatness of Thy power preserve those who are doomed to die.'

Someone might say that David wasn't using political power to assist Mephibosheth because that wasn't a political endeavor. But when David is thinking about deliverance from his political enemies, he doesn't revert to 'political' power there either. Rather, he calls upon the power of God: '...scatter them by Thy power, and bring them down, O Lord, our shield' (Psalm 59:11). Clearly there is but one power to accomplish all that is considered either sacred or secular. So what is Cal Thomas talking about? I believe he is reacting to the *abuse* of power he has witnessed among some fundamentalist believers in their attempt to change the culture through politics. But just because people will abuse God's power, doesn't mean there are two different powers.

The Unmentionable Issue
We also see the sacred/secular distinction in the life of the Church.

Just let a preacher mention politics from the average American pulpit and feel the electric shock rip through the congregation. The topic is about as welcome as a porcupine in a balloon factory. The sense you get is that although the point made by the preacher may be right, a worship service is clearly the wrong place to make it. The church is the place to discuss 'spiritual' things.

Several years ago I preached at a very large church in Northern Virginia, just outside Washington, D.C. A hefty percentage of this church was made up of employees of the Federal Government. My message was based on Matthew 22:21 where Jesus said to the Pharisees, 'Then render to Caesar the things that are Caesar's; and to God the things that are God's'. A good portion of my message focused on the Bible's view of limited government. Although I knew that the message would engender some hot discussion on the topic, I had absolutely no idea what a huge controversy laid ahead.

To make a long story short, a virtual war broke out over my sermon. Even many of those that favoured what I had to say approached me after the service to say that, although they agreed with many of my points, they felt that a Sunday morning sermon was *not* the appropriate forum. But I thought, 'God is Lord of all. Yet I can't talk about God's view of government?' Unfortunately the example of this church is widespread. The message is that God is Lord of all the nations, but not really. In reality, He's just the God of we suburbanite Christians who favour sermons on how to raise kids and have a positive outlook on life.

One of the great mistakes of the Israelites was that they reduced God to little more than a mere tribal deity. He was the God of Jewish religion, and nothing more. In *Decisive Issues Facing Christians Today*, John Stott reminds us how the Old Testament prophet, Amos, stunned the Israelite nation when he pronounced that the same power that delivered Israel from Egypt, brought the Philistines from Crete and the Arameans from Kir.[2] Evidently, God was bigger than faith and family.

We as Christians repeat the Israelite's error when, in our self-absorption, we think that God's main reason for being is to speak to us about religion and nothing more. *We forget that idolatry can be practiced two ways: by worshipping too many gods, or by making the one, true God too small.* But self-absorption will do this. If God is concerned about the world and all things in it, and He really does have an opinion about it, then let spirituality touch *all* of life.

Different Strokes?

The second point that needs to be assumed for the sacred/secular distinction to work is that both spheres would need to operate by different rules. What I mean by 'rules' is the codes of conduct people observe in their daily activities. The idea of rules, then, is closely tied to the idea of authority and power. Only a governing power can provide authoritative direction for any code of conduct.

Since there is but one governing power in the universe, it follows that there is no moral distinction between what God expects from Christians and unbelievers. It was the lack of this understanding that was so surprising to me during the Clinton/Lewinsky affair. One day I logged on to a Christian chat room. The topic was whether Bill Clinton should be held accountable for lying when it was *only* about sex and what should be done about it.

What surprised me was not that most of the participants felt that lying about sex was minor league. It was that even if found guilty, many believed that nothing should be done because the President is a 'secular' authority. One person commented that adultery was not a matter for the state to police. It was a 'moral' failing. And so what was the Congress expected to do – 'excommunicate the President?'

Cementing the view that Christians make a moral distinction between the sacred and the secular, the Barna Research Group released the results of a nation wide survey revealing that born-again Christians do not evaluate former President Clinton's character much differently than do other adults. The report is entitled 'President Clinton's Character is a Non-Issue to Born-Again Christians.' Nearly half of born-again adults said that Mr. Clinton could be deemed 'honest and trustworthy', compared to six out of ten other adults. George Barna commented, 'Surprisingly, the research shows that people's faith commitment makes only a small difference in their assessment of Mr. Clinton.'[3]

It doesn't take a rocket scientist to see that America is split on the issue of rules. We dance to different drummers. In fact, other national survey results reveal that up to 80percent of Americans claim to have a belief in God. And yet we as a society continue to demonstrate seeming intolerance to God's ways. One would expect the Church to be united on the issue of rules. We are not. Why is this? Clearly there is a disconnection between our public posturing about faith, and the way we live. It shouldn't come as a surprise, then, that Christians don't expect to see secular society operate by God's code of conduct, when they themselves aren't living by that same code of conduct seven days a week.

One God – One Standard

The Bible is clear that there is *one* set of rules for everyone to live by. God has given His rules to us in two ways: *natural and special revelation.* Let's go to Romans 1:18-20 where Paul discusses natural revelation: 'For the wrath of God is revealed from heaven against all ungodliness and unrighteousness of men, who suppress the truth in unrighteousness, because that which is known about God is evident within them; for God made it evident to them. For since the creation of the world His invisible attributes, His eternal power and divine nature, have been clearly seen, being understood through what has been made, so that they are without excuse.'

Paul says that the created order is all that is necessary to see that God exists. Creation is not enough to convey the finer points about salvation. But it does reveal enough about God to provide a foundation for moral absolutes and to hold us responsible for our lives. This is how Noah 'found favour in the eyes of the Lord' (Genesis 6:8), long before Moses delivered the ten Commandments to the nation of Israel.

Then we have the Bible – God's special revelation to us. Notice that Jesus did not say in the Sermon on the Mount, 'but I say to you, that every *Christian* who looks upon a woman to lust after her has committed adultery with her already in his heart.' No, in Jesus' words *everyone* is guilty of adultery of the heart under the conditions He describes (c.f. Matthew 5: 27-30).

When Jesus discusses murder he is clear that the *same* standards for breaking the 6th Commandment apply both before the altar and in the courtroom: 'But I say to you that everyone who is angry with his brother shall be guilty before the court; and whoever shall say to his brother, "Raca", shall be guilty before the supreme court; and whoever shall say, "You fool", shall be guilty enough to go into the fiery hell. If therefore you are presenting your offering at the altar, and there remember that your brother has something against you, leave your offering there before the altar, and go your way; first be reconciled to your brother, and then come and present your offering' (Matthew 5:22-24).

The President of the United States may not have been elected America's 'moral leader,' but one thing is certain. The President is a *moral agent.* God expects all secular authorities to live by the standards that nature and God's Word implore all men to live by. To expect anything less – to cut public officials some slack for no other reason than they are public servants and not priests in the house of God – is grading the secular on a curve God rejects.

Hitting the Cultural Pavement

I'll say it differently: the reason many believers are willing to accept another code of conduct for the world is that they have accepted another code of conduct for themselves. The sacred/secular distinction is the logical conclusion of those that differentiate the sacred from the secular in their *personal* lives. Christ is the Lord at the altar, but not in the boardroom, tennis club, and voting booth.

While I would love to sound erudite by grounding this false view of reality among believers in a modern-day 'platonic dualism' between the spiritual and the material world, in truth the problem is not as sophisticated as this. Rather, the sacred/secular distinction is the result of what Dietrich Bonhoeffer called, 'cheap grace.' This is grace one covets from the Church after the Lordship of Christ has been siphoned off. Believers' reluctance to incarnate Christ's Lordship in *all* that they do has created in their minds a greater distinction between God's standards and the world's behavior.

Because the Church has failed to hold itself and the world accountable to one standard of morality, rampant *pluralism* – the rejection of absolutes – prevails in our nation. Noted author George Grant comments, 'Pluralism has always been hard to define. Its topsy-turvy logic is often as unintelligible as medieval runes. In practice, it is an odd attempt to forge a cultural consensus on the idea that there can be no cultural consensus. It is the unspoken assumption that a happy and harmonious society can be maintained only so long as the only common belief is that there are no common beliefs. It is the reluctant affirmation that the only absolute is that there must not be any absolutes.'[4]

Do we dare think that America will skirt the consequences of rejecting God's moral standards? It hasn't up to now. Today suicide is the second leading cause of death for teens, up 300 percent in the last thirty years.[5] Between 1999 and 2001, a total of fifty-six children were murdered in U.S. public schools[6] – a fact which has earned American youth the undesirable label: the 'Columbine generation.'

Today America reminds me of a man standing atop a 60-story skyscraper prepared to jump. The man is fed up with rules. He says to himself, 'All I want to do is fly – fly and be free of all these rules!' So he throws all reason to the wind and jumps. What happens? For a very brief period of time the man is free. The wind whistles through his hair. For the first time in his life he has no constraints, no one to answer to, and no deadlines to meet. But then what? Wham! He hits the pavement. Unfortunately our subject has come into contact with authority – the harsh reality of breaking the rules.

No doubt – America is the man who has slammed into the pavement. Many have reasoned away God's law and now the consequences that God attached to the Law have fractured our temporary freedom through social rot. There was a day when the Church resisted society's ills. Soon, though, we came to tolerate it. Then we came to expect it. Now too many of us justify it. And we compound the whole matter when in our haste to excuse ourselves from our responsibility to hold society accountable, we offer this age-old social commentary: 'Well, it is a fallen world.' We forget that God placed us here to pick up the pieces and – in His power – to use the frame of a biblical worldview to rebuild the puzzle.

Two Tracks?

The third element that needs to be presupposed for the sacred/secular distinction to be viable is for the secular sphere of life to have a different destiny than that of the sacred. A friend of mine did a pretty good job of articulating this view when, in commenting about the Christian's responsibility to the culture, he said to me, ' But John, it's all going to burn up anyway!' My friend was expressing his view that a Christian is wasting time focusing on society's need for solid public policy, because the world is all going to wind up in the trash heap one way or the other. The radio preacher, Rev. J. Vernon McGee, expressed this view in the early 1950s, when he said, 'You don't polish brass on a sinking ship.'

This position is highly characteristic of what is called 'pietism.' What is pietism? While activists believe that the gospel should affect all of life, pietists contend that spirituality ends at the door of personal experience (American pietism is covered in detail in Chapter 7). Additionally, the common notion held by pietists is that the secular world is operating on a different track than the sacred world. The sacred world is headed for paradise, while the secular world is headed for the pit. So why bother impacting secular society for Christ?

Monkeying with God's Plan

One reason all Christians should trouble themselves to work to redeem secular society is that to do anything less produces the effects of *social Darwinism.* Let me explain. The name Charles Darwin should be quite familiar. In his works, *Origin of the Species* (1859) and *Descent of Man* (1871), Darwin propelled the theory of evolution into mainstream science. While Darwin was being published however, another movement was forming in America intending to eradicate orthodox Christian belief using Darwin's evolutionary theory.

Social Darwinism was rooted in the European rationalists who rejected the sinfulness of man and the sovereignty of God. Rather, they proposed that man was inherently good, and that because the 'fittest' only ever survive from one historical period to the next as Darwin supposed, man had it within himself to control history. Lester Frank Ward (1841-1913), a paleontologist and a founder of American sociology, helped America understand how this might work. Through his leadership Ward taught America's captains of industry how to apply social Darwinism to the nation's plans for economic advancement.

For Ward, the concept of 'acquired characteristics' held that a generation could acquire and pass on its positive characteristics to the next, guaranteeing economic and social betterment. Ward called his program 'Meliorism.' According to C. Gregg Singer, social Darwinists '...were charging that Calvinism was destructive of human freedom because of its reliance upon a sovereign God as the supreme sovereign in the affairs of man. Therefore Calvinism had to go and should be replaced by a philosophy of life more congenial to democracy and human liberty.'

At this point you are probably wondering what pietism has to do with social Darwinism. Now I have no doubt that Christian pietists haven't consciously given themselves to the philosophy of social Darwinism. The emphasis on personal spiritual growth, evangelism, and discipleship is not exactly what Charles Darwin had in mind when he introduced 'selective breeding'.

But Christians at Galatia didn't plan to stumble into heresy through the observance of the ceremonial law, nor did believers at Colosse intend to turn from Christ to ancient mysticism through the observance of ascetic rituals. But this was the danger in both cases. Remember, the greatest power of false teaching to influence Christian minds away from the 'whole counsel of God' is to package it as a way to enhance fellowship with God.

Having said this, now ask yourself what is the principle motivation among pietists to stay out of the 'culture-war?' It's to take the 'higher ground' and enjoy closer fellowship with God. The perception is that Christian lobbyists, pro-life advocates, and other evangelical, social activists who labour to redeem the culture, have opted for a *lesser* form of spirituality. Activists are 'fighting as the world fights.' How many times have you heard it said of applying the gospel to cultural issues, 'Well, that's not our ministry,' when what is really meant is

'That's no ministry at all.' But here is the point to consider. When Christians consciously decide which part of God's creation isn't worth redeeming, choosing instead the 'higher ground,' what happens to the *lower* ground? Unfortunately the culture is left for the moth and rust to destroy.

The result is that pietists practice their own sanctified brand of 'selective breeding'. The weak are left unattended, leaving only the 'strong' to survive. Future generations pass as the Church selects only those 'acquired characteristics' of the age it deems worthy of passing to the next. And here is the irony. Although it is the pietists who are forever criticizing activists for seeking heaven on earth, it is really the pietists who, under this philosophy, are guilty of attempting to create a Christian utopia!

A Right Perspective

So what is God's historical forecast for the secular? It helps to understand that God is *not* schizophrenic. He doesn't have one face for the sacred and another one for the secular. Paul says that '…all things have been created by Him and for Him' (Colossians 1:16). If 'all things' have been created for Jesus, obviously there is more for the Christian to include in his worldview than personal experience and morality. This includes God's plan for things like art, science, politics, music, the fashion industry, television, journalism, drama, medical research, economics and more. Sometimes we need to be reminded that 'everything created by God is good, and nothing is to be rejected, if it is received with gratitude; for it is sanctified by means of the word of God and prayer' (1 Timothy 4:4-5).

Given this, it's not the secular disciplines that are evil, but it's whether or not they are rendered to the glory of God that determines their usefulness in God's plan. For example, when God looked at His creation, He 'saw that it was good'. He placed man in the garden as His vice-regent to rule over the creation with Him. But today, man has scorched much of God's good creation through over-development and pollution.

The book of Revelation says that the musician and the craftsman will be included in Babylon's destruction, for they were a part of the great harlot's attempt to seduce the world (cf. Revelation 18:22). Yet the work of the Old Testament sanctuary could not have been completed without godly craftsmen (cf. Exodus 36:1), nor could God's plan for worship in the Davidic kingdom have been complete without gifted musicians (cf. I Chronicles 16:4-6).

Jesus was a carpenter. Paul was a tent-maker. In Acts 17, Paul easily found the common element in the work of the Athenian poets, revealing that all men are created in God's image. And God Himself used the work of a potter's hand as a sign to rebellious Israel that He is just in disciplining His people. No, there is *nothing* inherently evil about the secular. Not when it is sanctified for the Master's use. Paul writes, 'Whether, then, you eat or drink or whatever you do, do all to the glory of God' (I Corinthians 10:31).

To this point we have seen how God looks at the world only in terms of His *purpose* to restore all of life, and that nothing in the world is exempt. However, we have not looked at God's *plan* or strategy to achieve His goal. In the next chapter, I want to answer this question: 'What is God's master plan for restoring all of life?'

four

GOD'S MASTER PLAN TO RESTORE PLANET EARTH

In my hometown of Ft. Lauderdale, Florida is one of the most beautiful sanctuaries in all America. It belongs to the Coral Ridge Presbyterian Church. The senior minister of the church is the prominent Presbyterian – Dr. D. James Kennedy. If ever you're travelling either north or south on North US 1 in Ft. Lauderdale, the church is virtually impossible to miss. So is its ministry – it's worldwide. From Evangelism Explosion, to Coral Ridge Ministries, to its international television and radio outreach, Coral Ridge Presbyterian Church is a model of a church that is committed to helping restore all of life to the glory of God.

The world-reaching commitment of the Coral Ridge Presbyterian Church is clearly expressed in its vision statement: *'To glorify God by communicating the truth of Holy Scripture to our community while encouraging believers to become fully dependent on Jesus Christ and obedient to the Great Commission and the Cultural Mandate.'*

The vision statement of Coral Ridge Presbyterian Church represents perhaps the best statement I've ever read of what a practical, biblical worldview is all about. It captures the essence of God's strategy to reclaim planet earth. It is the plumline of Christian activism. In fact, all I will do here is simply reiterate the vision statement as a way of elaborating upon God's plan. *God's master plan for restoring the earth is to use His Church in obedience to the Cultural Mandate and the Great Commission.*

What is the Cultural Mandate? It is God's charge to the Church found in Genesis 1:28 to 'fill the earth and subdue it'. What is the Great Commission? It is Christ's charge to the Church found in Matthew 28:18-20 to reach the nations with the gospel of Jesus Christ through evangelism and discipleship. When we are active both in the Cultural Mandate and the Great Commission we are being both 'salt' and 'light' in the world (cf. Matthew 5:13-16). We are both *living* and *declaring* that 'the world and all that it contains is subject to the eternal purpose and plan of God'.

In his book *Led by the Carpenter*, Dr. D. James Kennedy remarks, 'God has given us His vision for His Church in the form of two great mandates: the Cultural Mandate and the Great Commission – the first commandment He gave our first parents in Eden and the last commandment Christ left to us before He departed this world. In these mandates, God has given us our assignment, our goal, our task. Because of the global and all-encompassing nature of these mandates, we cannot escape the fact that His purpose for the Church is global and all encompassing...Even more challenging than the scope of God's vision for the Church is the profound *depth* of this vision! We are not simply to advertise a message. We are not simply to announce that Jesus has come. We are to *fill the earth*, to *subdue it*, and to *have dominion over it!* God has called us not merely to win souls but to *claim Planet Earth* in His name!'[1]

The Ingrown Church

Sadly, although most Christians have heard about both the Cultural Mandate and the Great Commission, a large percentage of their knowledge is merely intellectual. Several years ago, I was a candidate for minister at a Presbyterian Church in California. I assumed that Californians were 'progressive' and would look forward to the challenge of taking on their community – and yes – the *world* for Christ. I was wrong.

The more I engaged church members about their vision for ministry, it became painfully obvious they weren't the least bit interested in anything but themselves. Then came the killer. During an interview with members of the congregation, one of the older women – a woman quite respected by the congregation – walked over to me, leaned over a bit, and said, 'We *are* your world.' I was absolutely stunned. What was even more shocking was that not a single person in the room attempted to correct her. Obviously, I didn't get the job – thankfully.

My experience in California served as a wake-up call. It showed me how correct the late Dr. Jack Miller of World Harvest Missions was when he observed that the Church is 'ingrown' in our day. So just to make sure we're all singing off the same song sheet, let me ask a couple of questions.

First, do you understand the purpose of both the Cultural Mandate and the Great Commission?

Second, are you actively engaged in fulfilling both of these essential mandates? If not, let's begin by looking at the technical definition of the Great Commission.

The Textbook Definition

One of the greatest personal evangelists of the modern era, is Dr. Bill Bright. Here's how he defines the Great Commission in his book, *Witnessing Without Fear*: 'What I do know is that God has made it crystal clear in His Word that every Christian is to "Go and make disciples in all nations...and then teach these new disciples to obey all the commands I have given you" (Matthew 28:19,20 TLB).'[2]

Elsewhere Bill Bright observes, 'Jesus Christ's last command to the Christian community was, "You are to go into all the world and preach the Good News to everyone, everywhere" (Mark 16:15, TLB). This command, which the church calls the Great Commission, was not intended merely for the eleven remaining disciples, or just for the gift of evangelism. This command is the duty of every man and woman who confesses Christ as Lord. We can not pick and choose which commands of our Lord we will follow.'[3]

Now that's the *technical* definition of the Great Commission. However, the congregation back in California understood the technical definition. What they were missing was something a bit less tangible. It's this 'something else' that's the *real crux of the issue* for getting believers *on fire* and engaged in evangelism. Pastors have tried teaching, encouraging, and in some cases 'guilt-tripping' their people into obeying the Great Commission with very little success in most cases.

I firmly believe that believers need to learn the Bible's instruction about the Great Commission. And for those that need to be swatted on the rump, perhaps a little guilt wouldn't be such a bad thing. But what the Church of today needs is *not* more teaching and cajoling about the Great Commission. What it needs is a *heart for the lost!* How can we get one? Let me share some of my own personal struggles in this area by way of example. My hope is that by seeing yourself in this story, God will help you gain *practical* understanding into the Great Commission.

An Evangelism Washout

I'll never forget the first time I tried to share my faith. I was a complete failure. To make matters worse, it happened while I was a student at Westminster Theological Seminary. Aren't seminarians supposed to know how to share the gospel? I didn't. I signed up for a class in evangelism my first year. Later I was surprised to discover the class met in a home in downtown Philadelphia. We were actually going to do evangelism! The problem was that I didn't want to *do* evangelism – I merely wanted to sit in a class and get some head-knowledge. Was I ever in for a surprise!

I suspect it was rather evident to the class instructor – the late Dr. Jack Miller – that I was only attending the class in mind and body, but not in spirit. One day he literally grabbed me by the arm and dragged me over to a young Hispanic boy. Jack looked at the boy and asked, 'What's your name?' He replied, 'Enrique.' Jack said, 'Enrique, this is John. John, this is Enrique. John, Go!' I knew what he meant. Dr. Miller wanted me to share the gospel with this fellow. I remember looking at Enrique with somewhat of a blank stare on my face. Then I thought that I'd better say something before Dr. Miller got the impression that I really didn't know how to share my faith.

So I started to talk. I said something about sin, a little something about Jesus, and muttered something else about faith. None of it made any sense. To make matters worse, I was absolutely scared out of my wits. And Enrique knew it. Finally Dr. Miller jumped in and bailed me out. He told Enrique about his spiritual need and all that Christ had done to reconcile him to his heavenly Father. Although Enrique didn't receive Christ that day, at least he heard a clear presentation of the gospel from Dr. Miller.

As I drove home, I couldn't get Enrique out of my mind. Where did I fail? Then it hit me. Although I hadn't yet learned how to articulate the gospel in a clear fashion, the *real* problem was deep in my heart – I didn't care about Enrique. *I had absolutely no heart for the lost.* After I got back to my rented room, I walked upstairs and lay on my bed. I began to cry. I prayed, 'God, here I am at one of the world's greatest seminaries. But deep down, I'm nothing but plastic. Please God, either make me real, or get me out!' Either God was going to fill me with a love for the lost, or I was committed to leaving seminary and never entering the ministry. I'm not sure exactly what happened, but at that moment, something warm came over me. I felt different.

Growing an Evangelist in the Pressure Cooker of Life

That summer I went home to Ft. Lauderdale. Although I needed a summer job, I was committed to finding a way to develop my new evangelism muscles. I didn't know when I would have the time to evangelize, because I needed to work a summer job in order to return to seminary. God really came through. Dr. Ross Bair hired me that summer to go door to door sharing the gospel in his community of Coral Springs, Florida as a representative of the Coral Springs Presbyterian Church. Wow! Not only did I find a job, I was actually hired to do evangelism! But I had no idea what I was in for.

Each day I woke to find myself gripped by the same fear that overcame me in the streets of Philadelphia. The difference was God had changed my heart. There was power to overcome the spirit of fear and timidity that stalked me daily. It was burning hot that summer as I trekked all over Coral Springs. I shared the gospel with people in front of stores, on sidewalks, and in restaurants.

I must have walked over 100 miles going door to door and telling anyone who would listen about Jesus. But as the weeks passed, it became all too obvious that no one had received Christ. Then late August came with my need to think about returning to seminary. But I was deeply troubled that no one had responded to the gospel. I asked God to move in someone's heart before I had to return to school.

I'll never forget my very last day in Coral Springs. It was literally the last hour of the last day of my summer job. I was walking down the middle of the road with homes on both sides – with my shirt sleeves rolled way up and sweat absolutely rolling down my face onto my already soaked shirt. I prayed, 'God, please – just one – let me see just one person accept you.' Then out of the corner of my eye, I noticed a man standing on his front lawn. He yelled, 'Hey, what are you doing?' I yelled back that I was with the Coral Springs Presbyterian Church and was out sharing good news with anyone who would listen. To my amazement, he actually seemed interested.

Without hesitation I stopped and introduced myself. He said, 'My name is Lindsay.' Slowly I turned the conversation to the gospel. Then all of a sudden Lindsay said, 'You know – I'm a pilot. And sometimes when I'm 30,000 feet in the air, I can't help but think about eternal things.' You could have knocked me over with a feather. But if that wasn't enough, Lindsay invited me into his home. As we talked about Jesus it was very clear God had prepared Lindsay for the gospel. In fact, I didn't even have to ask him if he wanted to receive Christ. Lindsay told me. We bowed our heads and prayed.

It was through these experiences and countless similar experiences, I've learned a valuable lesson. Christ never expected men to fully *understand* the Great Commission before obeying it. Much less did He ask us to treat it as a mere theological concept to be parsed and scrutinized – much like I planned to do as a seminarian. The Great Commission is to be *obeyed*. It is when we obey Christ's last directive to His Church that God begins to develop in us a love for the lost and the persevering hope for their salvation.

No didactic method can replace real-life experience for teaching us the meaning and all-importance of the Great Commission. Nor can the classroom substitute for revealing our ingrained resistance to sharing Christ. Until we obey our Lord's simple command to 'Go', we will not fully see our fears and prejudices that have kept us from becoming dynamic witnesses for Christ. Nor will we experience the power of God made available to us, which alone can overcome our fleshly insecurities and is able to transform us into men and women with hearts for the lost.

The First Command: the Cultural Mandate

The first command God gave to man – but second in our study – is the Cultural Mandate. This mandate is found in Genesis 1:28: 'And God blessed them; and God said to them, "Be fruitful and multiply, and fill the earth, and subdue it; and rule over the fish of the sea and over the birds of the sky, and over every living thing that moves on the earth."

God's order to the original couple represented a comprehensive directive to bring the primitive earth into submission to the will of man, as man himself served as God's representative, His 'viceroy.' Man is quite distinct from the rest of creation because he is the only creature that is created in the image of God. Man's unique relationship to God places him in the singular position to govern the earth on heaven's behalf. From the time of earliest man, humans have cultivated the soil, used the earth's produce to feed and clothe themselves, and have domesticated and harnessed animals into service. However, we must be careful not to take God's command to 'fill the earth and subdue it' in the passive sense only. In other words, we are to do more than merely spread out and occupy the earth until the Lord returns. As Meredith Kline has put it, this is a mandate for 'maximal global mastery.'[4] It is therefore from this command that the Church recognizes its *active* role to claim every area of culture to the glory of God – including politics, the fine arts, science, law, medical ethics, and more.

While this latter emphasis is part of the Cultural Mandate, it is not especially clear from Genesis 1:28. Some time ago, my wife Bonnie and I were discussing a political issue. At some point in the conversation I made reference to the Cultural Mandate. Bonnie said, 'Where is that in the Bible again?' I told her it was in Genesis 1. She thought for a minute and remarked, 'You know – I've often wondered about that text. How in the world did we get our responsibility to claim politics and other areas of culture for the glory of God from God's command to rule over the animals?' Good question.

The Cultural Mandate and Developing Nations
In time, man's progressive stewardship of the earth would lead him from his humble agrarian beginnings to using his ingenuity to develop all the earth's resources for the advancement of worldwide civilizations. The Scripture says, 'Then the Lord God took the man and put him into the garden of Eden to cultivate it and keep it' (Genesis 2:15). The word 'cultivate' (cf. Genesis 2:15), comes from the Latin root, *cultere*, meaning cultivator or planter. This root also gives us the word 'culture,' which is a general term we use to describe the ways of life associated with a people-group or civilization. This means that man's work of cultivating the earth is an all-inclusive concept that extends to every sphere of life where man's mind and hands are employed to control and utilize the processes of nature for the good of all. In his book, *Decisive Issues Facing Christians Today,* John R.W. Stott describes the scope of the Cultural Mandate: 'Developing tools and technology, farming the land, digging for minerals, extracting fuels, damming rivers for hydro-electric power, harnessing atomic energy — all are fulfillments of God's primeval command.'[5]

Nevertheless, because men have instinctively obeyed God's command to subdue the earth, it does not follow that every work performed by man in the cultivation process is a work God approves. The creation account records that man's job of cultivating the earth was to be an extension of the Maker's will for His creation, that it reflects His goodness.

The Scripture says, 'God saw all that He had made, and behold, it was very good' (Genesis 1:31). The creation was 'very good' not because it bore a goodness apart from God, but because it was made by a very good God. The inseparable connection between the goodness of God and His good creation means that the Cultural Mandate cannot be seen apart from the ethical concerns of the Creator. Man may only cultivate the earth within the bounds of how God defines 'very good.' Granted, God's curse upon the earth (in response to man's rebellion in the Garden), means that the earth has lost its unspoiled quality and is no longer 'very good'. However, God's unchanging goodness, as revealed in Scripture, still acts as the ultimate, ethical standard for man's labour in the culture and throughout the earth.

Nevertheless, the earth today abounds with the thorns and thistles of unethical men who are attempting to cultivate God's earth to the glory of Satan. This brings up an important question: Does the mandate to 'rule' over the earth include an additional prescription to *oppose* the evils of culture? In other words, is it enough to advance God's holy standards in culture, or are believers also called upon to *combat* unrighteousness when it threatens to destroy culture? The answer is that believers are indeed called to this more negative side of the mandate as well. Because the cultivation of the earth is to reflect the moral principles of the Creator, a redeemed people must *challenge* Satan's illegitimate grab for control of society and to bring the earth, and all it contains, into conformity with the express goodness of God. Thus, the cultivation process is more than the mere by-product of people seeking *subsistence*, but also must include their active *resistance* when society's norms run counter to God's claims.

In his book, *The Culture of Disbelief: How American Law and Politics Trivialize Religious Devotion*, Stephen Carter argues that even though faith is inherently at conflict with the prevailing culture, to deny believers access to the debate over what is best for society is to deny them the expression of their faith. Carter acknowledges the danger of mixing religious and political entities too closely, but adds that the larger threat comes when the Church's voice is no longer welcome in discussions affecting public life. Carter's position is that one cannot separate the secular from the religious, for believer's participation in civic affairs is itself a religious act. For him, society must uphold and defend the ability of citizens to practice their faith, even when that practice breaches the limits of political correctness.

I agree with most of Carter's points, especially that a consistent faith is one that is prone to resist the accepted norms of secular society. However, where I believe Carter is in error is in his assumption that the starting point for this resistance is faith itself. Faith is not the basis for the Church's stand in the culture. God is. This is the point communicated by my third building block of a biblical worldview: 'God is a jealous God. Because God is the source of all life, He insists on being included and worshipped in every area of life.'

We must not underestimate the importance of the above distinction. For if the elimination of the Church's voice from the cultural debate was nothing more than the suppression of people's faith, would not this suppression be justifiable, at least in those cases where faith had no public component?

For example, the Quakers have purposefully built a religious sub-culture, which allows them to argue that their faith would *not* be invalidated should someone attempt to silence their position on 'gays in the military', for instance. But God did not place an option clause on the Cultural Mandate, which says, 'Pietists need not obey.' To 'rule' the earth is a command. It is a mandate intended to further God's good purposes for the earth – those that reflect His righteous character. When God and His grand design for planet earth are seen as the justification for the Cultural Mandate, it is not the expression of our faith that is denied when the world attempts to marginalize the Church's voice in the public square. Rather, it is God Himself who is being denied His rightful role in all things.

Until Christ returns for His Bride, the Cultural Mandate remains the Church's prime directive to dress the earth in a beauty and splendor that befits the Creator. But where there is perversity, it remains our role as redeemed men and women to challenge it and to expose it for what it is – a vain attempt to dethrone the Creator.

How the Great Commission Serves the Cultural Mandate

Although many Christians have heard about the Cultural Mandate, perhaps less is known about it than the Great Commission. This is unfortunate. For had not our first parents fallen into transgression, the Cultural Mandate would have remained God's *only* directive to man regarding his role in the world. Put another way – Genesis 1:28 reveals the Cultural Mandate to be the *real* Great Commission for redeemed man! As a result, the Great Commission is not simply a means to populate heaven. Rather, Christ gave us the Great Commission as a way to gather an army of redeemed men and women for the work of the Cultural Mandate.

Dr. D. James Kennedy told a story before a Baptist assembly about a woman who asked him what he planned to do with all the people he was leading to Christ. The question caused him to pause and think. Over time, an answer began to formulate in his mind. The mission would be to lead as many people as he could to Christ and then enlist them into the work of transforming the culture for the glory of Christ. This is an important concept.

How the Cultural Mandate Serves the Great Commission

Now we have seen how the Great Commission serves the Cultural Mandate. Yet, there is also a way in which the reverse is true: the Cultural Mandate serves the Great Commission. In 1997, I wrote *Do You Have a Biblical Worldview?* The small booklet takes all the major themes associated with biblical worldview and boils them down to the size of a gospel tract. One Southern Baptist pastor was particularly interested in the booklet. However, he let me know right off the bat he was leery about the Cultural Mandate. He said, 'I don't want anything to do with that theology that says we're going to restore the world to a point, and then turn it over to Jesus when He returns.' The pastor was referring to what is popularly known as Dominion, or Kingdom theology. Some people call it Christian Reconstructionism, or Theonomy. It holds that the Church's job is to turn over a *near-perfect* world to the Lord at His return, who shall then make all things *absolutely* perfect.

At any rate, not only did I manage to convince the Southern Baptist pastor that I wasn't a theonomist, I even excited him about the booklet to the point he ordered several hundred! What did I say that calmed his fears?

I shared that the Cultural Mandate is God's instrument to create a flourishing context for the reception of the gospel in the world, not a means to usher in the millennial reign of Christ. To prove my point, I took him to Acts 17, where we find Paul addressing the Athenians at Mars Hill. The 'Areopagus' was a court where questions of a religious nature were discussed and decisions were reached. However, by the time Paul arrived in Athens, the court had degenerated into a place where all the Athenians did was debate, argue, and discuss the latest religious fad. Decisions were a thing of the past. Verse 21 says the Athenians 'used to spend their time in nothing other than telling or hearing something new'. The Athenians were not prepared for what they were to hear from Paul. His message was more than just another 'twist on life.' His was the gospel of Jesus Christ.

Part way into Paul's sermon he says, 'and He made from one, every nation of mankind to live on all the face of the earth, having determined their appointed times, and the boundaries of their habitation, that they should seek God, if perhaps they might grope for Him and find Him though He is not far from each one of us; for in Him we live and move and exist, as even some of your own poets have said, "for we also are His offspring" (Acts 17:26-27). Paul is saying to the Athenians that the Creator is responsible for placing all order and design in the world. Although scholars are split over the exact meaning of Paul's use of 'appointed times' and 'boundaries of their habitation', clearly Paul is here describing a highly organized world that owes its design features to the Creator.

However, important as this is, it is the *purpose* Paul assigns to this order that is our interest. Paul says the reason God placed order in the world is so we 'should seek God'. In other words, God has established order to better facilitate man's coming to God. The fact is that anarchy does not provide an environment conducive to honest religious inquiry. There's just too much flying around. However, where there is order and our surroundings are not fighting for our attention, our hearts and minds are free to focus on the more important issues bearing eternal weight.

In both Genesis 1:28 and 9:1-7, God intends the Cultural Mandate to serve as His directive to redeemed man to maintain the order God placed in His world, better enabling all men to seek the truth. It is in this sense of upholding and conserving the creation in its balance and design, that the Cultural Mandate serves the Great Commission. For where there is lack of order, men are preoccupied with non-order. But where there is peace, men are free to discern the meaning behind their liberty. They are free to both hear and respond to the call of God upon their lives.

Let me illustrate. In 1992, Hurricane Andrew hit South Florida displacing literally thousands of people. Within hours of the devastation, well meaning friends of mine wanted to run down to Homestead to pass out gospel tracts. But I implored them to wait until at least a modicum of order returned to the area. My fear was that people would be so upset they would not be able to give the evangelists any attention. My recommendation to my friends was first to practice the Cultural Mandate. I said, 'Help clear the rubble and just be "salt" in Homestead until order is re-established. Then after things have calmed down a bit – begin to practice the Great Commission.'

A Circular Argument

Now the question becomes, 'How does God define *order*?' By His standards found in the Bible. When culture is operating by God's standards, it helps to fulfill God's eternal plan of salvation. Thus, we are faced with a circular argument. God's plan includes using you to share the gospel so that people will receive Christ. This is the Great Commission. But it doesn't end there. God will then use you to shape culture – indeed *every* area of life – according to His standards. This is the Cultural Mandate. As God's standards are applied to the world, order is preserved creating conditions that contribute to *more* people receiving Christ. And on it goes.

Between the Great Commission serving the Cultural Mandate, and the Cultural Mandate serving the Great Commission, I contend that the latter relationship is the more important one. Unless the Cultural Mandate is principally seen as a *servant* of the Great Commission, we will run the risk of allowing the Church's earthly agenda to over-shadow its heavenly agenda. The Cultural Mandate is not an end in itself. It is a means toward an end – the building of God's *spiritual* kingdom on earth.

Now let's look at the principle *means* that God has chosen for His Church to use in fulfilling His twin mandates.

five

REACHING THE
WORLD GOD'S WAY

I'll never forget the summer of 1989. Each year, a group of churches that are part of my denomination run a youth camp near the New Jersey shore. I was invited to be the guest speaker that summer and James Ward performed a concert the final night. I was both excited and terribly nervous. Although I had preached in many different settings, I had never spent an entire week speaking to a hundred or so middle school and high school students.

As I spoke to groups of kids day and night, I began to wonder if I was really connecting. A few kids were quite gracious to tell me how much they appreciated my words, while others walked away with a look of indifference. One evening, everyone – kids and staff – was expected to gather in the main auditorium for a special evangelistic service. Again, I was the speaker. But mere hours before I was to speak, the thought popped into my head to forget my prepared message. I reasoned, 'Why on earth am I even contemplating not doing my message? It's the only thing I know for tonight.' But somehow I knew to drop my prepared words.

The problem was I didn't have anything else on my heart to share that evening. After flipping through the pages of the Bible, I landed in I John. I began to read and meditate. But the only thing running through my mind was that I John was written in large part to refute the destructive teachings of the Gnostics. I thought, 'I can't go up in front of a swarm of young people and expect to keep their attention speaking about first century Gnosticism!' But something told me that was exactly what I was supposed to do. I prepared a few notes, said a prayer, and headed for the auditorium – all the while thinking, 'There's absolutely *no way* this is going to work.'

The evening started with announcements and singing. I had preached in churches, tents, revival meetings, on street corners in the snow, and in the parking lots of New England factories in freezing cold conditions. But nothing had prepared me for how frightened I felt that night. In my flesh, I was fully convinced the message I was about to deliver was going to bomb, and the kids were going to sit in their seats like concrete statues during the altar call. Then suddenly, as I was mulling over my options, I heard, 'and now our speaker for tonight – John Barber.'

I don't remember much about my less-than-memorable talk on Gnosticism, other than stressing the need to live righteously in our bodies, as well as in our hearts and minds. And I did preach Christ, although rather feebly, I thought. But I do recall the close. Most of the kids were either talking or looking like they couldn't have cared less about my message. I thought, 'I knew this was going nowhere. Why didn't I stick to my prepared speech?' In rather uncharacteristic fashion, I mumbled my way through a call to the group to come forward for prayer – either for salvation or any personal needs. No one moved. I asked again. As I expected, not a single kid moved. Then a couple of 'cut-ups' began to snicker and laugh. It was all a big joke to them. However, I was feeling a sense of dread and embarrassment.

Then it happened. A young boy stood and came forward. I recognized him immediately. It seemed that the young man was slightly handicapped – so I was told. He was a good boy with a big heart. But his mannerisms – and the bit of saliva that was almost constantly swimming on his lower lip – were a little hard for some kids to work through. Each day I witnessed him trying hard to get the others to accept him and invite him into whatever they were doing. When that didn't work, he'd just butt in on conversations, act a little crazy – anything to attract attention. But his actions only made matters worse.

A few kids from his church showed great compassion for him, but most of the group really didn't have time.

Well – there he was – walking to the front with every eye glued to him. Even the laughing stopped. But because he wasn't familiar with 'altar calls', instead of facing me, the young man turned and faced the auditorium full of kids. In fact, he stood so close to me, his left shoulder actually touched mine. What happened next was one of the most amazing things I've ever had the pleasure to witness.

There was something compelling about the fact that the young man made eye contact with the other kids – many of whom had shunned him so openly that week. I honestly believe that had he faced me, the effect would not have been the same. The kids could see the sincerity in his eyes – eyes that throughout the week had a glazed and confused look. But now the young man's eyes appeared clear and the kids could see the difference. Soon a softening of hearts began to move through the room. It began at the front, and made its way through the first several rows of seats, and didn't stop until every kid in the auditorium had been touched by it.

I gave one more invitation and it happened. Suddenly, the chairs began to empty. Not just a couple, not just a few, but row after row came forward to call upon the Lord. I stood in absolute awe and amazement. As soon as kids came up, tears would begin rolling down their faces. Several girls to my immediate left were weeping so hard they had to be helped back to their seats. Some kids were kneeling. Other were holding each other. Then I looked out across the auditorium and there was not a single young person still sitting. The only reason some couldn't come forward was because there simply wasn't room enough at the front. I put the microphone to my mouth to say a few words and I thought, 'No – just let them talk to God.'

Honestly, I don't recall everything that happened that night. But I do know this: God was glorified. Many young people accepted Christ that night, while backslidden teens got right. Repentance filled the room. A young man even approached me to ask for forgiveness. He had apparently said some things about my teaching that week that were less than complimentary. He looked at me, motioned his hand across the room, and said, 'But look at this.' I knew what he meant.

God reinforced two important lessons to me that night. First, Christ has *all authority* in salvation. God really didn't need my scripted speech to win a room full of lost kids. All He required of me was to preach the gospel. As the fourth building block of a biblical worldview makes clear, 'God is all-powerful.' He is the One who 'spoke, and it was done; He commanded, and it stood fast' (Psalm 33:9).

Second, God has chosen the *preaching* of the Word as the principal means to win the lost to Himself. Paul writes, 'God was well pleased through the foolishness of the message preached to save those who believe' (I Corinthians 1:21). Undoubtedly God used that young man to help 'break the ice' for other kids to come forward, but in the final analysis, it was the power of the gospel that melted their hearts. As we shall soon see, it is the first building block of a biblical worldview, God's self-existence, that assists us in gaining insight into 'why' God has chosen the foolishness of preaching to save people.

The Authority to Proclaim

In the last chapter we saw that God's *strategy* to achieve His goal of restoring all of life includes both the Cultural Mandate and the Great Commission. Now we need to examine the principal *means* God has ordained to carry out His dual strategy. Building upon the two lessons reinforced in me back at the Jersey shore, let's focus first on the Great Commission, and the principle of *authority and the preaching of the Word.* (Note: here it is not my purpose to restate points about the Great Commission that are currently available in other fine books and articles. I only wish to focus on what is weak among us – what is lacking. Yet, with respect to the Great Commission, what is lacking today may be the most important element.)

Christ begins His commission to His Church saying, 'All authority has been given to me in heaven and on earth' (Matthew 28:18). Jesus' last words to His disciples remind us of His first words calling men to become His disciples, 'Repent, for the kingdom of heaven is at hand' (Matthew 4:17). The kingdom of heaven came with power and authority to challenge Satan's domain. Now, according to Jesus, His authority is complete – having conquered sin, death, and the grave in the flesh.

That Jesus is now in complete charge of heaven and earth means the Great Commission is first and foremost a matter of *authority.* The presentation and teaching of the gospel should convey that *every* person belongs to Christ and He alone holds exclusive rights over all creation. It is not in keeping with the gospel of the kingdom to tell men, as the French thinker Blaise Pascal suggested, that deep in their hearts is a 'God-shaped vacuum', only Christ can fill. Sin has rendered the *whole man* empty. His life – if it can be called that – is like the crumpled wreck of a stolen car left by the thieves after it has been stripped for parts. But Jesus purchases the mass of metal and freely offers to restore it *only* if it is understood that He is the sole owner with exclusive rights to drive the car whenever, and wherever He wants.

But we need to do more than tell people *about* Christ's authority. It is *in* His authority that the evangelism/discipleship task is completed. God does not, nor does He expect us to, use bait-and-switch tactics or non-threatening worship environments to turn men to the cross of Jesus. Only Christ's authority – His power – is able to regenerate the hearts of men dead in sin and trespasses and bring them to salvation. No man, no manner of conversation, and no contemporary worship service can replace the sovereign authority of Christ that changes men from enemies of God into His friends.

A Prophet in Training

The fact that Christ – by His authority alone – is able to change hearts was central in God's instruction to Ezekiel. The vision of the valley of dry bones should be a familiar story. The Bible says, 'The hand of the Lord was upon me, and He brought me out by the Spirit of the Lord and set me down in the middle of the valley; and it was full of bones. And He caused me to pass among them round about, and behold, there were very many on the surface of the valley; and lo, they were very dry' (Ezekiel 37:1-2).

Here we find the Lord literally compelling the prophet into the valley to look upon the dead, dry bones. The Bible says that Ezekiel concluded that the bones were indeed very dry. Why would the Lord insist that Ezekiel look at the bones to see that they were dry? God is planning to use Ezekiel to prophesy over the bones and raise them anew.

What real difference does it make that Ezekiel knows the true condition of the bones if his only role is that of prophet? *Unless Ezekiel fully appreciates the extent of the problem, he will never fully appreciate the extent of the answer.* Therefore, the self-existent God placed Ezekiel in the valley to 'see the world the way God sees it' (first building block of a biblical worldview), in all its sin, death, and complete hopelessness. By showing the world as a valley of dry bones, God made His point to the prophet that it would take something with a *supernatural* element in it for the bones to live again. Only when Ezekiel had fully internalized this truth was God ready to use the Prophet – and not a moment sooner. But has the Church of today forgotten this all-important lesson? Have we come to trust in our own human efforts to win the lost?

Medicine for the Dead?

Today, far too many Christians have become desensitized to the true spiritual condition of the world. Things are no better in the pulpit. With the slow erosion of American social mores has come a slacking of profound insights and dynamic preaching on sin and salvation from many American pulpits. Although it is difficult to trace the problem, I believe preaching begins to fail with the notion that things in the world are not as bad as they appear. When this happens, the supernatural element that accompanies the preaching of the gospel is replaced with human innovations to reach unbelievers.

Although the theological position of many ministers of the gospel today is that man is dead in sin – a valley of dry bones – they preach *as if* he were just sick and weary, in need of a doctor rather than the *Lord* of life. What he needs is advice, encouragement, and therapy. Where the therapeutic approach fails, it's not because people are flat out dead in sin. No, it's because we live in a 'post-Christian' era – a time when truth is no longer appreciated as truth and when it takes meaningful friendships to prepare people to accept Christ. But the world is far worse than post-Christian. It is dead.

Philosopher Jeremy Bentham was the father of utilitarianism. When Bentham died, he gave orders that his entire estate be given to the University College Hospital in London. However, there was one condition. His body was to be preserved and placed in attendance at all the hospital's board meetings. This was duly carried out, and for many years Bentham was wheeled up to the board table and the chairman said, 'Jeremy Bentham, present but not voting.'[1]

Bentham's deceased condition is the sinner's condition. Although the sinner is among us, he is incapable of casting a vote in favour of Christ. Paul writes, 'And you were dead in your trespasses and sins' (Ephesians 2:1). It is from this verse, and from many others, that we learn of man's 'total depravity'. With regard to man's relationship with God, he is spiritually dead and therefore unable to do anything for his salvation. In his commentary on Ephesians 2:1, D. Martin Lloyd-Jones compares sinners to zombies. 'Life for the non-Christian is a living death...You cannot say anything beyond saying that a man is dead. It is not 'almost dead', he is actually dead; it is not 'desperately ill', it is 'dead'.'[2] Sinners are literally dead men walking. Not just dead men walking, but stinking, decaying, and putrefying dead men.

When will the Church come to grips with what it means to be dead in sin? *Everything* from the crown of a sinner's head to the tip of his toes is *ethically* dead and separated from God. Thus, the born-again experience cannot come at the end of a sinner's honest inquiry or spiritual journey. The new life Christ imparts happens through *resurrection*. It takes place the second Christ raises a spiritually dead heart to life through His power and authority. It is *this* power and authority we should seek in our evangelism and continue to seek in discipleship.

The present attitude in the Church that men are dead in sin – but not really – fails the biblical test. There is no special music, no church drama, no twenty-minute pep talk on faith and family, and no church picnic that has the power to make sinners anything less than graveyard dead. The valley of dry bones says that apart from the raw power and authority of Christ working directly upon the hearts of men bringing them from spiritual death to life, man and all of his modern devices is totally incapable of providing a reasonable substitute.

Any method of evangelism built upon the premise that all men need is a little something more, or a little something less, to help them reach a decision for Christ is a house built upon an unsure foundation. The only thing that can win men back from the dead is the all-powerful gospel, backed by the authority of Christ, applied directly to the problem of sin. The evangelistic method or church service that reflects less than this truth stems from a non-biblical view of the nature of man.

The Church would not be in need of Christ's authority if men were not dead in sin. Then we would need every earthly technique at our disposal to convince men of their need for Christ. But because men are dead in sin, the *only thing* capable of addressing their need is an authority *greater* than death. That authority is found only in Christ who conquered death by rising from the dead. Now we arrive at what is God's principal means on earth to carry out the Great Commission.

All the Trimmings Without the Bird

The Word of God preached is Christ's principal means to win the lost. The proclamation of the gospel is the *spearhead* of the Great Commission. The relationship between Christ's authority and preaching is this: the gospel is never proclaimed without being joined to the Spirit of the Lord who has the authority to raise sinners to new life. The authority of Christ to raise the spiritually dead is the key to understanding preaching and vice-versa. If men were not dead in sin, there would be no need for preaching. We could make do with prayers, hymn singing, and liturgical dance in our services, and counseling sessions would make up our evangelism. But because men are dead in sin, a supernatural element must be introduced into the equation if spiritual life is going to come out of death. In evangelism, preaching meets this challenge because biblical, Spirit-filled preaching is Christ speaking. And when Christ speaks, the dead rise.

Indeed, each step of Ezekiel's ministry is accomplished through prophecy (prophecy and preaching are identical in as much as both are means to proclaim God's Word). He is to prophesy that the bones hear the Word of the Lord (Ezekiel 37:4). He is to prophesy that breath enter the newly formed bodies (vs.9). And he is to prophesy the restoration of these new lives to the land of Israel (vs.12). At each point, it is the words of the prophet, along with the Spirit of the Lord, which provide the catalyst for change among the dead bones.

It is with this understanding of the power of the Word preached, together with the Spirit of Christ working to raise the dead, that Paul writes, 'How then shall they call upon Him in whom they have not believed? And how shall they believe in Him whom they have not heard? And how shall they hear without a preacher?' (Romans10:14)? Paul doesn't say *drama*. He doesn't say *personal evangelist*. He doesn't even say *teacher*. No, he says 'preacher'.

In his commentary on Romans, the late Dr. James Montgomery Boice draws our attention to an important mistake in the New International Version of the Bible: 'The New International Version is mistaken when it adds the word "of" so the text reads, 'believe in the one *of whom* they have not heard.' What it actually says is: 'believe in the one *whom* they have not heard.' The point is that it is Christ himself who speaks to the individual, and that it is hearing him that leads first to belief and then to calling on His name in salvation.'[3] Boice, then, in citing the great New Testament scholar Leon Morris, goes on to say how Christ is heard – through the preaching of God's Word by God's messengers: 'This means that the "word" of Christ is not whatever you might choose to make it. Rather it is the content of Christian doctrine as taught by qualified and appointed preachers. 'The point,' says Morris, 'is that Christ is present in the preachers; to hear them is to hear him."[4]

That there are other means to assist the Great Commission is clear. Not everyone is a preacher. You can use personal witness, films, books, and videos – *whatever* conveys the message of Christ clearly. But here's the problem. Years ago we began to tell laymen they didn't need to be a golden orator to be involved in evangelism. It worked! But now the pendulum has swung to the opposite extreme. Now the task is to convince the Church once again of the necessity of the preacher in the job of evangelism. Today whole evangelistic organizations and missions agencies are at work for the Great Commission in America – and around the world – that have absolutely no time for preachers. In fact, preachers are discouraged from joining many evangelism and missions agencies today for fear that their preaching will not be 'innovative' or that it might upset the apple cart and dissuade sinners from the gospel.

In late 1998, I was discussing this very issue with a prominent church leader. He told me the spread of the early church could be traced in Scripture to laymen sharing their faith and not to 'professional preachers'. To support his position he pointed to Acts 8 where the Bible tells of a great persecution that rose up against the believers in Jerusalem, scattering all except the apostles. The 'laymen', as he put it, then went about evangelizing the regions of Judea and Samaria through personal witness.

It's true that the first evangelistic thrust into Judea and Samaria was lay-driven. However – and as I pointed out to the gentleman – believers in Acts 8 were not simply practicing the art of personal witness, as if all they were doing was talking with people one-on-one about Christ. Rather, the Bible says, 'those who had been scattered went about *preaching* the word' (Acts 8:4, italics added). The persecuted laymen of Acts 8 may not have been professional preachers, but 'preaching' is *exactly* what they did in reaching the lost for Christ!

Today the Church's plan for revival includes praying it in, uniting the clergy, mobilizing key missions organizations for the harvest, and racial reconciliation – everything *but* the singular most effective tool God has given the Church to call the lost to Himself – preaching. But throughout Scripture the proclamation of the Word of God is His *predominant* means for calling nations and individuals to obedient trust. To either eliminate or downplay preaching in any strategy for evangelism is equivalent to inviting people over for Thanksgiving dinner, minus the turkey!

Now let's shift to the Cultural Mandate and examine God's principal means for its accomplishment – *the power of a transformed life.*

Taking Care of What's Important to God

1985 was a difficult year. I was still recovering from back surgery, having broken my back in a weight lifting accident. Somehow I managed to graduate from Yale with a Master of Divinity degree and then start New England Evangelistic Ministries shortly thereafter. The forming of the ministry came at some expense to my ego. I started like so many others. I rented a small office in North Haven, Connecticut, chose a name for my ministry, printed stationary and business cards, and started making phone calls.

My immediate goal was to jump right into the itinerant ministry, focusing on the great spiritual need of New England, and preaching evangelistic meetings throughout the five states. The problem was that very few churches were willing to have an evangelist come to preach for several days. This was the time when 'spiritual life' conferences were beginning to push evangelistic crusades to the back. Even fewer churches were willing to work together with other churches on an area-wide crusade meeting, particularly if the evangelist was anyone other than Billy Graham.

The days turned into weeks and there were no meetings. My short-term debts were beginning to mount. I trusted that my income would be provided, in part, through the churches that requested my ministry. But there were no churches. Then came the day I sat in my office staring at an outstanding bill for a little more than $200. I was literally down to pocket-change. Suddenly I was gripped by a feeling of despair and panic. 'Where was I going to get the money, and why wasn't God using me?' I began to pray.

Within seconds I felt God telling me to take my last few cents, give it away, and He would bless. I reached into my pocket and pulled out a whopping $2.87! I had more than I thought. I tried to reason with God, but to no avail. He impressed upon me the thought that as long as I waited for evangelism to come to me, I would be waiting forever. My ministry was to begin in the world.

I got into my car and headed for downtown New Haven. Soon I walked into a MacDonalds and purchased whatever $2.87 would buy – it wasn't much. Then I proceeded out the door and found a man walking by who really looked like he could use something to eat. I walked right up to him, stuck the bag out, and said, 'Sir, I want you to have this.' With a stunned look on his face he slowly reached for the bag of food. And almost as if he thought it was all a prank, he pulled back his hand. I said, 'No, no, it's really for you – take it please.' He took it. Then with a look of gratitude, he said something in a language

I didn't understand. I replied, 'What does that mean?' He responded, 'That's Aramaic for, "God is with you."' I knew I had the right guy!

I got back in my car and headed to my office. When I arrived, I noticed a message on my answering machine. It was from a local businessman whom I had met several weeks earlier. When we met we shared about ourselves, and I told him my plans for starting the New England ministry. He seemed impressed. I didn't see him again. But here was a message from him. To my amazement, he said that he had written me a $250 check the day after meeting me, but didn't have an address to send it to. He had asked people all over town for my whereabouts or my phone number, in that my listing hadn't yet come out. I called him immediately and went to pick up the check. Within days my bill was paid. What was God saying to me through that experience? It was – *if you take care of what's important to God, God will take care of what's important to you.*

The following weeks would find me right back in the streets of New Haven taking care of what was important to God. Slowly I moved from handing out food to sharing the gospel. I bought a little loud speaker, set it up, and began to preach. I remember one winter in particular standing in front of a nativity scene located near a bus stop and a shopping mall. It worked well for me. I used the scene as a backdrop for the gospel. Many passers-by thought I was part of the display.

I told the Christmas story over and over – in snow, sleet, and rain. For hours I was out in the cold telling anyone who cared to listen about the baby Jesus, and that He alone was the world's promised Messiah. Soon thereafter two young men – Eric Brockway and John Velleco – joined me, and New England Evangelistic Ministries became a reality. The ministry purchased a large gospel tent and we began to hold evangelistic crusades.

Over the next few years I preached approximately 200 evangelistic services in all the New England states, including New York and New Jersey. Did my vision for evangelism become a reality in New England? I believe so. But only after I was first willing to take care of what was important to God.

Walking the Talk

Christ's brilliant summary of the law to 'love the Lord your God with all your heart, and with all your soul, and with all your mind', and to 'love your neighbour as yourself', also summarizes the scope of the Cultural Mandate. Whether we offer food to a less fortunate person, or use our God-given, musical gift in the context of a professional, symphony orchestra, transformed lives demonstrate our love both for God and neighbour, and as a result, help to bring the creation a little closer to the will of the Creator.

It has been said, 'You are the only Bible a person will ever read.' When the world observes our Christian lives, it should see the reality of the gospel, not only in word, but also in deed. By obeying the Cultural Mandate we demonstrate the power of the gospel in deed — in our work, government, society, nation, and world.

The Cultural Mandate, God's first command to man, and the Great Commission, Christ's last directive to His Church, represent God's two-fold strategy to restore all of life unto His glory. We must not emphasize or diminish one to the exclusion of the other. The Church must obey both. We can look at this truth however we like — salt and light, word and deed, Cultural Mandate and Great Commission. But however we look at it, we must live it. We cannot afford to let history pass and let Christ say at the judgment seat we failed to exemplify His heart for His world in its totality while we were yet in it.

Before I tell you where we're going from this point, let's review a few things we've covered so far:

The Sovereignty of God Teaches...

The World and all that it contains is subject to the eternal purpose and plan of God.

God's Purpose for the World is...

To restore everything that was lost at the fall — both in man and in the rest of creation — to its proper role of worshipping and glorifying Him.

God's Master Plan for Achieving His Goal is...

To use His Church in obedience to the Cultural Mandate and the Great Commission.

A Biblical Worldview is...

Seeing the world as God sees it. It is thinking God's thoughts after Him in ALL areas of life.

Building Blocks of a Biblical Worldview are...

1. God's self-existence:
   Necessary for seeing the world the way God sees it.
2. God's unity and simplicity:
   Holds all of life together as a platform for faith.
3. God is a jealous God:
   Because God is the source of all life, He insists on being included and worshipped in every area of life.
4. God is all-powerful:
   God reigns and rules over all of life. Satan can do nothing apart from the sovereign will of God.
5. God's gospel is concerned with the restoration of the whole of life: Everything exists for the glory of God, to which the gospel is committed.

Where We're Headed

Today the Church is divided in its commitment. Typically, Christian, social activists are committed to the Cultural Mandate, while generally Christian pietists are dedicated to the Great Commission. Activists stress institutional change, while pietists contend that real change in society is only possible to the degree that human hearts are changed. While one stresses the earth's needs, the other focuses on the demands of a kingdom not of this world. Like two men – one holding the trunk of an elephant, the other grasping its tail – activists and pietists are failing to appreciate God's *whole* plan to restore planet earth. The result is a lack of biblical balance in both camps.

I propose that the Church, in order to be part of God's purpose to restore all of life unto His glory, must integrate in its life and worship the needs for *both* cultural restoration *and* spiritual discipleship. We must combine the Cultural Mandate and the Great Commission. By merging both mandates, with a view toward restoring all of life unto the Creator's praise, we will produce what I envision as a *new Christian activism*. In the next three chapters, I want to set this new movement in context by way of a critique of both Christian, social activism in America, and its counterpart, American pietism. We begin with the Christian, social activist movement.

Six

THE CHRISTIAN SOCIAL ACTIVIST MOVEMENT

'In May 1979 I called a group of conservative leaders to meet in my office in Lynchburg, to talk about the future and to organize for the long, hard struggle ahead. In spite of everything we were doing to turn the nation back to God, to morality, and to conservative patriotism, the national crisis was growing quickly out of hand!'[1] – so writes Dr. Jerry Falwell about the start of The Moral Majority in his autobiography.

I don't know what you were doing in May 1979, but I certainly wasn't thinking about America's growing moral crisis and what steps could be taken to reverse it. Like so many others, I was focused on my future. If you asked my opinion in 1979 about America's growing intolerance to the notion of moral absolutes, I would have stated quite clearly that we were a nation awash in sin. But what was I doing about it? Nothing. This is one reason I have great respect for men like Jerry Falwell. He is one of the 'doers of the Word', not just a hearer.

Joining Jerry Falwell to form the first board of directors of The Moral Majority were other 'doers', including D. James Kennedy, pastor of the Coral Ridge Presbyterian Church in Ft. Lauderdale, Florida; Charles Stanley, pastor of the First Baptist Church in Atlanta, Georgia; Tim LaHaye, then pastor of the Scott Memorial Baptist Church in El

Cajon, California; and Greg Dixon, pastor of the Indianapolis Baptist Temple.

Yet some twenty years later, Cal Thomas and Ed Dobson – two figures also instrumental in the Moral Majority – wrote a cynical book criticizing the vision and work of the organization and similar organizations birthed shortly after its founding. In the belief that the effort to reclaim American culture has failed, *Blinded By Might*, is a clear shot across the bow of the same conservative, Christian leaders both authors worked closely with in the past. Cal Thomas writes, 'In perhaps the biggest and costliest battle waged by conservative Christians, twenty years of fighting has won nothing.'[2]

I firmly disagree with Cal Thomas and will address his remark in a bit. But now I will offer my own pros and cons of the Christian, social activist movement in America. I believe you'll find my pros more positive and my cons not nearly as condemnatory as those espoused in *Blinded by Might*. Let's begin with the cons.

The evangelical, activist movement is over-dependent on family values as a means to forward the Christian message in America. Even the casual observer of the American political scene has become familiar with the phrase, 'traditional family values'. This oft quoted, yet hotly debated, subject has become the backdrop for Christian conservatives' call for a return to biblical principles in American culture. So important has the cause of family become in our day, that we find the word 'family' in the names of several of the more notable organizations that carried on after the close of the Moral Majority – The Family Research Council, Focus on the Family, and The Traditional Family Values Coalition.

The perception of the family as the cornerstone of Christian, political activism today is commendable. But have we leaned too heavily upon the institution of the family as the standard by which so much that is wrong with America is to be judged? I think so. The problem began with the mistaken assumption that the family is a criterion for righteousness, against which, the values of a culture can be judged.

Although the institution of the family is *the* most important building block within society, only God and His kingdom may act as the standard for righteousness in a nation. Biblically speaking the family has values. However, it's better to say the family *is* a value of a higher truth – the kingdom of God. The family must always be seen as an extension of God's sovereign rule on earth and never presented as a values bearer in its own right. The Bible says of the kingdom of God, 'Thy throne, O God, is forever and ever; A scepter of uprightness is the scepter of Thy kingdom' (Psalm 45:6).

In this regard, the kingdom of God judges the family. The kingdom is also the ultimate standard for all the Church does in the area of politics affecting the family. Only God and His kingdom are the criterion for righteousness in a nation, not the family. This is seen in Psalm 51:4, 'Against Thee, Thee only, have I sinned, and done this evil in Thy sight, So that Thou art justified when Thou dost speak.' Although there is no clearer affront to the institution of the family than adultery, David did *not* say his adultery with Bathsheba was a sin against the family. Rather, David said his sin was *only* against God and nothing else.

In Genesis 9, God didn't make His covenant with the family – although this would have been the perfect opportunity to do so, in that Noah and his family were the only family on earth at that time. The Bible says, 'And God said, "This is the sign of the covenant which I am making between Me and you and every living creature that is with you, for all successive generations; I set My bow in the cloud, and it shall be for a sign of a covenant between Me and the earth" (Genesis 9:12-13).

Although God's covenant with Noah resulted in many blessings to his family, the scope of the covenant is general, including all of nature. Hence, it is called the 'universal covenant' or the 'covenant with nature'. Additionally, it is 'man', not the family that forms the basis of the injunction against murder (vs.6). Even in the Abrahamic covenant, the reference to 'seed' – although it includes Abraham's descendants – is to Christ (cf. Genesis 17:7 KJV; Galatians 3:16). Indeed, the word 'descendents' does not refer to Abraham's physical progeny, but rather to his *spiritual* descendants (cf. Galatians 3:7).

In Scripture, God's grace poured out on families always results from the more important issue of God's faithfulness in His covenants, which serve the still larger purpose of establishing His kingdom on earth. For example, 2 Kings 4 records a family in trouble. A prophet who worked under Elisha died and left his wife and children with a large, unpaid debt. As the story unfolds, God helps the widow, but not merely because He was committed to helping families in distress. God remained faithful to this family because He was committed to His covenant with David. This family lived during the reign of King Jehoram of Israel, meaning that the nation was under the Davidic covenant. Thus, the scriptural foundation for God's mercy to this widow is found in Psalm 146:9, 'The Lord protects the strangers; He supports the fatherless and the widow.' God 'supports' the fatherless and the widow only so far as relieving suffering is a means to establishing David's throne forever (cf. 2 Samuel 7:10-17).

Getting the Horse Before the Cart

What is the purpose of the family? Throughout the Bible, the family is *not* a standard to which a nation's social mores are called to conform. Rather, *the family is a vehicle through which God's righteous standards are manifested in the world and the biblical doctrine of dominion is achieved.* For too long believers have complained that television, movies, and the government are not 'family-oriented.' But God does *not* expect the culture to orient to the family. *God expects the family to orient the culture to Christ!* In the new Christian activism, the family will be seen as a *catalyst* for change in an immoral world. It will act as one of God's principle instruments for subduing the earth in righteousness through the Great Commission, as parents raise up and disciple their children, and through the Cultural Mandate, as godly families help to transform every sphere of society and culture.

Where the Movement Really Went Wrong

Typically, those critical of Christian, social activism charge that activists are building the 'wrong kingdom'. Instead of using spiritual weapons to build God's eternal kingdom, they are trying to use political power to fashion a shiny, Christian kingdom on earth. I reject this criticism. I've never known a Christian activist whose motive was to use political power to build the wrong kingdom.

Here is the *real* problem. By 1979, disgust and concern over the declining state of American culture had reached a boiling point among a majority of evangelical Christians. Unfortunately, many of these people lacked a solid theological base for constructing a plan to address the needs of the culture. This deficiency forced people to rally around concepts they did understand, such as 'family values', 'decency', and 'America's Christian heritage'. It was these concepts which supplied the plank for a true grass-roots movement of social conservatives.

However, language has meaning and with meaning comes substance. Once the social-oriented agenda took shape, it forced the larger and more important issues of the kingdom of God to the rear. When this happened, the spiritual principles, which the movement stood for, began to suffer beneath the weight of the pragmatism that marked its true climb to prominence.

It was assumed by many within the movement that whatever was good for the family, was good for the kingdom of God. But in Christianity, what's good for the goose, isn't always good for the gander. This is something no one foresaw. Jesus said, 'Do not think that I came to bring peace on the earth; I did not come to bring peace, but a sword. For I came to set a man against his father, and a daughter against her mother, and a daughter-in-law against her mother-in-law; and a man's enemies will be the members of his household. He who loves father or mother more than Me; and he who loves son or daughter more than Me is not worthy of Me' (Matthew 10:34-37). According to Jesus, not everything that is friendly to the family is friendly to the kingdom of God.

The second problem I see with the Christian, conservative movement is the insistence that because something is deemed sinful – it threatens the Judeo-Christian value system upon which America was built – it's automatically assumed to be against God's will. This includes everything from punk music to gun control. Personally, I can think of a hundred music groups I'd rather listen to than the Dead Kennedys. And I believe the *real* agenda of many 'gun safety' advocates, like Rosie O'Donnell, was exposed when she said, 'Sorry. It is 1999. We have had enough as a nation. You are not allowed to own a gun, and if you do own a gun, I think you should go to prison.'[3]

However, let me make this point. There comes a time when the Church must acknowledge what God is doing to achieve His master-plan for planet earth — not only through righteous men — but also through the sinful intents of men's hearts. The fact is God is all-powerful (See fourth building block of a biblical worldview). God's power was clearly demonstrated when He hardened the heart of Pharoah as a way to glorify Himself through signs and wonders in Egypt (cf. Exodus 7:3). Paul writes, 'For we know that God causes all things to work together for good, to those who love God, to those who are called according to His purpose' (Romans 8:28). God would not be God unless He was able to work *both* the good and the bad together to accomplish His will.

Although God is not the 'author' of sin, the Bible is replete with examples of God using sin to serve Him. What if God was working His will through a specific sin in America, but the Church opposed it to such a degree we failed to submit to His will? Would we not be fighting God? Here's an example from Scripture to consider.

In I Kings 12, Rehoboam, King of Judah — already blinded by power — rejects godly counsel from the elders who served Solomon, his father, and instead takes the advice of ungodly, less qualified men. The issue revolved around alleged abuses under Solomon, including excessive taxation and the relief people sought from the new king. Rehoboam's rejection of godly advice in the matter was disastrous, leading to the loss of his throne and a divided kingdom. Jeroboam became king in Israel and Rehoboam became king in Judah. But then notice what happens? Rehoboam has a son named Abijah, who becomes king in Judah, who has a son named Asa, who also becomes one of Judah's kings. It is Asa who brings reforms to the nation of Judah, and, along with Rehoboam and Abijah, becomes a major figure in Jesus' family tree (cf. Matthew 1).

Do you see how God used a bad situation to produce good? God used Rehoboam's sin to move him out of Israel into Judah, where there his grandson, Asa, would bring revival and also become a major link in the history of redemption leading to the birth of Christ. God proved Himself sovereign throughout — even in Rehoboam's sin! Indeed, 'the world and all that it contains is subject to the eternal purpose and plan of God'. But if this situation happened today, adjusting for democracy, conservatives would send a delegation intent on getting the president to accept godly counsel. What if he agreed? Would a modern-day 'Asa' be kept from leading a great national revival?

Wisdom: the Activist's Key to an Effective Strategy

What is required on our part is *wisdom* to know how to balance resistance to sin in America, with how God might be using it to further both His temporal and eternal purposes. The first building block of a biblical worldview, God's self-existence, can be of help here. Frankly, left to my own wisdom, I could never discern how God might be using a particular sin to His ultimate advantage. But because God is the self-existent, sovereign Creator of the universe, He has the ultimate 'bird's-eye' view of the issues confronting the Church and the world. He is not part of the problem. He is THE solution. Thus, I can trust in Him. This is why the Bible says, 'But if any of you lacks wisdom, let him ask of God, who gives to all men generously and without reproach, and it will be given to him' (James 1:5). What can wisdom teach us?

Wisdom may tell us to limit our activism to prayer. In essence this is what Jesus did with Peter. The apostle denied Jesus three times in the garden at Gethsemene. Jesus predicted both Peter's denials and the discipline that soon would follow. Satan would sift Peter like wheat. Anyone would have done anything to stop Satan from ravaging the life of his friend. After all, Jesus spent His entire ministry 'doing good, and healing all who were oppressed by the devil; for God was with Him' (Acts 10:38).

However, this was a different situation. Jesus recognized His Father's sovereign hand in the coming discipline upon Peter's life. The only thing Christ purposed to do for his friend was pray: 'but I have prayed for you, that your faith not fail; and you, when once you have turned again, strengthen your brothers' (Luke 21:32). What Christian activism must understand is not everything that goes bump in the night needs to be met with a flurry of phone calls to Congress. There are times when Jesus wants us to do nothing more than pray.

Today there are many areas of American society under God's disciplining hand. Many of my close friends believe that former

President Bill Clinton was not leading America toward God's wrath and chastisement – rather he *was* God's judgment on America! I don't agree, but it demonstrates my friends were at least thinking in the right direction. If they are correct, then following Christ's pattern with Peter, Bill Clinton's alleged misdeeds as President would have provided an opportunity for the Church to limit its activism to prayer.

Wisdom may tell us to take no action. This is an option only if we are convinced it's God's will to permit Satan full sway into something – a movement or an institution – in order to sacrifice it. This is a decision that requires much prayer. And in most cases the decision will require the Church to build new, parallel movements or institutions.

While Jesus hung upon the cross, He was pierced for our transgressions. He was crushed for our iniquities. But the Bible says Jesus did nothing to help Himself. He submitted to His Father's will. He did not even offer a prayer to relieve His condition. Instead, 'He was oppressed and afflicted, Yet He did not open His mouth' (Isaiah 53:7). Do Christians understand that if God wants the Church to sacrifice an area of American culture, submission to His will is more important than mass-mailings designed to turn things around?

A Guide for All Occasions

Regardless of what form of action the Church takes when addressing specific cultural issues, Scripture offers clear counsel on how to deal with all of life's challenges: 'Submit therefore to God. Resist the devil and he will flee from you' (James 4:7). The entire history of modern Christian pietism and activism in America can be balanced on this single verse. For where pietists are inclined to *submit to God,* activists are prone to *resist the devil.*

Pietism assumes that all power in the world – whether good or evil – derives from God, and we are to submit to it regardless of its purpose. Passive resistance, in whatever form it takes, is the only legitimate response to abuse of power. Activism assumes that only that power that is used to reward the righteous and punish evildoers is of God. Proactive initiatives and overt resistance are legitimate responses to oppressive government and cultural malaise. Which is correct?

Both are. Good or bad, God is the 'first cause' for everything that happens in the world (cf. Romans 8:28-30). But the Bible also teaches that the devil seeks to devour us (cf. I Peter 5:8). So, when faced with a trial, how can one possibly know what to do? Should one submit to God, or resist the devil? According to James, we are to *both* submit to God *and* resist the devil in any and all circumstances. This includes Satan's attacks in our personal lives and at every level of culture. This means that on the cultural level we are to submit to God's hand in teen suicide, euthanasia, abortion, lascivious art, and the homosexual agenda – *while at the same time* – standing firm against the devil with all spiritual might. The result is that Satan will flee!

The third difficulty I see with the evangelical, activist movement is its over-dependence on an American political system that provides only short-term gains. Although this book is sympathetic to the goals of Christian, social activism, I readily admit that as a movement, it has leaned too heavily upon the political system as a way to affect the culture. In their zeal for the Cultural Mandate many activists have failed to appreciate what the Great Commission can do to change lives and the role that those lives can play in transforming a nation from within. It's not my belief that Christians shouldn't be involved in politics. Rather, we have come to *depend* far too much upon public policy and not enough upon the power of evangelism to cure the nation's ills.

Politics offers a solution that's only good until it's overturned by a future vote. The gospel changes lives forever. Some time ago, a close friend and Christian lobbyist said to me, 'The political gains we make can be reversed by the next vote, the strike of the pen, or by a liberal judge.' Proving my friend's point, a partial-birth abortion ban was overturned by a liberal judge in Virginia in 1999. Shortly after the judge's bad decision, The Center for Reproductive Law and Policy (CRLP), released this announcement: 'In a victory for pro-choice advocates, today U.S. District Judge Robert E. Payne found Virginia's so-called "partial birth abortion" ban unconstitutional, and issued an order permanently blocking enforcement of the law.'[4]

The CRLP also states, 'Partial-birth abortion laws have been blocked or severely limited in 20 states. Permanent injunctions have been issued in 12 states, including Iowa, Kentucky, Nebraska, and New Jersey, where the statutory definition of 'partial-birth abortion' is very similar to that in the Virginia law. Seven states (Arkansas, Illinois, Iowa, Kentucky, Louisiana, Nebraska, and New Jersey) have appealed final decisions to U.S. Courts of Appeal in the 3rd, 5th, 6th, 7th, and 8th circuits. Abortion providers have appealed a federal court's decision upholding Wisconsin's ban to the 7th Circuit. A narrower ban on certain methods of abortion was permanently enjoined in Ohio. The U.S. Supreme Court denied a petition to hear that case in March, 1998.[5]

This is the world of flip-flop politics. Not only does it affect lobbyists, but also professional politicians. Winston Churchill observed, 'The main qualification for political office is the ability to foretell what is going to happen tomorrow, next week, next month, and next year – and to have the ability afterwards to explain why it didn't happen.'[6] Clearly the Christian would be wise not to put too many of his eggs into the political 'basket'.

Reconciling an Eternal Kingdom with Infernal Politics

I'm convinced the source of much frustration and anxiety among Christian political activists – and for believers in general who support an active Church in politics – comes from more than mere dissatisfaction with the 'system'. The real problem comes from never having reconciled how to fight for an eternal kingdom within a system that only offers a fix for the interim. What is the solution? In the 'new' Christian activism, we must always bear in mind the eternal nature of God's kingdom and fix our eyes on Jesus – the 'author and perfecter of faith'.

The Bible says God's plan to restore all of life began before the foundations of the world (cf. Ephesians 1:4) and will not be complete until all things have been subjected to Christ (cf. I Corinthians 15:26-28). But the point is God's plan *will* be complete! This means the kingdom of God doesn't rise and fall with every congressional vote or strike of the president's veto pen. 'The Lord has established His throne in the heavens; and His sovereignty rules over all' (Psalms 103:19). God's plan for the ages – that He will someday bring all things under subjection to Christ – is as true the day Congress votes to ban partial-birth abortion, as it is the following week when the president may veto it.

Never forget that before the gospel is 'good news', it is first bad news. It reveals a world that has been 'made subject to futility' by God, who has promised to redeem it in hope. Each perceived setback in applying Christ's Lordship to the culture is one more opportunity to 'feel' its futility. But as we learned in our brief study of Ezekiel's experience in the valley of dry bones, God who transforms the world also transforms us. Dashed expectations in our work in the Cultural Mandate and the Great Commission only serve to help us 'see the world the way God sees it' (first building block of a biblical worldview), and to trust Him.

Holding Back the Flood

Now let's move to what I believe is the greatest success of evangelical, social activism. *It has provided a powerful vehicle to restrain evil in America, providing the gospel greater opportunity for advancement.* In Chapter 4, I spoke about the relationship between the Cultural Mandate and the Great Commission. I said, 'It is in this sense of *upholding* and *conserving* the creation in its balance and design, that the Cultural Mandate serves the Great Commission.'

Notice I did not say 'upholding and *preserving* the creation'. As a consequence of man's rebellion in Eden, the rest of the created order was affected. It would no longer yield its bounty easily. God said, 'Cursed is the ground because of you; in toil you shall eat of it all the days of your life. Both thorns and thistles it shall grow for you; and you shall eat the plants of the field; by the sweat of your face you shall eat bread, till you return to the ground, because from it you were taken; for you are dust, and to dust you shall return' (Genesis 3:17-19).

The curse, which God placed both upon man and the earth, including other living creatures, means that the creation is on a 'downhill' slope. It is therefore not possible to 'preserve' the creation as it was in its original state, only conserve it. Put in the language of social activism, it is not possible to eliminate societies' sin, only restrain it.

A few years ago, I was in a car with a Christian lobbyist who worked in Washington, D.C. I asked him what he felt was his role in the kingdom of God. He surprised me. He said, 'All I am is a little boy with his finger in the dike – holding things back while you guys can go out and preach the gospel.' This was one of the more wholesome descriptions of Christian political activism I've heard. But his point was well-taken. Political activism is not a way to save the world. But it plays a *part* in God's plan to save it. It's a non-negotiable part – a way to facilitate the Cultural Mandate by holding back the flood of evil.

Critics charge that Christian engagement in the culture-war has been a colossal flop. Abortion has not been turned back. Public education still doesn't want God in the classroom. And the war to eliminate immorality and vulgarity on prime-time television has produced only more homosexual or lesbian characters. But this is what the critics are missing. What if the Christian influence hadn't been there at all? Can you imagine where we'd be in America today had people like D. James Kennedy, Jerry Falwell, Jim Dobson, and Tim and Beverly LaHaye, not fought to steer the ship away from the rocks? No, they haven't led America into calm waters, but their valiant efforts have certainly spared this nation from a fate far worse!

What if the Moral Majority Had Never Been Born?

People who say over twenty years of activism produced nothing, should look again. Since 1979 America has witnessed a precipitous rise in Christian radio, television, church planting, and mercy ministries. If we think for a second that all this would have happened without culture-minded Christians with their 'finger in the dike', holding back the flood of hedonism and debauchery in our land, we are dead wrong. I tremble to think what egregious inroads enemies of the gospel would have made in the hearts and minds of countless Americans – many of whom have since come to Christ – had activists not stood in the gap to challenge their evil devices.

The media was not favourable to us, but we sure got their attention. They were forced to reckon with our message. During an episode of

'Phil Donahue', Jerry Falwell was a guest along with a woman representing the homosexual/lesbian agenda. At a point where the woman felt Donahue was deferring to Falwell too often, she exclaimed, 'Why are we allowing this man to set the agenda?' Donahue replied, 'Because he is setting the agenda.' Restraining evil by standing in the gap and setting the agenda — just what it means to be 'salt'.

The Salt of the Earth

Jesus said, 'You are the salt of the earth; but if the salt has become tasteless, how will it be made salty again? It is good for nothing anymore, except to be thrown out and trampled under foot by men' (Matthew 5:13). In commenting on what he considers the lamentable product of Christian conservatives in the public square, Cal Thomas writes, 'Politically conservative Christians like to use the salt metaphor as the rationalization for their political involvement. They say that political activism is part of the "salting", or preserving process. But this is not entirely true, perhaps not even mainly true. Salt does its primary work when it is invisible, not when it's seen. Salt preserves, not while in a shaker or in a box on a store shelf, but only when it penetrates the meat or other substance that would spoil without its application. Salt only slows down the spoilage process; it does not preserve forever.'[7]

I believe Cal Thomas is expressing his concern that Christians should spend more time letting their unseen presence be felt in the culture and less time in politics or battling the liberal establishment — at least that's what I think he means. But here's what Matthew 5:13 does mean.

The words of Jesus were spoken during the Sermon on the Mount (Matthew 5-7). Exhortations and warnings from Christ to His followers precede the beatitudes (5:13-16). The sermon as a whole presents a vivid picture of the world as a place of tremendous beauty and design where God superintends His creation by dressing the lilies of the field and arranging each blade of grass (6:27-34). Yet the same creation is tempered by great ugliness. Men have logs protruding from their eyes (7:1-5). Their hypocrisy is so great they are not content to point their fingers while justifying themselves, but their rivalry quickly turns to hate, and hate to murder. For Jesus, there is no distinction between the cause and the effect. Both the inner condition of the heart and the outward act violate God's law (5:20-22). The same applies to adultery and divorce (vv.27-32).

Jesus solves the spiraling threat to society in a single line saying, 'Therefore, however you want people to treat you, so treat them, for this is the Law and the Prophets' (7:12). Some have suggested that Christian, political activists offer overly simplistic solutions to complex issues. If so, then Jesus was the first to lead the way. Crime, the break-up of the family, teen suicide, and more would be stood on their heads if everyone followed this simple verse in the Bible. But Jesus knew men would continue to 'practice lawlessness' (vs.23) until the day of judgment. So, early in His sermon, Jesus exhorts His followers to be 'salt' and 'light' (5:13-16), that the same men with murder in their hearts might turn to God as they see the Church's good works and glorify the Father who is in heaven. What exactly does it mean to be 'salt?'

Politically conservative Christians do *not* 'like to use the salt metaphor as a rationalization for their political involvement,' as Cal Thomas supposes. Christ *compels* us to use it. We don't have a choice. Neither do we have a choice in how, where, and when we are to be salt. God's creation is a complex entity. It includes people, institutions, and forces. The sweeping inclusion of *every* area of life on planet earth in Christ's sermon requires the Church to salt the earth at every level and in every way. There are no modifiers. *'Salt' is a catch-all word that refers to doing whatever it takes – within the bounds of the law of God – to conserve the creation and restrain the putrefying effect of sin in God's world.* The effect is to benefit the spread of the gospel of Jesus Christ, with a view toward global evangelization. Cal Thomas is right that 'salt only slows down the spoilage process'. But it wouldn't matter if it *hastened* the process. If Jesus says to be salt, we must be salt!

Another thing salt does is act as an irritant. Have you ever heard someone say, You're putting 'salt in the wound'? A person once said to me, 'John, all that these Christian groups do is get people mad. Christians should just love others and quit starting wars.' But the world is at war. Jesus never compared the world to 'meat' as Cal Thomas suggests. The overall message of the Sermon on the Mount compares the world to an *open wound*. If salt is applied to a festering wound, don't be surprised when you hear a scream. *The Church is not responsible for the 'war' in culture-war. Warfare is the result of the world's attempt to remove the salt!* Since 1979, restraining the putrefying effect of sin in the world for the benefit of the gospel, is precisely what Christian, social activists have done for all Americans — and they have done a pretty good job.

Now let's look at the pietists.

Seven

IN THE SWEET BY AND BY: AN ANALYSIS OF AMERICAN PIETISM

On the opposite end of the spectrum from the Christian, social activist movement is American pietism. The restricted social activism of pietism is built upon the basic assumption that discipleship is mainly limited to both personal experience and soul winning. In other words, pietists hold that there is no direct application of the Lordship of Christ to either culture or society at large. Therefore, it is always best to take a 'passive' posture toward political and social corruption. After all, as I stated in Chapter 3 in my discussion on the sacred/secular distinction, the pietists' view is that God is only interested in 'religious' things. It is this faulty theological base which serves to encourage the pietist to obey the Great Commission to the virtual exclusion of the Cultural Mandate. This chapter is written to further refute errant pietism. By the way, I feel qualified to refute it because I used to be a practicing pietist.

A Turning-Point
By 1986, New England Evangelistic Ministries was making an impact. Although some invitations to preach came from churches, most of them resulted from initiating contact with pastors and lay church leaders. In 1986, I approached three churches – a Baptist Church, an

Evangelical Free Church, and a Bible Church in North Haven, Connecticut with the idea of sponsoring an evangelistic crusade. All three responded positively. Because I had experience in securing permits from local townships for the purpose of erecting our tent and using school auditoriums to hold our meetings, I volunteered to go to the North Haven Town Hall to get the permit. Our plan was to use the auditorium located in the city's Parks and Recreation facility. I filed the application and waited.

Shortly afterward the city's response arrived. We were turned down! I couldn't believe it. Why were we denied? The letter stated, in no uncertain terms, the town of North Haven no longer granted permits for the use of public space to 'religious' groups and cited a city statue to that effect. I was stunned. I shared the bad news with the leadership of the three churches. At first we didn't know what to do. We talked through several options, but no one seemed to have a handle on a solution. This was the first time any of us had been confronted with such a dilemma.

I had always believed it was wrong to resist secular authority. I based my belief on Romans 13:1, 'Let every person be in subjection to the governing authorities. For there is no authority except from God, and those which exist are established by God', and I Peter 2:13, 'Submit yourselves for the Lord's sake to every human institution, whether to a king as one in authority, or to governors as sent by him for the punishment of evildoers and the praise of those who do right.' But here I was having my view put to the test.

It was during that time Pat Robertson was readying his run for the presidency of the United States. As providence would have it, he was invited to speak at the Yale Law School in neighbouring New Haven. I don't know what prompted me to go, but I went to hear him. His subject was the Supreme Court and its usurpation of authority, particularly as its decisions have affected the right-to-life and the freedom-of-religion movements in America. To my astonishment, I found myself hearing something for the first time.

I had assumed the Supreme Court was a 'human institution' as outlined in I Peter 2:13 and by default had God's approval to speak on any issue. But Pat Robertson spoke about the 'limits' of authority from both the Bible and the U.S. Constitution. His basic thesis was that God has granted to the state the role of securing our natural rights to life, liberty, and the pursuit of happiness, not to be a catalyst for a new social order. Pat Robertson believed the Court had crossed this line citing 'Roe v. Wade' (1973), the landmark decision effecting legal abortion, and 'Engel v. Vitale' (1962), where the Court held that under the First Amendment a state may not sponsor prayers in its public schools.

Although Pat Robertson was speaking on a national level, it only took a second to apply his words to the situation I was facing in North Haven. Instantly I could see the city didn't err by rendering a *wrong* decision on the part of the churches, but by rendering a decision *at all*. It hit me that freedom of religion is not the bailiwick of the state, regardless of where it is expressed – in a church or in the public square. Freedom to worship is an unalienable right from God. The role of the state is to acknowledge it, not to sanction it, much less disapprove it. John the 'activist' was born.

Fighting City Hall

The following day, I contacted leaders from the three churches and urged them to fight North Haven's decision. After a few weeks, it became clear that two churches were not up to the fight, and from the third, only a single elder, Joe Dapino, cared enough to stand with me. I contacted the Rutherford Institute, which put us in contact with attorney Joe Secola. A lawsuit was soon filed against the town of North Haven.

To say that seeing the lawsuit through was difficult is an understatement. Not only unbelievers, but also Christians let me know our stand was unwelcome. Moderates didn't like our 'rock the boat' mentality, while the pious rejected our effort as fighting a 'worldly' battle. A woman who believed prayer was the only remedy to fight injustice said to me, 'We've been praying for eight years for the town of North Haven to change its policy and along you come and bust down the doors!' I replied, 'Ma'am, your prayers have been answered!'

Twenty months later we won the suit, and the town of North Haven was forced to make the statute it used against us constitutional, setting a legal precedent in the State of Connecticut. And how gratifying it was years later to run into people from North Haven who expressed their thanks and told me how often the town's parks and recreational facilities were being used for Christian events to the glory of God.

The Real Beginning of a Worldview

It was my experience with the town of North Haven, Connecticut that sharpened my thinking on the Christian's role in society. An activist Christian is one who is deeply committed to personal piety and who expresses his love for Christ in the world through personal witness. However, is a believer's role in the world complete without addressing the broader issues of culture and society? The answer is no. Not everyone agrees, however. Pietism believes that both cultural and social issues and institutions should not be addressed directly by the Church. Rather, our role is to allow our Christian influence to be felt in society and to lead others to Christ, whereby they too will allow their presence to be felt. Permeating the world with the love of Christ, the pietist concludes, is the best and only biblical way to transform society at large.

There are two main reasons pietists use to justify their philosophy of social disengagement. *First, the Church has no jurisdictional authority in public policy issues. And second, believers are called to be like Jesus, who demonstrated passive resistance to hostile government.* Let's begin with the question of *jurisdictional authority.*

Render Unto Caesar

The view I espoused prior to my North Haven 'awakening' was that government possessed a fundamental right to say and do anything about what goes on in society. But it stands to reason that extending to government broad jurisdiction in all matters pertaining to the common good of man would conversely limit the role of the Church in the same. You simply can't have it both ways. You can't say, for example, that it's the job of the Church and parents to educate children, while at the same time say education is the job of educrats and bureaucrats in Washington, D.C. Certainly the state can facilitate parents in the education of their children, but it is not the right of the state to claim a 'we know best' posture which reduces children to 'wards' of the state and parents to 'field workers'.

The last twenty or so years in particular have witnessed a precipitous rise in the state's encroachment and usurpation of jurisdiction into what are at heart spiritual matters. We are living in a time when both elected and appointed public officials seem less interested in protecting the God-given rights of citizens and are more concerned with heralding the benefits of the 'compassionate state'. Government wants to care for the homeless, provide for the disadvantaged, and level the economic playing field in order to eliminate poverty. While solving moral dilemmas is indeed a noble cause, God has not given this responsibility to the state. Rather, He has called His Church to minister to people's spiritual and physical needs. Because the Church has largely abdicated its healing role in society, the state has been able to turn moral and spiritual matters into public policy issues.

You've heard it said, 'Public policy issues are not the concern of the Church.' But the main reason many issues have become public policy issues in our day is that for many years, the Church did not provide leadership in those areas and thus allowed its issues to be taken over by the world's bully pulpit. So then, when we speak about 'reclaiming America for Christ' or 'restoring all of life to the glory of God', we're not talking about imposing a Christian agenda upon poor, unsuspecting people. Rather, we are simply trying to take back issues and institutions the world stole from us!

Someone might argue that the protestant doctrine of 'common grace' (God's restraint of sin so that unbelievers can do good things for society, but not things that merit God's favor), allows for flexibility on this issue, and to this I would agree. Certainly God can use even a pagan state to do things that are beneficial to its citizens. But this doesn't imply that the state should take charge of welfare or education any more than that it should take over the press or the church. Ultimately, this is a question of competence and jurisdiction. While it is a blessing to live under a government that is seeking to help the poor and seek justice for all, we need to recognize that the historical pattern is that of a state crossing jurisdictional lines because the Church has neglected its God-given mandate. While the State is doing 'good,' God is not receiving the glory for it – how much better it would be if the Church led the way in creating a just society to the glory of our God.

Today the Church as a whole is failing to see it is selling off its birthright for a pot of stew. To permit the state to usurp authority and jurisdiction in areas reserved exclusively by God for the Church to superintend is to turn over the kingdom of God to Caesar. Not only is it the duty of the Church to oversee areas of life that fall within its jurisdiction, but it is also the responsibility of the Church to confront the world when it steals its issues and impersonates the Body of Christ. Now you're probably looking for more examples of how jurisdictional lines between church and state have blurred in America. I'm going to give you some, but first a little theology and history.

Back to the Garden

Let's look once more at the Cultural Mandate: 'And God blessed them; and God said to them, "Be fruitful and multiply, and fill the earth, and subdue it; and rule over the fish of the sea and over the birds of the sky, and over every living thing that moves on the earth"' (Genesis 1:28).

In addition to meaning what I have previously stated, the Cultural Mandate charges man with building and maintaining a civil society that reflects the moral principles of the Creator. Under God's covenant with Adam the family was the only form of human government. Everything was fine until the fall, and sin entered into the world, making civil society reflect the evil heart of man as much as the righteous standards of God. From then on all civil societies would be marked by a tug-of-war between sin and righteousness for dominion over the human race.

To insure that God's will for mankind would prevail over the sinful intents of men's hearts, God instituted formal human government in Genesis 9:5-6. In addition to this negative goal, human government also had a positive goal. The maintaining of civil order was meant to create a peaceable environment for men's practice of *self*-governance in submission to their Creator. Any actions resulting from the institution of human government that either detracted from, or encroached upon, these twin goals, men were to change or remove.

We find, then, there is a biblical basis for limited government. Jesus expressed this fact in concise terms: 'Then render to Caesar the things that are Caesar's; and unto God the things that are God's' (Matthew 22:21). *With respect to balancing our obligation to both God and to government, Jesus meant we should render all that belongs to God and nothing less and to render only that which belongs to the state and nothing more.* The other meaning of this verse is to place before human government a restriction that it not meander into spiritual issues reserved exclusively for the kingdom of God to address. To acquiesce to government's claim over such areas would be the same as demonstrating obedience to a man impersonating a police officer. He has no right or authority.

Perhaps the clearest example of the state going beyond its intended, restrictive role of maintaining civil order is found in I Samuel 13. Israel was confronted by a huge Philistine army camped at Michmash, preparing to fight. As was customary, the priest – in this case Samuel – was to offer sacrifices unto the Lord so Israel would be successful in battle. The problem was that Samuel was detained. Saul waited seven days for Samuel to arrive to no avail. Thus, in the 'interests of the state', Saul offered the sacrifices himself. This was a terrible mistake. Saul, a secular official, took upon himself a priestly role, thus usurping authority and jurisdiction in spiritual matters God never gave to him.

This event marked the beginning of the end of Saul's reign as king. Eventually, the priest arrived at Gilgal, 'And Samuel said to Saul "You have acted foolishly; you have not kept the commandment of the Lord your God, which He commanded you, for now the Lord would have established your kingdom over Israel forever"' (I Samuel 13:13). Saul's compromise of his kingship led to rank corruption (cf. 15:1-9). God's replacement of Saul as king with David was soon to follow. In our day, examples abound of the state usurping jurisdiction over spiritual concerns. Before we look at some, let's look at how the principle of jurisdictional authority is embodied in the Declaration of Independence.

Dependence Upon God Means Independence From Human Restraint

It is the principle of self-government under the Creator that was written into America's Declaration of Independence: 'We hold these truths to be self evident that all men are created equal, that they are endowed by their Creator with certain unalienable rights that among these are life, liberty and the pursuit of happiness.' To illustrate the meaning of the Declaration of Independence, imagine three sacred pathways relating man to God. They are life, liberty, and the pursuit of happiness.

Because God is the author of life, only God has sole authority and jurisdiction in all matters and questions pertaining to life. Because God created the conscience, and Thomas Jefferson was quite clear that liberty first meant liberty of conscience, only God has jurisdiction over the conscience of man. Because the Creator has endowed us with the pursuit of happiness, our greatest degree of happiness is defined by our seeking a deeper relationship with God. Where does the state come in? To protect the rights of its citizen's to life, liberty, and the pursuit of happiness, and to insure that no external force, including government itself, will ever impose its will upon a people who are practicing their Creator-endowed rights. *For this is the essence of liberty: freedom from externally imposed government.* What are some practical examples of the state crossing the line?

Crossing the Line

The trend in American government, both local and federal, is to exceed its God-mandated limits by attempting to assume more of our lives under its authority. Government that fails to recognize the supremacy of God is by its very nature *utopian.* It wants to save everybody. Acting upon this inclination, it believes it, not God, has sole jurisdiction over areas of life, liberty, and the pursuit of happiness.

The result is that life, rather than understood as that which comes from the hand of God, has been redefined by the state as some slime that crawled up a tree and became a man. This evolutionary view of man has led to an evolutionary view of the U.S. Constitution. In 1973, Justice Harry Blackmun was able to discover a 'penumbra' in the Constitution paving the way for a woman to take the life of her unborn child. In 1994, this 'survival of the fittest' mentality led the state of Oregon to be the first to pass legislation permitting a physician to assist in suicide.

The state has also recreated liberty in its own image. Today's government no longer interprets liberty as liberty *to serve* God, but rather as liberty *from* God. It began when government viewed itself as the answer to solving society's moral ills. In order for the state to effectively deal with moral problems, it must control the areas where those problems are found. Inevitably, government's intervention results in a lessening of our freedoms. The sad history of intrusive government is that it always starts as a remedy for social decay, but ends in the suppression of individual liberties.

Thus, government sees the First Amendment to the Constitution less as a protection of religious liberty, and more as a means to scour Christianity from America. In keeping with the message of Old Testament Baal worship that 'the State is your God', the federal government now tries to socialize us. Government employees have been subjected to 'diversity day' training. FAA employees have received indoctrination into mysticism and new-age theology. The Department of Education has pushed God aside, claiming jurisdiction over the conscience of children by handing out condoms and mentally and spiritually programming kids with outcome-based education that destroys the distinction between right and wrong.

Then there is the pursuit of happiness. Jesus never promised happiness. But He did promise the pursuit of happiness. Referring to His commandments, Jesus said, 'If you know these things, happy are you if you do them' (John 13:17 KJV). However, government that rejects God's commands is never satisfied to insure merely the pursuit of happiness. Instead it wants to *guarantee* happiness. Thus we have welfare, affirmative action, and reams of entitlements. We have entire departments of the federal government whose sole job is to minimize risk in business and to insure that everybody plays according to a level playing field. And we have tons of spending programs that transfer wealth from the private sector to the non-capital generating public sector.

The above examples reveal the state's brazen attempt to be Christ in the lives of countless Americans. John warns the Church of the coming of the spirit of Antichrist, 'Who is the liar but the one who denies that Jesus is the Christ? This is the antichrist, the one who denies the Father and the Son' (I John 2:22). We live in a day when many church leaders are calling for revival. *In the new Christian activism the goal of revival will not only be to awaken the Church to do more, but also to get the state to do less.* For how can the Church fulfill its role in the world when the state is already doing it?

Americans need to embrace a valuable lesson taught by Abraham Kuyper, a 19th century Dutch theologian and statesman. Kuyper taught a principle he called 'sphere sovereignty'. His view was that government receives its sovereignty directly from God and that this sovereignty includes a defined role. The state must fulfill its God-given mandate to protect its citizens and uphold justice, and not presume to undertake additional functions. Doing otherwise, warned Kuyper, results in governmental corruption and the repression of personal liberties.

He wrote, 'With great earnestness and force it is necessary not only to protest against the alleged omnipotence of the state, but also to resist it. That alleged omnipotence of the state is the most unbearable tyranny that can be imagined. A group of men of coercive temper, by flattery and deception, by beglamouring with promises, discovers how to obtain support from the masses, and promptly seats itself on the throne of God and conducts itself as though omnipotent, in order to give free reign to love of power and to covetousness. ...we are exposed to the great danger, under the high sounding name of state sovereignty, that progressive inroads are made on our personal and social liberty.'[1]

During Kuyper's life, virtually all of Holland was in church on Sunday. Bible literacy was the highest of any nation. But unfortunately, the Dutch government failed to heed the warning of its prophet. It continued to seize more and more authority and control over people's lives. Today, Holland is awash in sin. Its coalition government has leaned toward communism for years. Its military is ill-equipped, and its economy is a slave to European and global interests. This must not happen in America.

The second reason pietists give to justify their theory of social disengagement is that Jesus was a pacifist and we are to be like Him. In 1999, I was blessed to have a series of e-mail dialogues with noted pastor and author Francis Frangipane. Although we talked about a lot of things, the focus of our discussions was the Christian's proper response to moral and political corruption, with special emphasis on Bill Clinton. It was a stimulating give-and-take with me, the activist, on one end, and Francis Frangipane, whom I consider more of a pietist, on the other.

In one e-mail Francis Frangipane wrote these rather moving words, 'Life has reduced me to one focus; I want to be like Jesus was in the gospels. All my eggs are in one basket; the way before me is very narrow. In truth, I am committed to never deviate from the straight path of how to act, pray or reveal Jesus in the midst of this crooked world. Yes, I tell people the truth, but when they do not heed my words, I must follow Christ's example: I must intercede; and when wounded, I must pray for forgiveness for my enemies.'

WWJD?

Being like Jesus should be the singular quest of every believer. Where Francis Frangipane and I disagree is on the Christian's role in society. He believes that if Christians are to *be* like Jesus, we must *do* as Jesus did in the Gospels. We must limit our response to evil to only speaking out on the issues, but where that doesn't work we are obliged to model holiness, intercede, pray, and nothing more. But is this all we can glean from what Jesus lived and taught?

It's fair to say that if we limit our inquiry to the Gospels of what Jesus would do in the face of political decay, we're going to come away with very little evidence of an activist mentality in our Lord. For example, Jesus never confronted secular rulers with graft, greed, and vice. There's not a shred of biblical evidence He ever called a godless magistrate to step down. We never find Him organizing a movement to replace the Roman Empire with a form of government that reflected God's righteous rule. No voter-guides. No calls to withhold funding from hedonistic Roman artists. No campaigns to curb the homosexual threat to the family. Nothing. Jesus summarized His entire philosophy of social activism by saying, 'But I say to you, do not resist him who is evil; but whoever slaps you on your right cheek, turn to him the other also' (Matthew 5:39). Case closed? Not quite.

The fact is the attitudes and actions of Christ toward civil government and culture generally cannot be narrowly defined from either His public words or His interactions with secular leaders. Jesus Christ did not come into the world to remove rotten politicians. The Bible says, 'just as the Son of man did not come to be served, but to serve, and to give His life a ransom for many' (Matthew 20: 28). Jesus Christ came into the world to die for sinners. Nothing could have been more contrary to His plan to die upon a cross and provide the ultimate sacrifice for sin, than to take down the Roman Empire and to install a theocracy under His rule. Jesus had a better plan.

We would do well to remember that Christ's death, burial, and resurrection did more to destroy the power and persuasion of crooked politicians than any voter registration drive could have accomplished. Jesus didn't bother removing one bad apple for another. He went right to the source of their power and pulled the plug! Listen to Paul describing what Christ accomplished at the cross: 'When He [Christ] had disarmed the rulers and authorities, He made a public display of them, having triumphed over them through Him' (Colossians 2:15). All the spiritual powers, which had fuelled Satan's insidious attempts to overthrow the kingdom of God through political force and prowess, were paraded on the shoulders of Christ-the-victor at the cross. All that remained was for Christ to send His disciples into the world to effect His victory.

Redemption: Accomplished and Applied

The reason we don't see Jesus directly confronting the political 'fat cats' of His day is that His life and ministry occupied a special part in God's redemptive plan. This plan included past, present, and future aspects. The *prophecies* connected with God's redemption in Christ and the coming judgment of His enemies are found in the Old Testament. Redemption and judgment *accomplished* are found in the Gospel accounts of Jesus Christ. Redemption and judgment *applied* begin in the book of Acts and are not complete until the final judgment and the consummation of all things.

Certainly the Church of Jesus Christ is to pray and intercede for wayward politicians. However, the Church now sits in that period between *God's redemption accomplished* in Christ, when the spiritual strongholds over God's people were broken, and the *physical destruction* of the same, which is to take place at the end of the age. It is the job of the Church not only to be a praying, spiritual kingdom, but a vehicle through which the grand design of Christ is to be finally realized. The more the Church sheds abroad the glorious riches of Christ unto salvation, the more it must contend face to face with the powers of darkness in their *spiritual* (cf. Ephesians 6:10-20) and *physical* capacities (cf. Acts 13:6-13).

As in everything related to the kingdom of God, the spiritual precedes the physical. Sin brings spiritual death before it brings physical death. Redemption brings spiritual life before it brings the resurrection of the dead. Likewise, Jesus dealt with the spiritual side of sin, death, and the grave in His selfless sacrifice at the cross, whereas He is now calling His followers to confirm His triumph in the world. Unless we are willing to apply the Lordship of Christ to everything that makes up the world, His death was in vain. *If all Christ wanted was a praying people who were called to holy living, He already had that under the Old Covenant. What Christ purchased through His shed blood under the New Covenant was a people who would bring the kingdom of God to earth (cf. Matthew 5:9-15), thus transforming every sphere of life to the praise of His glory.* Given pietism's argument that being like Jesus automatically excludes social activism, let's look at another reason Christians need to be involved in the world.

What Does It Mean To be Like Jesus?

Perhaps the strongest argument in favour of the believer's involvement in questions affecting society has to do with the nature of sanctification. The Bible teaches that sanctification is a process (cf. Philippians 1:6). It reveals that although all men are created in the image of the triune God (cf. Genesis 1:26-28), the believer is both remade and conformed to the image of Christ in his daily living (cf. Romans 8:29). One might think that upon conversion men would be remade in the image of the triune God in whose likeness they were formed. Not so. According to Paul, all the fullness of the Trinity dwelled in Jesus in bodily form. Thus to be conformed to Christ, is to be made complete. Paul writes, 'For in Him all the fullness of Deity dwells in bodily form, and in Him you have been made complete, and He is the head over all rule and authority' (Colossians 2:9-10).

If being like Jesus meant nothing more than a life of holiness and prayer, then the pietist is correct in his theory of social disengagement. But notice in verse 10 Paul says '...and He is the head over all rule and authority'. Does this mean that in addition to being called to a life of piety, believers are to rule with Christ in the world? Affirmative. Returning to Genesis 1:28 (the Cultural Mandate), we know that the man who was created in the image of God was to rule over the earth. Included in Paul's point is that to be completed in Christ, is to be returned to one's rightful role of having worldwide dominion. Therefore, and this is the most important point for the pietist, the man who says He wants nothing more than to be like Jesus, has automatically enlisted himself into the Cultural Mandate!

The fact is man, in the image of God, is a *ruler*. He is as much a ruler on earth as he is a citizen of the 'sweet by and by.' Man's dominion over the earth is a responsibility delegated to him by his King. Man, as a viceroy, is subject to Christ's absolute authority under which he lives and rules. A viceroy that leaves politics, the arts and sciences, and indeed every area of society, uncultivated by the will of the King has abdicated his role as caretaker over His Master's property.

In the next chapter, I wish to speak on the need for *realistic expectations* in the culture-war.

Eight

THE CULTURE–WAR AND REALISTIC EXPECTATIONS

There is no doubt that many Christian activists are not witnessing the pace of progress toward cultural reform they once hoped to see when Ronald Reagan was first elected president. Paul Weyrich is president of the Free Congress Foundation and a man who was instrumental in the formation of the Moral Majority. Weyrich created a storm of controversy in March 1999, when, in an article for the *Washington Post*, he called conservatives to abandon attempts to reclaim the culture. He writes, 'For several decades, cultural conservatives' strategy has been to elect conservatives to office and then to rely on their help to retake society's institutions: not only government but also the public schools, the universities, the media, the entertainment industry and so on. I was an architect of that strategy, and in a narrow, political sense, it won some major victories. Through massive mobilization of grass-roots cultural conservatives, Ronald Reagan was elected in 1980, along with some culturally conservative senators such as Charles Grassley. In 1994, the same strategy gave the Republicans control of the House of Representatives for the first time in 40 years. But in terms of the culture war, this strategy failed. The culture has continued to deteriorate. Today, the old rules of conduct are not merely broken, they are scorned.'[1]

Based upon his assessment of conservatism's failure to change American culture for the better, Paul Weyrich challenged the movement to replicate the pattern of our American forefathers. 'What should we do about it? What our ancestors did: Declare our cultural independence. Just as they separated themselves from King George, royal governors and Stamp Act, so we should separate ourselves from Jerry Springer, public schools and the dictates of political correctness.'[2]

Obviously Paul Weyrich sounded disappointed. The strategy he helped to create – the retaking of society's institutions through electoral politics – failed to meet expectations. But were Paul Weyrich's expectations realistic? I think not. Yet realistic expectations are essential in any plan of action. When people set out to represent Christ in culture, they need to know what cultural transformation looks like and what the Lord expects. A false barometer always gives a wrong reading.

A new Christian activism calls cultural conservatives to reassess the way we have engaged the culture if we're going to avoid further disappointment and experience success in the future. With that in mind, I wish to address the need for *realistic expectations* in the culture-war. Our expectations of what we can achieve in culture quickly become unrealistic in proportion to two things.

First is confusion over the Christian's relationship to the world. I have great respect for Paul Weyrich. But I disagree with his earlier assertion that electing conservatives to office is enough to retake America's cultural institutions. This reveals that in Weyrich's mind, involvement and trust in the world-system took precedence over separateness from it early on. But with Weyrich's call to a new 'cultural independence' the pendulum has swung to the opposite extreme. Now separateness from the world is taking precedence over involvement in it. The way to stop this polarization is to *balance* separateness from the world with involvement in it.

Second is a misconception of what cultural transformation looks like. I disagree with Paul Weyrich's position that success in the culture-war requires wholesale change at the institutional level, or else we must go underground. Developing a biblical picture of what a restored earth looks like will bring balance to this issue as well. Now let's return to addressing the first problem with this question...

Who Are We?

The Bible is full of vivid metaphors describing the Christian in terms of his *separateness* from the world. Although Jesus sends us 'into the world', we are not 'of the world'. As a result the Bible says we are 'strangers,' 'aliens', and 'pilgrims'. Because Christians, as the Apostle Paul says, have been 'raised up with Christ' we have already been made separate in principle from the ideology of 'political correctness' which Paul Weyrich would now like to see us separate from in practice. The real challenge for us is to live what we already are in principle.

In this regard, separateness must always be balanced with *involvement*. Nowhere does the Bible cast the Christian's separateness in a light that would allow him to remain unengaged from the world. The fact that the Christian is *ethically* separated from the world is all the more reason he must *physically* go into the world to claim it for the glory of God. The life of the Apostle Paul is a vivid example. He said of himself, 'I have been crucified with Christ; and it is no longer I who live, but Christ lives in me; and the life which I now live in the flesh I live by faith in the Son of God, who loved me, and delivered himself up for me' (Galatians 2:20).

Here we see both separateness and involvement held in perfect balance. Paul had given up everything from his former manner of life as Saul of Tarsus in order to love and serve Jesus Christ. What did Paul's new life look like as a result of having Christ living within him? He was an apostle. He laboured as an evangelist, discipler, and church planter. He defended the faith before secular authorities taking 'every thought captive' to the obedience of Christ Jesus. By the end of Paul's life his labour had left a growing movement of Christian expansion that eventually turned the entire Mediterranean world on it's head.

The Bible gives three descriptions of the life of Paul that balance separateness with involvement and help form a biblical concept of who we are as representatives of Jesus Christ. The descriptions are of a prophet, an ambassador, and an apologist. First, the prophet.

Our Prophetic Role

Paul never used the word 'prophet' to describe himself. However, he often stood in the role of the prophet: 'If anyone thinks he is a prophet or spiritually gifted, let him acknowledge that what I am writing to you is the Lord's commandment' (I Corinthians 14:37). The Church takes on a prophetic role whenever it confronts the world's rejection of God's standards. No, we don't deliver new commands from God. Nor can we predict the future. But the Church does have a prophetic ministry to fulfill.

Even a cursory overview of the prophet in Scripture reveals that they were deeply involved in national life. Theirs was a heartbreaking message of doom to stiff-necked people who needed to hear that a return to God was the only way to avoid judgment and calamity. History demonstrates that not too many people listened to the prophets of old. Isaiah preached for over fifty years and only a small remnant responded. Jeremiah laboured for more than forty years and where did it get him? He was hated by his countrymen, placed on trial by the priests and prophets in Jerusalem, put in stocks, made a public laughing stock, and if all that wasn't enough, he was imprisoned in a cistern full of mud and left to die.

How did the Old Testament prophets manage to continue under such unbearable circumstances without declaring their 'cultural independence'? In part, they knew what to expect. God said to Isaiah 'Go, and tell this people; Keep on listening, but do not perceive; Keep on looking, but do not understand. Render the hearts of this people insensitive, Their ears dull, And their eyes dim, Lest they see with their eyes, Hear with their ears, Understand with their hearts, And return and be healed' (Isaiah 6:9-10).

To Jeremiah, God revealed He would destroy Judah: 'Lift up a standard toward Zion! Seek refuge, do not stand still, For I am bringing evil from the north, And great destruction' (Jeremiah 4:6). Later God revealed He would seek His people in captivity and restore them: 'Behold, I am going to send for many fishermen, declares the Lord, and they will fish for them; and afterwards I shall send for many hunters, and they will hunt them from every mountain and every hill, and from the clefts of the rocks' (16:16).

And yet Isaiah, Jeremiah, and the rest of the Old Testament prophets had more going for them than realistic expectations. There was a *spiritual balance* to their lives that enabled them to keep their expectations focused. On the one hand, they were men who deeply cared about the welfare of their people. As a result, the prophets faced the daily temptation of caring *too much* about how both they and their messages were received. On the other hand, they were nothing more than mouthpieces, separated unto God, who dared not allow concern over human opinion, or even empathy with their people, to dull the razor-sharp message God had entrusted to them.

Jeremiah suffered more than the rest. He had a big heart. His passionate concern for Judah is seen in his tears and laments that cover every page of his prophecies. But God warns him not to allow his big heart to overshadow his role as God's mouthpiece in calling Judah to repentance: 'Now, gird up your loins, and arise, and speak to them all which I command you. Do not be dismayed before them, lest I dismay you before them' (Jeremiah 1:17).

Nevertheless, concern over human opinion has become a mark of the modern-day Church. We care too much what others think. Overall, where fatigue has not turned us cynical, lust for numbers has caused the few with energy left to become selective in their preaching – emphasizing consolation without the condemnation and hope without the horror. But the day is coming when God's patience will run out, and with it, time for America and the world to repent. The Church must return to being separate from the world, while remaining actively involved in it, and declare God's message to individuals, families, cultures, and nations that time is short. This is the job of the prophet. It is our job too.

Representing Two Realms

Next, we are *ambassadors for Christ*. Paul writes, 'Therefore, we are ambassadors for Christ, as though God were entreating through us; we beg you on behalf of Christ, be reconciled to God' (2 Corinthians 5:20). The *Merriam-Webster Dictionary* defines 'ambassador' as 'an official envoy; especially: a diplomatic agent of the highest rank accredited to a foreign government or sovereign as the resident representative of his own government'.[3]

The role of an ambassador is really twofold. He is charged with representing the interests of his home nation or kingdom in a foreign land. But he is also under orders to remain keenly interested in the peace and security of the land he labours in. Instability in the region may threaten his nation's vital interests in the area. Working to secure a just and lasting peace between a foreign nation and its neighbours is a key priority of any nation's overall foreign policy.

Likewise, the Christian ambassador has two jobs. He is commissioned to represent Christ and His kingdom in the world. In this regard he maintains a *separate* and autonomous identity from the world to which he is sent. But he must also be attentive to the peace and security needs of the world. Remember my point in Chapter 4? Disorder and unrest in the world can quickly turn to anarchy, and anarchy is a threat to the type of environment God prefers for people to seek Him. The Christian ambassador must be *involved* in the dialogue over what is best for culture and the broader questions that affect society. He must always bear in mind that his purpose is never to serve the interests of the world, but *only* the eternal interests of the higher kingdom he represents.

This means *the Christian is not an ambassador for family values, religious liberties, the Framers' understanding of the Constitution of the United States of America, or even America's Christian heritage. The Christian represents Jesus and His kingdom.* The degree to which a person loses sight of this, is the degree to which he will develop false expectations and quickly find himself entangled in a worldly war aimed at winning a worldly peace.

I cannot help to think that Paul Weyrich became entangled in a worldly war. Regarding conservatism's failure to win back the culture, he writes, 'So what is to be done? Continuing with a strategy that has failed is folly and guarantees defeat. Instead of attempting to use politics to retake existing institutions, my proposal is that we cultural conservatives build new institutions for ourselves: schools, universities, media, entertainment, everything — a complete, separate, parallel structure. In every respect but politics, we should in effect, build a new nation among the ruins of the old.'[4]

I agree with Paul Weyrich that cultural conservatives cannot continue to depend upon politics to win back American culture. But I disagree that we should do so in order to avoid 'defeat'. The main problem among Christian activists as a group is their insistence on 'winning' the culture-war, rather than glorifying God. They have failed to treat their passion for the culture as a forum for worship, but instead have allowed their calling to degenerate into a worldly grudge-match where it's 'us against them'.

The Apostle Paul says, 'and pray on my behalf, that utterance may be given to me in the opening of my mouth, to make known with boldness the mystery of the gospel, for which I am an ambassador in chains; that in proclaiming it I may speak boldly, as I ought to speak' (Ephesians 6:19-20). Paul's only concern was heaven's interests and that he might represent Christ and his gospel fearlessly in the world. He was not concerned with winning, but with remaining obedient. It was the prayers of the saints that enabled Paul to balance his active involvement as an ambassador for Christ in the world with the fact he was a citizen of heaven.

Defenders of the Faith

And last, we are *apologists*. An apologist is simply a person who defends something or someone, either in writing or in speech. So stirring was Paul's defense before King Agrippa, the King replied, 'In a short time you will persuade me to become a Christian' (Acts 26:28).

I remember learning about apologetics at Westminster Theological Seminary many years ago. One day as I was chatting with a group of students, our apologetics instructor, Professor John Frame, walked up. As if he could see the fear in us over what was coming in the course, he said, 'Relax. Presuppositional apologetics can be boiled down to two points taken from the teachings of Paul in Romans 1: first, that all men undeniably know the truth but suppress it in unrighteousness, and second, that the only way to approach them is to pull the rug right out from under them.'

'Presuppositional apologetics' is a method used to defend the Christian faith. It assumes that the image of God in man – although it has been marred by sin – continues to act as a testimony to men that they belong to the Creator and need to return immediately to His loving care. In this approach there is 'no neutrality'. The Christian apologist must not meet the sinner halfway and attempt to use reason in order to convince him of the truth of the gospel. Instead, one must assume that all men possess a general knowledge of the existence of God, but due to the deceitfulness of their hearts, are suppressing it. Thus, whether in personal evangelism or in defending Christian principles as they relate to the culture, the right approach is to appeal to the sinner's innate knowledge of God by simply telling him the truth as it is revealed in Scripture. The next step is to defer to the sovereign Spirit of God as the change-agent.

This is good news to the Christian apologist. The power to conform people's thinking to truth does *not* lie in human arguments. Rather, it lies within the *power of the Holy Spirit* who uses what natural truth there is in man to His advantage. Paul writes, 'Where is the wise man? Where is the scholar? Where is the philosopher of this age? Has not God made foolish the wisdom of the world?' (I Corinthians 1:20).

Nevertheless, many Christians are not making full use of the apologetic method I have just outlined. Instead of 'pulling the rug right out from under them', many of us went into the culture-war using the world's 'bat and ball'. It began years ago when we *assumed* that John Q. Public was silently outraged over America's slide toward Sodom and was ready to respond to a common-sense plan to restore the culture. So while on secular TV and radio, we followed our opponents, using language designed to fuel the outrage of the public without getting them outraged at us. What did we find?

We talked about faith and family, only to discover that homosexuals could do the same. We held up liberty and freedom in the context of 1st Amendment rights, only for People for the American Way to turn our own message against us. We reasonably demonstrated the inconsistency of our opponent's viewpoint by comparing his support for abortion with his disdain for the death penalty, only for him to paint us as hypocrites for opposing violence in movies while supporting the right to bear arms.

Then to our great surprise we discovered that, from the start, the liberal establishment, including the major media, was never interested in allowing us a forum to debate the truth. No, it was looking to *smash* the truth and us with it. The 'world' is not interested in truth. It is bent on *force*. And it will use whatever force is within its grasp to destroy the truth. Once we figured this out it was too late for many of the issues we felt so passionately about.

In the new Christian activism we're going to depend a bit less upon 'setting the record straight' and more upon the power of God's truth. This doesn't mean that our defense on particular issues must be limited to quoting Bible verses. But 'speaking the truth in love' does require us to articulate a biblical worldview in a straightforward and caring manner. For example, if while discussing gay marriage, someone exclaims, 'But don't you teach tolerance to your children?' you should reply, 'No, I teach my children righteousness. If they understand righteousness, they will tolerate what God tolerates.' This answer pulls the rug out from under your antagonist and leaves him nowhere to go, except to some serious self-examination. And it opens the door for sharing the gospel.

Remember, a good lifeguard never jumps into the pool to save a drowning victim or else both will drown. Rather, he stands at the edge of the pool and throws out the 'lifeline'. Likewise, the effective Christian apologist never defends the truth from a point of neutrality. Rather, he stands upon the 'solid rock' and speaks the truth in love. In this way he balances involvement in the dialogue while not sacrificing the objective truth.

The Earth God Sees

The second question I wish to address in helping to develop realistic expectations for what the Church can accomplish in culture, is *what does a restored earth look like?* Throughout this book I refer to God's purpose to 'restore' all of life on planet earth. Traditionally the word 'restore', when used in a Christian context invokes among believers the thought of a return to the idyllic conditions of the Garden of

Eden. Unbelievers, on the other hand, envision an American-style theocracy with some right-wing dictator at the top. At no time have I argued we can expect to witness the dawning of a 'Christian utopia' where the Church reigns and rules over the inhabitants of the earth prior to the return of our Lord. A restored earth means something far different.

The Lord's Prayer: a Guide to the Future

There are *three signs,* taken from the Lord's Prayer that reveal what a restored earth will look like. These three signs also act as our guides, telling us if our labour for Christ is leading toward the restoration of all things. Jesus said, 'Pray, then, in this way: Our Father who art in heaven, Hallowed be Thy name. Thy kingdom come. Thy will be done, On earth as it is in heaven. Give us this day our daily bread. And forgive us our debts, as we also have forgiven our debtors. And do not lead us into temptation, but deliver us from evil. For Thine is the kingdom, and the power, and the glory, forever. Amen' (Matthew 6:9-15).

What are the three signs? They are the coming of the kingdom of God to earth, the realization of God's will on earth, and the filling of the earth with God's glory. The last verse of Christ's prayer clearly summarizes the three signs: 'the kingdom, and the power, and the glory' (vs.13). Let's look at the first sign.

The first sign of the restoration of all things is the coming of the kingdom of God. Jesus said, 'Thy kingdom come' (Matthew 6:10). Jesus' request to His heavenly Father included a charge to His disciples to be actively engaged in spreading the kingdom of God on earth. At the outset this sounds like an impossible task. But don't feel overwhelmed. One reason we instinctively flinch at the thought of such an undertaking is because after Jesus said 'Thy will be done', He then said, 'as it is in heaven'. The result is that most people believe Jesus was calling the Church to create conditions on earth that reflect current conditions in heaven.

Jesus did have heaven-like conditions in mind, but only in the distant future, when the present age has ended. Then all things will be *completely* restored. Until then, 'Thy kingdom come', is a declaration of fact that God intends to have his *complete way* in the world, just as He does in heaven. Not a single person, institution, or thing will have been left untouched by God's kingdom by the time Christ returns. This does not mean that everything on earth will be affected for the better. The advance of God's kingdom in the world will redeem some men and harden others. Not all things will be changed for good, but all things will be prepared for the final judgment. The result is that God's kingdom will affect the whole earth, fashioning it into the exact state God has predetermined best suits the larger purpose of Christ's glorious return.

This is an important concept for the Church to grasp. Pietists correctly view the kingdom of God as spiritual but are resistant to the idea that its approach should directly affect conditions on earth at the institutional level. While activists, who understand the all-embracing significance of the kingdom, struggle to rectify their theology with real life conditions on earth. But 'Thy kingdom come' does not refer to the 'rapture' or to the sanctioning of God's kingdom by the world. Rather, the reference is to God's *rule* or *administration* over all things unto their appointed end.

What does this mean for the work of the Church in the world? The bottom line is that until the kingdom comes in all its fullness, it will always affect the world with *mixed results.* In terms of the culture, we can therefore expect to see *degrees* of change, but not *wholesale* change. Wholesale change will come at the return of Christ. Until then, we may be able to stave off homosexual marriage, for example, but unable to eliminate federal funding for the National Endowment for the Arts (NEA). Nonetheless, the part of culture that proves resistant to being reformed still works for God toward the *final* restoration of all things.

Why do many Christians labour with false expectations regarding what they can do to change the culture? Principally, it is because they confuse the kingdom of God with the Church. If the Church and the kingdom were the same, then one would be inclined to interpret cultural transformation in light of the pattern of beliefs one has become accustomed to at the local church where one worships. So, if one regularly attends an activist-oriented church, then one would expect the kingdom to transform culture along the lines of religious liberties. But if one were a monk, then one would not be adverse to the idea of the coming of the kingdom precipitating culture's deterioration, because for him, this only facilitates the privatization of religion.

However, a simple comparison between the kingdom and the Church will prove that although there is overlap, the two are not the same. The kingdom of God is purely spiritual (cf. John 18:36). But the Church is partly spiritual and partly physical. It has people. The kingdom is composed of every level and dimension of spiritual blessing at once and without variance (cf. Matthew 6:10). While in the Church, Christ distributes spiritual gifts to each one according to the measure of faith God has given them (cf. Romans 12:3-21).

We know that the kingdom came down to earth with Jesus Christ (cf. Matthew 4:17). It can be said that the kingdom 'fills' the Church (cf. Ephesians 4:10). Or perhaps that the priceless benefits of the kingdom are 'given' to those who are born of the water and the Spirit (cf. Matthew 13:11; John 3:1-5). The kingdom is perfect. It simply 'is'. While on earth the Church is imperfect. Thus the Church is 'becoming'. What does this comparison teach us?

The spiritual and transcendent nature of God's kingdom infers that it cannot be reduced to a political or religious agenda. The kingdom is not the penthouse suite of the Church. It is the light whose rays fill the building. Thus, the kingdom cannot be wrapped in a flag or hidden in a prayer closet. Its ability to touch lives is not limited to the voting booth or to the monastery. Rather, 'The wind blows where it wishes and you hear the sound of it, but do not know where it comes from and where it is going...' (John 3:8).

The state of absolute purity and perfection of the kingdom emphasizes the Bible's position that the kingdom, in all its fullness, must be ushered in at the end of the age, not turned over to Christ at His return. In Christ's parable of the mustard seed (Matthew 13:31-32), He presents the kingdom as an emerging order. A man plants the smallest of all seeds, a mustard seed, only for it to become larger than all his other garden plants. The point is that, although the kingdom of God begins with the planting of Christ in human hearts, its final state overcomes all the kingdoms of the world. The picture of birds of the air nesting in the tree's branches, is a reference to Christ. Daniel foretold this when, in interpreting Belteshazzar's dream, he predicted the coming of a kingdom that would put to an end the world system of Babylon (cf. Daniel 4:19-27). Christian pietists that limit the scope of the gospel to the threshold of personal morality, do so in flagrant denial of Christ's teaching.

On the other hand, Christian activists should not infer that because the kingdom is an 'emerging order,' that they are to *prepare* the earth so Christ can reign properly at His return. Instead, our goal should be to shape the earth in such a way that it is a *preview* of what's to come. In commenting on the relationship between the Cultural Mandate and the kingdom of God, pastor/author Peter J. Leithhart, explains, 'Adam and Eve, with their descendants, were to construct on earth a glorious replica of the heavenly dwelling of God. I emphasize the use of the word replica.' The earth was to become like heaven, but never by the efforts of even sinless human hands could it actually become heaven. The goal was progressively to approximate God's eschatological order. Even without sin, the fulfillment of the creation would have come to man as a gift. "Replica" does not, however, capture the dynamic relationship that God intended to exist between heaven and earth. Earth was not merely to become "like" heaven, but it was to become more and more an "expectation" or "foretaste" of the glorified eschatological order. Earth was not merely to "mirror" heaven; it was to "grow up into" heaven, without in fact becoming heaven.'[5]

I glean from pastor Leithhart's observation that although the Church is to create a 'foretaste of the glorified eschatological order' on earth there are limits to what we can, and should, seek to achieve. It will be helpful if we can remember that the biblical picture of the earth just prior to the return of Christ is a place where both good and evil will exist *simultaneously.* The gospel will enjoy a season of productivity unmatched anywhere in history (Matthew 24:14). While at the same time the earth will be marked by apostasy (2 Timothy 3:1-5).

The second sign of the restoration of all things is the realization of God's will on earth. Jesus said, 'Thy kingdom come. Thy will be done, On earth as it is in heaven' (Matthew 6:10). When Martin Luther's daughter, Magdelena, was fourteen years old, she became sick and lay dying. Luther prayed, 'O God, I love her so, but nevertheless, Thy will be done.' Then he turned to his daughter and said, 'Magdelena, would you rather be with me, or would you rather go and be with your Father in heaven?' And the girl said, 'Father, as God wills.' Luther held her in his arms as she passed away, and as they laid her to rest, he said, 'Oh my dear Magdelenachen, you will rise and shine like the stars in the sun. How strange to be so sorrowful and yet to know that all is at peace, that all is well.'[6]

The story of Magdalena is quite touching. Yet it points to a profound truth. God's will, like God's kingdom, is a mystery. There are times when God's will produces lighthearted joy in our lives. While at other times, like in Luther's case, God's will comes at a great price. Nonetheless, even in his darkest hour of despair, the believer can rejoice that his sovereign God always knows what is best and that someday, perhaps in heaven, he will understand the 'why' of life.

'Thy will be done' is a phrase that today invites every conceivable opinion regarding its meaning. The pietist concludes it is a reference for God's children to lead holy lives. While some activists look for the establishment of the theocratic reign of Christ on earth, where the Church will make unbelievers 'knuckle under' and live like Christians. Both are wrong. Christ anticipated a world that was similar to the life experience of Martin Luther. He saw a world that, although tremendously impacted by the Word of God, would also be stung by evil and acquainted with suffering.

That God Has His Way in the World

Theologians make several distinctions in the will of God. The most common is between the 'secret' and the 'revealed' will of God. The *secret* will of God refers to His hidden decisions or 'decrees'. These decrees affect everything God wills to do or permit and which is permanent. For example, God's decrees may speak of those who are to be included in salvation (cf. Romans 9:18-19), to God's purposes among the kings of the world (cf. Daniel 4:17, 25, 32, 35), to those things God simply wants to do without telling anyone (cf. Psalm 115: 3), or to suffering, such as the taking home of Luther's 14-year-old daughter, Magdalena. (cf. Job 1:18-19).

The *revealed* will of God, on the other hand, comes to us by precept and is revealed in the Law and the gospel. God's revealed will also pertains to man's responsibility before Him and details how he can experience the blessings of God in full.

So when the Lord's Prayer says, 'Thy will be done', does it mean the secret or the revealed will of God? If it's the former, then our role is somewhat reduced, because God always accomplishes His secret will without telling anyone what He is doing. And you may as well forget asking Him what He's doing, because it's a secret. But if it's the revealed will of God, then we have our work cut out. Spreading the kingdom of God would mean seeing to it that the moral law – the Ten Commandments – becomes the rule of faith and practice for every nation on earth.

Fortunately, although the Lord's Prayer emphasizes the revealed will of God, it also includes his secret will. R.T. France comments, '*Thy will be done* can apply both to men's obedience to God's will in the world today and to the ultimate working out of God's purpose for the world.'[7] This is good news for Christian workers! It means we don't have to create heaven on earth in order to help establish God's will.

With the inclusion of God's secret will, 'Thy will be done', refers equally to the *rejection* of the gospel as well as its *acceptance* (See Isaiah 6:9-10; Romans 9:6-16 and John 3:16), the *confounding* of secular authorities as well as their *repentance* (See Exodus 7:3; Daniel 4:34-37), and His *patient judgment* upon sin as well as His *swift execution* (See Ecclesiastes 9:11; Genesis 19). The Lord's Prayer anticipates a world where God's will, in all it's shades of meaning, is being fully accomplished. It is a place where good and evil, sin and salvation, blessing and suffering co-exist (See Matthew 5:10-12).

How do these facts help inform the expectations of Christian activists today? It means that flourishing cultures and upward trends in society are insufficient alone to gauge progress toward establishing God's will on earth. Thus, when believers say 'Thy will be done' in the context of cultural reform, they must understand that is a *statement of faith* in the God of culture, not a request for God to rubber-stamp their agenda.

What is our role in facilitating God's *secret* will? *Obedience.* Although God does not inform us of His secret will, he does use us to accomplish much of it. Daniel suffered. However, had he not recognized God's sovereign hand in his life and remained obedient to God in Babylon, he would not have become Nebuchadnezzar's trusted confidant, capable of interpreting the King's dream. Isaiah suffered. Yet had he not comprehended that he was only a part of God's ultimate plan, Isaiah would not have persevered in proclaiming God's Word to disobedient Israel.

How can we accomplish God's *revealed* will? The prophet Micah said, 'He has told you, O man, what is good; And what does the Lord require of you But to do justice, to love kindness, And to walk humbly with your God?' (Micah 6:8), What satisfies God's justice? When we come to Him in repentance and faith and bring others to His forgiving care. What satisfies God's kindness? When we make Christ our kindred brother and introduce others to the family of God. What satisfies God's humility? When we come on bended knee before the Judge with nothing to plead as our own and say 'yes' to Him and His commission to represent His cause in the world.

His Glory Shall Fill the Earth

The third sign of the restoration of all things is the filling of the whole earth with the glory of God. Jesus said, 'For Thine is the kingdom, and the power, and the glory, forever. Amen' (Matthew 6:13). As I previously mentioned in Chapter 3, the glory of God is inseparably linked to the gospel. Jesus clearly said the day is coming when the gospel will be preached throughout the whole earth (Matthew 24:14). This doesn't mean that everyone on earth will someday be a penitent believer. Rather, Jesus predicted a time when all the elect will have been *reached* (Matthew 24:22), and every nation will have been *affected* by the gospel (vs.14).

The day is coming when, through the worldwide preaching of the gospel, the glory of God will fill the earth in a very practical way. As of this writing, the *JESUS* Film Project, a ministry of Campus Crusade for Christ International, has translated the film into over 600 languages, reaching more than 4 billion people worldwide.[8] Wycliffe Bible

Translators has completed nearly 500 Scripture translations, making God's Word available to more than 35 million people.[9] We are close to seeing God's glory take hold of every nation on earth!

More Than Conquerors

As the glory of God fills the earth, we should expect the Church to suffer persecution in unprecedented proportions. Paul writes, 'We are afflicted in every way, but not crushed; perplexed, but not despairing; persecuted, but not forsaken; struck down, but not destroyed; always carrying about in the body the dying of Jesus, that the life of Jesus also may be manifested in our body...For all things are for your sakes, that the grace which is spreading to more and more people may cause the giving of thanks to abound to the glory of God' (2 Corinthians 4:8-11, 15).

Xu Yongze is the founder of the Born Again movement in China. He is known as China's most famous house church prisoner. Xu was rewarded for his Christian commitment by being forced to serve three years in a Chinese labour camp. He said, 'I came to feel how Jesus must have felt on the cross.' He was arrested in 1997 when police raided a meeting of house church leaders in central China. He said that during the first months of his detention, he was slapped hundreds of times, handcuffed with both arms behind his back, and pulled up in midair to be beaten. Xu served his sentence in a camp where each prisoner had to string 2,500 Christmas tree bulbs every day with a thin wire. Sources say these decorative lights are exported to the United States. Once freed, Xu reported he had been tortured during interrogation sessions. He also had both arms handcuffed to an iron gate and was stretched up off the ground in a cross position when the gates were opened.[10]

Praise God that Xu Yongze was not murdered. Unfortunately, only heaven knows the number of saints who have suffered martyrdom down through the ages. So great will the number of those be that have fallen to persecution, that John remarked, 'And I saw the woman drunk with the blood of the martyrs and with the blood of the witnesses of Jesus' (Revelation 17:6). Since Cain slew Able the 'blood of the martyrs is the seedbed of the Church'. Historically, it has always been true that the Church is never stronger than in the winepress of suffering.

However, the Church is full of men and women who become indignant when their 'rights' are threatened. But this too is our right: 'For to you it has been granted for Christ's sake, not only to believe in Him, but also to suffer for His sake' (Philippians 1:29). Since its birth, the Church has been faced with the challenge of living in a delicate balance between fighting for its rights, while being careful not to fight God. It is somewhere in the 'balance' that His glory fills the earth.

The Bible also says, 'We are more than conquerors through Him that loved us' (Romans 8:37, KJV). Note it doesn't say, 'we are conquerors'. It says, 'we are *more* than conquerors'. Do not expect God to conquer all vice and depravity in the world in *practice* before Christ's return. If God were to do this then the Church would only be made up of mere conquerors, not unlike the champions of the world that seek an earthly throne. But we are children of the King who shall someday reign with Him in glory. It is in this context that Christ appeals to his Church, first to say that His is not a battle for control of the world, for this He already has, but that the world might know Him. And second to express that it pleases Him when His Body, in pursuit of this goal, is willing to trade its earthly life through persecution for a better glory.

Recap

The challenge before the Church is big, but not impossible. This chapter's purpose is to point out that false expectations in Christian service can easily lead to fatigue and retreat, and to further equip you with a theological foundation for what you can rightly expect in building God's kingdom on earth. The quiet attitude of many is that unless massive, wholesale change occurs across the board in American culture and the world, the Christian agenda is failing. Not only is this untrue, it is not even close to the truth. By balancing *separateness* with *involvement* and remembering we are not charged with erecting a Christian utopia, but with *representing the transcendent kingdom of*

God on earth that has the power to affect all of life, our labour for Christ will be marked by realistic, attainable goals that will be reached.

In the last three chapters, we have taken a critical look at a number of errors that have contributed to the failure of both activism and pietism to restore the earth to the glory of God. In the following chapters, I wish to elaborate upon my position that the answer to this dilemma must be sought in a 'new Christian activism' that seeks to combine the activists' stress upon the Cultural Mandate and the pietists' stress upon the Great Commission. We need the best of *both* worlds: a dual-emphasis upon the cultural restoration and evangelism, which together, will work to achieve God's master plan for His world.

To stimulate further thinking toward this end, I have selected six key-areas (representing both pietism and activism) the Church must address as part of its uniform plan to restore all things. Different points of a biblical worldview from chapters 1 and 2 support my thinking in each area. The first two areas are prayer and church unity, which pietists underscore in the work of the Great Commission. The last four areas are the fine arts, immigration and related international affairs, the environment, and politics, which activists stress in the work of the Cultural Mandate.

Interestingly, not only is the Church called to labour in both the Great Commission and the Cultural Mandate, but as we examine challenges that arise in each of the above areas, we also shall see that, in many cases, answers are to be sought in a combination of the Great Commission and the Cultural Mandate. This is not an exhaustive list. Many more areas, both within the life of the Church and in the culture, require our work and refinement. However, I believe these represent the areas of greatest need. We begin with prayer.

Nine

PRAYER – THE ULTIMATE WARFARE

The section of practical Christianity where pietism has made the largest contribution to the Church is in the area of prayer. We who address the culture with the claims of Christ would do well to remember that Christianity's public face is little more than a hollow mask when our lives are not filled with an abiding, personal relationship with Christ through prayer. Moreover, prayer stands at the crossroads of everything the Holy Spirit produces in the believer in order to prepare him for spiritual warfare in the world. *Prayer is the most important discipline a Christian must practice on a daily basis in order to be effective in helping to fulfill the Cultural Mandate and the Great Commission.*

Yet prayer is undoubtedly one of the most widely misunderstood disciplines of the Christian faith. To many Christian social activists, prayer is a means to *transform* the world for Christ. The average believer, however, views prayer as a power *over and against* the world. And a growing number of pietists, such as Ed Silvoso, view prayer as a means to *evangelize the lost.* Although prayer invites all the above, from a biblical perspective, prayer is really something much different. Prayer is *conflict with God.* Therefore, a new Christian activism will require some change, both in the way many believers view prayer and in the way prayer is being practiced in some parts of the Church. Let's begin with a look into the Old Testament at the life of Jacob.

Learning Grace in the Trenches

During the patriarchal period of the Jewish people we find the life of Jacob as recorded in the book of Genesis. Despite the fact he was a chosen instrument of God and was destined to be blessed, Jacob spent the greater part of his life attempting to take by deception what would have been his anyway if he had only been willing to wait for it.

The first place we see hints of Jacob's spiritual struggle is when he was in his mother's womb. It seems that Rebekah had a difficult pregnancy because the Bible says that the children 'struggled' within her. So she inquired of the Lord and was told that 'two nations are in your womb, And two peoples shall be separated from your body; And one people shall be stronger than the other; And the older shall serve the younger' (Genesis 25:23).

As the two boys grew up, Jacob must not have believed that he would be the stronger of the two and that the nation he represented would rule over the nation his brother Esau represented. Because he lacked faith that God was able to fulfill the promise to Rebekah, Jacob felt that if he were to 'get his due', it would have to be through cunning manipulation and self-effort.

One day Issac, now blind and near death, sent Esau out to hunt. Evidently Issac was going to give his final blessing to his sons on a full stomach. Once Esau returned home faint with hunger, Jacob was able to trick his older brother into giving him the promise of his birthright in exchange for a mere bowl of soup. Then Jacob, now joined by his mother Rebekah, tricked Isaac into bestowing upon him the greater blessing, predicting that Jacob would be Lord over his brothers. Jacob, whose name meant 'supplanter' had now won by human effort what God had intended to give him all along.

This brings us to Genesis 32 where we find Jacob on the verge of entering Canaan where God plans to bless him. But this time things are going to be different. Before Jacob can steal this blessing, God decides to break him of his trickery and fleshly determination. Verse 24 says, 'Then Jacob was left alone, and a man wrestled with him until daybreak.'

The traditional view of this verse is to interpret Jacob's 'wrestling' as a wrestling in prayer. This is correct. In fact, the picture of Jacob wrestling with God has filled the imaginations of believers with the potential of prayer. Jacob, according to many people, presents us with a heroic struggle. Even after being crippled by God in the hip and exhausted, Jacob is still able to overcome even the Almighty and get from Him what he wants. Therefore, the challenge as many see it is this: Do we truly understand the power of prayer — that we, through fervent and persevering prayer, can prevail over God and get from Him the blessings we so urgently desire for ourselves, our families, and our nation? What a fantastic thought! But is it true? Not really.

The Battle You Want To Lose

Verse 24 doesn't say that Jacob wrestled with God. Rather, it says that God wrestled 'with him' until daybreak. In other words, Jacob didn't wrestle with God as a result of his own choosing. He was forced to wrestle. God's greatest desire was to bless Jacob and to use him as an instrument of His grace. But Jacob would have to learn the hard way that God's blessings do not come as a result of human will, but rather come in God's own time and in His own way.

Yet Jacob proved to be so strong-willed that even after God was forced to dislocate his hip as a way of getting his attention, he continued to struggle. It wasn't until God threatened to give up on him that Jacob came to his senses and cried out, 'I will not let you go unless you bless me' (v.26). With the word 'you' Jacob identified the source of all blessings as God. Jacob was through taking God's blessings by stealth. He now committed Himself to living in total dependence upon God and His grace as the wellspring of all blessings.

One of God's blessings to Jacob resulted in a change of name. 'Your name shall no longer be Jacob, but Israel; for you have striven with God and with men and have prevailed' (v.28). No longer was he to be known as the 'supplanter', but as Israel, which means, 'he who strives with God'.

Yet, not only had Jacob striven with God, but also he had 'prevailed' over God. But to prevail over God, in this sense of the word, doesn't mean that he beat God. Rather, it means that God beat him. It means that in prayer, he finally submitted his whole life to God so that He could bless him according to His timetable. Having been taught this valuable lesson through an intense battle with the Almighty, Jacob was a man who was literally *slain by grace*.

The story of Jacob teaches that although there are many battles you as a believer are expected to win, prayer is the one field of battle where God expects you to lose. But it's in losing your whole life to God in prayer that you place yourself in the best position to receive all the blessings He has prepared for you. Jesus said, 'If anyone wishes to come after Me, let him deny himself, and take up his cross, and follow Me. For whoever wishes to save his life shall lose it; but whoever loses his life for My sake and the gospel's shall save it' (Mark 8:34-35).

The picture of God wrestling with Jacob calls for a renaissance in the Church's thinking concerning the relationship of corporate and private prayer to the Cultural Mandate and the Great Commission. I will begin by looking at the matter of corporate prayer.

The Church needs to rethink the forum it is increasingly using for its prayer gatherings, which may be helping to turn a sacred experience into an event. National and statewide prayer gatherings, such as those facilitated by Concerts of Prayer International, are bringing together scores of believers who are calling upon the Lord to send spiritual awakening and revival to America. Some of these events are televised.

While I personally recognize many positive benefits to these organized meetings, I feel we must consider the opinion of Jim Cymbala, pastor of the Brooklyn Tabernacle and author of *Fresh Wind, Fresh Fire*, who said, 'Prayer is not for televised events.'[1] I interpret Jim Cymbala's remark as not merely challenging the legitimacy of 'televised' prayer rallies, but also as questioning any effort to coordinate prayer into an 'event'. Corporate prayer is not an event. It is a holy experience with God where believers are confronted with the undeniable fact of their sinfulness and their desperate need for God's continuing grace. And where together, as the Body of Christ, they submit their lives in full to God's sovereign will and implore His miracle-working power. If the intensely hallowed nature of corporate prayer simply does not lend itself to being 'showcased', then we should consider ways to make this particular approach to corporate prayer more biblical.

The Church needs to re-examine the philosophy of corporate prayer reflected in many of its prayer gatherings. Revival is a sovereign act of God. However, the current thinking on the part of many believers is to use corporate prayer the way an obstetrician uses pitocin. Prayer is what you use to 'induce' God to awaken a nation or revive a church. Certainly believers should join together to seek God on the issue of revival. But convincing God to birth the next Great Awakening is not the principle purpose behind corporate prayer. Rather, corporate prayer is a supernatural forum God uses to bring His Body into conformity with His plans for awakening and revival!

In Acts 2, Peter, having been filled with the Holy Spirit, boldly proclaimed the meaning of Pentecost to thousands of people who were in Jerusalem for the Jewish Feast of Weeks. He declared, 'But this is what was spoken of through the prophet Joel: "And it shall be in the last days", God says, "That I will pour forth of My Spirit upon all mankind; and your sons and your daughters shall prophesy, and your young men shall see visions, and your old men shall dream dreams" (Acts 2:16-17).

According to Peter, God's pouring forth of His Spirit on the day of Pentecost was not in response to the prayers of the disciples in the upper room, but rather was an event subject to the sovereign will and timing of God who, hundreds of years earlier, had revealed His plan through the prophet Joel. This tells us that epochal spiritual events in history are God-driven, not prayer-driven. God, through His Spirit, is the one who enters into history, turns the heart of the king, explodes on the scene with spiritual power, and decides the beginning and the ending of the ages. Prayer is the primary way the Church submits to God, keeps in step with what He is doing, and is blessed. I'll say it differently: corporate prayer is not an event to which God must respond. Rather, it is the sovereign God who decides the events of history, of which the Church, as God moves His people to prayer, becomes the primary beneficiary.

The Church needs to cultivate a proper attitude in corporate prayer — one that reflects a biblical understanding of the sovereignty of God. Several years ago I was invited to preach an evangelistic crusade in northern Connecticut. Several pastors associated with the crusade held a prayer meeting in order to lift it up before God. For almost thirty minutes I was pleased to hear wonderful, Spirit-filled prayers being offered up to heaven's throne by some truly godly men.

Then another pastor closed the time in prayer. It only took a second for the pitch and volume of his voice to approach near ear-shattering levels. He literally screamed his prayer for nearly five minutes. Once the meeting had concluded, one of my associates asked me, 'Is God deaf?' My unspoken thought was, 'He is now.' Later I asked the pastor why he prayed the way he did. He responded, 'Sometimes you've got to storm the gates of heaven to move God.' But later I thought, 'Is this the Lord of the harvest? A slumbering general who has to be rudely awakened from His nap for Him to lead His troops into battle?'

The Bible says, 'Since therefore, brethren, we have confidence to enter the holy place by the blood of Jesus, by a new and living way which He inaugurated for us through the veil, that is, His flesh, and since we have a great priest over the house of God, let us draw near with a sincere heart in full assurance of faith, having our hearts sprinkled clean from an evil conscience and our bodies washed with pure water' (Hebrews 10:19-22). It's really unnecessary for any Christian soldier to 'storm' heaven. Jesus' blood and righteousness have already provided full access before the throne of grace.

However, we must also guard against too much soberness in prayer. I'll never forget a night very early in my itinerant evangelism days in New England. At the conclusion of an evangelistic service an elderly saint walked up to me and said, 'Son, you preach like a man on fire for God. But you pray like a man whose belt's a little too tight.' Point taken. The fact that Jesus has provided the way of reconciliation with the Father, means that access before the throne of grace is not to be treated with graveness. In our prayers we should not yell at God, but neither should we bore Him to tears.

No doubt the prototype for prayer that Jesus established with His disciples, what we call the Lord's Prayer, appears on the surface to offer little room for emotion. But the pattern of Scripture also indicates that whenever people are in the presence of a Holy God, either directly or through angelic visitations, their whole beings are affected. Adam hid himself. Jacob was crippled. Moses' face shined. Isaiah trembled in repentance. Mary declared herself a 'bondslave of the Lord'. The shepherds were terribly frightened. The apostles in the upper room spoke in tongues. Cornelius could not take his eyes away. Is it possible to be in the presence of a Holy God and not be equally moved in body, mind, soul, and strength? I think not.

In his book *Joy Unspeakable*, Dr. Martin Lloyd-Jones recounts the powerful effect prayer had in the ministry of yet another great Calvinistic preacher, Robert Murray McCheyne, who, after spending time with God in prayer, merely had to face his congregation and a spirit of repentance would sweep the room. 'It has been authenticated so many, many times, that Robert Murray McCheyne had simply to enter the pulpit and before he had opened his mouth people used to begin to weep and were convicted of sin. He had not uttered a word. Why? Well, the explanation was that this man had come from the presence of God and the Spirit was poured forth.'[2]

I am examining both the overly aggressive posture as well as the too timid approach in prayer because Jacob's sin can be seen in both. Jacob was a 'control freak'. His self-reliance stood in the way of his trusting God to fully produce the blessings in his life. When we pray too hard we infer that God is napping and it is up to us to take up the slack. But prayer that is faint-hearted reduces God to little more than a religious ritual that is impotent in dealing with real-life issues.

Perhaps like Jacob of old you too are a 'control freak'. You believe in God's promises. But because you are much better at walking by sight than by faith, you live in constant fear and anxiety over the future. But prayer brings us into the presence of the Sovereign Lord where we see this attitude as foolishness. Prayer is the ultimate self-examination before the Holy Spirit who reveals that God and His timetable for our lives and the world He has created are perfectly on schedule.

We can live as though there is no Holy Spirit in the world until we go to prayer. There we can no longer defend our accusation against God that He hasn't got the slightest idea of what He is doing with our lives. In prayer the Holy Spirit uproots our faithlessness and reveals to us all those things we have propped up in our lives as 'God' that are the real source of our confusion and anxiety. In prayer we are stripped naked before the Lord of life who reveals to us that our fear about tomorrow is fused to the selfish pride that constantly feeds our rebellious opposition to God.

Ray C. Stedman remarked, 'We must either be praying or fainting – there is no other alternative. The purpose of all faith is to bring us into direct, personal touch with God. True prayer is an awareness of our helpless need, an acknowledgment of divine adequacy. For Jesus, prayer was as necessary as breathing, the very breath of His life. Although God certainly knows all our needs, praying for them changes our attitude from complaint to praise, and enables us to participate in God's personal plans for our lives.'[3] Now let's consider private prayer.

Like corporate prayer, private prayer must always remain dependent upon the sovereign grace of God. Paul's own prayer for the church at Ephesus shows the extent to which all that we ask of God cannot possibly come close to what our gracious God can perform. He says, 'Now to Him who is able to do exceeding abundantly beyond all that we ask or think, according to the power that works within us' (Ephesians 3:20).

Yet one of the tendencies in many believers is to view their prayer life as a 'work'. I recall a young guy who was going through difficult times said to me, 'I'm going to chain myself to the altar and pray and not get up until God hears and answers.' This fellow's attitude is characteristic of so many people who will pray over a single issue for hours in the hopes that their diligent striving will merit God's attention. But prayer is no different from any other area of Christian living. Just as you cannot earn salvation through good works, you cannot earn a physical healing, a financial blessing, or even a single answer to prayer. All of it is by grace through faith. A prayer's intensity or length is no substitute for humble faith before a gracious and giving God.

Someone might say, 'But we are called to persevere in prayer!' This is true. However, persevering prayer is not a forum where the good gifts of God are attained through determined self-effort. The Bible says that God hears and answers our prayers the second they go up to heaven. John writes, 'And this is the confidence which we have before Him, that, if we ask anything according to His will, He hears us. And if we know that He hears us in whatever we ask, we know that we have the requests which we have asked from Him' (1 John 5:14-15).

Persevering prayer is much like our experience of abiding in Christ. It is a time of spiritual communion with the Father, who, having answered our prayer within a breath of its utterance, now works to soften and shape our hearts into vessels suitable to contain the answer.

Nevertheless, it remains the practice of many believers to 'pray through' on important issues. 'Praying through' describes an activity where one continues in prayer until one senses he has reached a solution. But often the way a person knows he has attained a solution to his problem through prayer is not rooted in the Bible's declaration that 'if we ask anything according to His will, He hears us'. Rather, it is based in the achievement of emotional release and a subjective sense of wellbeing. A sense of peace should accompany the believer in every area of his life, but the fact remains that God hears and answers our prayers according to His sovereign will, not according to how we 'feel'.

The truth that God is intimately involved in every aspect of His creation ought to suggest to us that God is not a cosmic wizard who can only be reached by a tortuous journey of 'praying through'. On the contrary, your heavenly Father has entered into a covenant with you. His promise is to bless you. God wrote His covenant in the very blood of Jesus Christ. And He has sealed His promises in the Holy Spirit. They are readily available to all who submit to His will and walk by faith.

Prayer should be infused with the truth that God is in control of all things for our good. Let's take a deeper look into the relationship of the sovereignty of God to private prayer by way of Paul's letter to the Philippian believers. Paul writes, 'Be anxious for nothing, but in everything by prayer and supplication with thanksgiving let your requests be made known to God. And the peace of God, which surpasses all comprehension, shall guard your hearts and your minds in Christ Jesus' (Philippians 4:6-7).

The reason Paul can challenge his readers to lay their cares aside is because God is in control. If God is in control, why worry? Notice that Paul doesn't encourage prayer as a means of getting rid of anxiety. Rather we are to 'Be anxious for nothing'. In other words, the absence of worry in a believer's life should be a 'state of being'. This state of being is not achieved through prayer, but rather is the result of faith.

Once our hearts are calm before the Lord, then it is time to pray. I often liken prayer to dialing up a radio station. God is not to be found at the higher frequencies where fear and anxiety live. Rather He is to be sought at the lower frequencies of rest, peace, and contentment — all of which comes by faith.

Worry is sin. Ask a group of believers, 'Who worried last week?' And watch all the hands go up. But then ask, 'Now who committed adultery last week?' And no hands go up. Why? It's because we make the distinction between acceptable and non-acceptable sin. Yes, many believers' prayers are hindered due to the presence of sin in their lives. But most people's sins are rarely the obvious ones like murder, adultery, and cheating. The great sin in most of our lives is worry. But the Bible says don't worry, just pray.

Prayer must always be united with supplication. What is supplication? It is an old English word that, like a diamond, has many facets to its meaning. One meaning that relates directly to the sovereignty of God suggests that when we pray, our absolute focus should be on God and nothing else. Perhaps you're like me. There are many things on my mind, so when I pray I often find it difficult to keep my mind focused on God. But to pray with supplication means that our hearts and minds are focused on the face of God like a laser beam.

I don't wish to mix metaphors; however, another way to describe supplication is to say that if prayer is the throne room of God, supplication is closing the door behind you. All the cares and distractions of life are now shut out as your full attention is directed toward God.

In fact, Paul offers his own definition of supplication in Philippians 4:8: 'Finally, brethren, whatever is true, whatever is honorable, whatever is right, whatever is pure, whatever is lovely, whatever is of good repute, if there is any excellence and if anything worthy of praise, let your mind dwell on these things.' Can you think of anything more true, honorable, right, pure, lovely, good, excellent, and worthy of praise than God?

But the fact that God is to be the absolute focus of our hearts and minds in prayer points to a major reason why many people find it difficult to practice supplication. Sadly, many people are so mad at God over their problems they refuse to look Him in the face. Is that you? Do you secretly blame God for something? Your failed expectations? A health problem? The fact you're still single?

I've heard so many excuses why people don't pray. A woman once told me she was so worn out that she couldn't even find the strength to pray. But after sharing her situation with me it became painfully obvious that her real problem was the bitterness she harboured in her heart toward God. Have you ever been so mad at someone you didn't want to be in the same room with him? This lady was so infuriated with God over her problems she refused to enter the throne room because she knew He would be there.

But this is where the sovereignty of God helps. God is not like a cat that plays with we little mice until He has finally had enough and kills us. He loves us. His sovereign control over all people, places, and events is aimed at His highest glory. But God's desire to receive all glory does not come at the expense of our happiness. Jesus promises an abundant life. He said, 'I came that they might have life, and have it abundantly' (John 10:10).

And Paul reminds us that everything that happens in life – including our problems – is subject to the sovereign working of God who has our ultimate good in view. He writes, 'And we know that God causes all things to work together for good to those who love God, to those who are called according to His purpose' (Romans 8:28).

When you don't feel like praying is the time you must pray. Reluctance to pray is a sign you haven't yet come to the place of total surrender before the sovereign God. Blaming God and making yourself out to be a victim illustrates how much you are still a part of the world system under the control of Satan.

But God is prepared to do mighty miracles in your life if you would fully surrender your life to Him. My little girl Haley once asked me, 'Daddy, why do people at church raise their hands when they sing?' I told her the story of Moses and the parting of the Red Sea. As long as Moses lifted his hands and staff in the air, the waters of the Red Sea remained parted, providing the way of escape for the Hebrews from Pharoah. I then explained that Moses' outstretched arms represented the universal sign of surrender. Likewise, lifting hands in worship is one way we demonstrate to God that our lives are fully surrendered to Him. It is then that God performs mighty wonders in our lives as He did with Moses.

Regardless of our circumstances, prayer must always be joined with thanksgiving. Is God in control in the lean times? When you've lost your job? After the miscarriage? Are you able to thank Him in all things? Permit me to share some examples of how I believe prayer can reflect the sovereignty of God in the new Christian activism. This example comes from my own personal struggle with joining prayer to thanksgiving in the midst of difficult circumstances. It all took place when my labour for the Great Commission involved helping to plant churches.

After several hard years of ministering in New England, I moved in 1989 to the Washington, D.C. area. A year later I was asked to become part of a church planting team that was focusing its efforts on the western parts of Virginia and West Virginia.

The first place I was sent to help start a mission church was Leesburg, Virginia. I'll never forget my first meeting with the small core group who had already been gathering in a funeral home on Sundays for prayer and Bible study. There were eight of us, not including the corpse that was waiting in the wings for the one o'clock funeral!

Within several months the core group grew to approximately thirty people and we were able to rent the sanctuary of a local Seventh-Day Adventist Church. Increasing to thirty people took no small effort. Personal evangelism proved difficult in this rural town, and visitors to the church often did not stay. Each time a visitor chose not to return, I would literally cringe inside.

Eventually the Lord spoke to me through His Word, saying that unless I could pray and thank Him for each person that left our church I would be ruined as a minister of the gospel. So I started to thank Him and over time I witnessed God pour out His blessings on our struggling group. I recommended we call the mission Potomac Hills Presbyterian Church. Everyone agreed. After eighteen months the mission was stable enough to call a full-time pastor. In time, the mission became a full-fledged Presbyterian Church. This freed me to go to the next spot, Winchester, Virginia, where I was to help to start another mission church.

To say that getting the core-group in Winchester off the ground was hard would be an understatement. After two failed evangelistic outreaches, I sought God for wisdom, and again the Lord confronted me with my need to thank Him for the fact that no one was responding to the evangelism intended to facilitate the church plant. It was truly amazing, but as I began to pray and thank Him, God really provided me with supernatural strength to keep the vision for the mission church alive.

Although all the factors weighed against it, shortly thereafter I decided to just jump in and start church services. I rented the Seventh-Day Adventist Church in Winchester and called the first service for 6 December 1992. To encourage the church not to grow weary as I had, I named it Eagle Heights Presbyterian, based on Isaiah 40:31, 'Yet those who wait for the Lord will gain new strength; they will mount up with wings like eagles, they will run and not get tired, they will walk and not become weary.' Today Eagle Heights Presbyterian is a thriving body in the northern part of Virginia's Shenandoah Valley.

The next place I went was Charles Town, West Virginia, the site where John Brown was hung after being captured just a few miles north at Harper's Ferry. This time the Seventh-Day Adventist building and every local school facility were unavailable for use. So I rented a 140-year-old Methodist Church building on Route 9. Talk about difficult conditions! Through the weeks of planning and meeting together, it looked like the mission might succeed. However, after several months it became increasingly clear that it was not God's time for a Presbyterian Church in Charles Town.

One evening I arrived early for our weekly Bible study, which was held in a trailer parked outside the old Methodist building. I remember pacing up and down inside that trailer for several minutes, frantically praying that God would bring the people we needed to plant a solid church. Then God reminded me once again that I was to thank Him, even for the fact the mission was failing. If ever there was a time my prayers embodied the idea of 'conflict with God', that was it.

In all the time I laboured to plant churches in the Shenandoah Valley, that was the hardest thing God ever asked me to do. But once I thanked Him, I was able to see it was His church, not mine, and that it was His prerogative to do with it what He wanted. It was then that I turned the mission over to God. What happened to the Charles Town mission? It failed. But it failed because God wanted it to fail. And for that I thank Him. Friends, be sure to thank God in all things. For unless you are able to thank Him in the midst of all your circumstances, you have not yet come to the place of total surrender.

So now we have come full circle. For total surrender was Jacob's hard-earned lesson. Yet it is this very lesson that God is still teaching His people today. We pray for revival, awakening, and God's rich blessing upon our nation and the world. We seek His face that He might provide resources for our ministries, money to pay the bills, healing for our time-worn bodies, and strength for the journey. All of these prayers are biblical. Nonetheless, until we learn that prayer is first and foremost the most important way to tell God that, should He choose not to provide any of these things for us, we will still love Him, we will not have learned the lesson of total surrender.

Now let's focus on another important area of 'Body life' that if practiced, can strengthen and assist the Church in its labour in the Cultural Mandate and the Great Commission — church unity.

Ten

THAT THEY MAY KNOW WE ARE CHRISTIANS

Have you ever wondered what makes the difference between a spotlight and a laser beam? How can a medium-power laser burn through steel in a matter of seconds, while the most powerful spotlight can only make it warm? Both have the same electrical power requirements. The difference is unity.

A laser can be simply described as a medium of excited molecules with mirrors at each end. Some of the excited molecules naturally decay into a less excited state. In the decay process they release a photon, a particle of light. It is here that the unique process of the laser begins. The photon moves along and 'tickles' another molecule, inviting another photon to join him on his journey.

Then these two photons 'tickle' two more molecules and invite two more photons to join the parade. Soon there is a huge army of photons marching in step with each other. It is this unity that gives the laser its power. A spotlight may have just as many photons, but each is going its own independent way, occasionally interfering with other photons. As a result, much of its power is wasted and cannot be focused to do any useful work. However, the laser, because of its unity, is like an army marching in tight formation and is able to focus all its power on its objective.

The way the laser beam utilizes 'unity' to focus its power illustrates another area where I believe pietism has offered much needed direction to the Church in recent years. It is the area of *church unity*. Francis Frangipane observes, 'The Spirit of Christ who dwells within us is pleading for our unity. How can we be so deaf to His desires, so cold toward His passions? How can we say we love Him and not keep His commandments or embrace His vision for us?'[1] Francis Frangipane bases his remarks upon Jesus' words: 'Holy Father, keep them in Thy name, the name which Thou hast given Me, that they may be one, even as we are one' (John 17:11). So important was the issue of unity to Jesus that He said the discernible imprint on our lives that we are His followers would be the love we shared in the bond of unity. He said, 'By this all men will know that you are My Disciples, if you have love for one another' (John 13:35).

Today, Jesus' disciples live during an exciting time when much is being written on the subjects of personal evangelism, church planting, church growth, and Christian, social activism. Nevertheless, there remains an 'Achilles' heel' in the life of the Church that is curtailing its efforts in reaching the world for Christ. The Church is divided. By 'divided' I don't mean to suggest that our divisions fall merely along theological and denominational lines. Rather, I'm referring to the overall lack of *Christ-like love and unity* that exists between many members of the Church.

When Jesus said the world would recognize us by our love for each other, He wasn't comparing Christian love to an 'identification badge'. Jesus prayed, 'That they may all be one; even as Thou, Father, art in Me, and I in Thee, that they also may be in Us; *that the world may believe that Thou didst send Me*' (John 17:21, italics added). Self-denying love shared between God's children is a persuasive truth that God Himself lives in the midst of them which, in turn, draws unbelievers to His side. This love and unity is more than a way the world has to single out the children of God, but rather, as it finds its source in the Father's love, bears an *attraction* to the world to come to the cross of Jesus Christ.

Nevertheless, many believers have traditionally underestimated the benefit of church unity to the work of reaching the world for Christ. What accounts for the lack of unity among believers?

Many Christians fear that efforts at church unity will lead to a weakening of doctrinal standards. Increasingly, believers are suspicious whenever they hear a call to unity. And indeed, there is justification for their mistrust. Today we live in what Dr. John MacArthur calls an 'age of tolerance'.[2] It is a time when, according to Dr. R.C. Sproul, 'relationships are more important than truth'.[3] There should be little doubt that the world's ability to overlook truth is an outgrowth of its disdain for it. One might expect the Church to be different. But as history demonstrates, once Satan is able to convince Christ's followers that the Church is built, not upon the rock of revelation, but upon the sand of relationships, the Church then begins to exhibit the same contempt for truth that marks the world.

Beginning in 1992, a group of prominent evangelical and Roman Catholic leaders began to map out a unified statement called, 'Evangelicals and Catholics Together: The Christian Mission in the Third Millennium (ECT)', that in the opinion of many, represents an assault upon the Christian gospel for the sake of creating a unified front in the work of the Great Commission in third-world nations. Many people that believe in the 'doctrine of cobelligerancy' – the idea that believers of diverse theological and denominational backgrounds must fight together against a common enemy – do *not* believe that ECT meets the doctrine's criteria that the nature of the alliance not call upon believers to refute the fundamentals of the gospel. They contend that ECT fails this test because it asserts a unity of mission between evangelicals and Roman Catholics in the midst of disagreement over the *foundation* of the Christian mission – that forgiveness of sins and reconciliation with God has been made available to the world based upon the merits of Christ, and Christ alone.

On the other hand, believers must also be vigilant to avoid allowing the pendulum to swing to the opposite extreme, where the mere mention of church unity is viewed as joining the One World Church and following the Antichrist. Paul writes, 'Being diligent to preserve the unity of the Spirit in the bond of peace. There is one body and one Spirit, just as also you were called in one hope of your calling; one Lord, one faith, one baptism, one God and Father of all who is over all and through all and in all' (Ephesians 4:3-6). The type of unity Paul encourages is not a 'unity for unity's sake'. Nor can meeting at the Howard Johnson's on Wednesday mornings for the evangelical pastor's prayer breakfast attain it. Rather, unity is of the *nature* of the Church. Like the spots on a leopard, unity is part and parcel of what makes the Church the Body of Christ. Thus, we do not work to obtain unity. Rather, we are to be diligent to 'preserve' the unity of the Church. Paul can affirm the unity of the Church because it arises from the unity of God (see second building block of a biblical worldview).

In his commentary on Ephesians, John R. W. Stott observes, 'Indeed, we can go further. We must assert that there can be only one Christian family, only one Christian faith, hope and baptism, and only one Christian body, because there is only one God, Father, Son, and Holy Spirit. You can no more multiply churches than you can multiply gods. Is there only one God? Then he has only one church. Is the unity of God inviolable? Then so is the unity of the church. The unity of the church is as indestructible as the unity of God Himself. It is no more possible to split the church than it is possible to split the Godhead.'[4] Because the Church is one, believers must strive to practice biblical unity even where a level of theological and denominational division exists.

One church believes in infant baptism; another believes that being filled with the Holy Spirit is a second work of grace. Where do believers draw the line in their willingness to practice church unity? *Whenever Christians are pressed to accept unity at the expense of the essentials of orthodox Christian belief, they must decline the offer.*

St. Augustine allegedly coined this epigram as a basis for agreement between believers of different Christian communities whenever questions of doctrine arise: 'In essentials, unity; in non-essentials, liberty; in all things, charity.'[5] This is an excellent criteria to use when judging the legitimacy of a call to church unity.

Petty jealousy and backbiting has created a major source of discord and disunity among church members and also among church leaders, which is hindering the effective outreach of many local churches. As long as church members are fighting; as long as rivalry, pride, and jealousy are in our midst, God is simply not going to bless the Church's outreach.

One of the principle problems among the Philippian believers was disunity. The issue revolved around two women named Euodia and Syntyche (cf. 4:1-3), both of whom had helped Paul in the ministry. Although conservative commentators are at a loss over the details of the dispute, the majority agrees that over time an unhealthy rivalry emerged between the two women resulting in a fight over who should receive the greater credit for assisting Paul in his ministry. Soon sides began to form in the church. Bickering and self-aggrandizement then took center stage in the church, taking the focus off of Christ. Therefore, Paul writes the church to say that only in Christ can believers restore unity and develop a singleness of mind and purpose.

Although Christ is the central message of Philippians, 'joy in the Lord' surfaces very early in the letter as the *practical* remedy for its disunity. So pervasive is the theme of joy throughout Paul's letter that Philippians has been called the 'Epistle of Joy'. Someone might say, 'You're silly to think that something as superficial as joy in the Christian life can help heal major divisions within a church. There must be another answer.' Afraid not. At a time when local churches are more and more looking to 'experts' to solve their problems, 'joy in the Lord' remains God's prescription for internal strife among believers. I recall Dr. Henry Krabbandam, professor at Covenant College, who at the time was speaking on the subject of the sin of disunity among believers, say, 'Either sin will kill your joy, or joy will kill your sin.' How does this work?

The type of joy Paul speaks of is not to be confused with a 'good feeling.' Instead, Paul encourages joy 'in the Lord'. Joy, as a fruit of the Spirit, is not emotion-based. It is *person-based*. Joy finds its source in the person of Jesus Christ and the work of redemption, which He has accomplished on our behalf. Joy stands as the all-inclusive sign that the *fullness* of salvation is evident in a believer's life. Thus, a believer who is full of Christ is one who has 'crucified the flesh with its passions and desires' (Galatians 5:24), and who simply does not have the will to 'become boastful, challenging one another, envying one another' (v.26), which is the root of disunity. When your life is full of joy, you do not have room in your heart for the spirit of envy and strife. You have neither the time, nor the inclination, to fight and quarrel.

The sin of envy is also evident among church leaders. Pastors are busy building and growing new churches, but underlying many of their individual efforts is a professional rivalry that is fueled by a thirst for personal acknowledgment in the ministry.

One minister describes his jealousy over the success of a fellow minister this way: 'I shall never forget the sense of guilt and sin that possessed me over that business. I was miserable. I was practically saying to the Lord Jesus, "Unless the prosperity of thy church and people comes in this neighbourhood by me, success had better not come". Was I really showing inability to rejoice in another worker's service? I felt that it was sin of a very hateful character. I never asked the Lord to take away my life either before or since, but I did then, unless his grace gave me victory over this foul image of jealousy.'[6] Praise God this man of God *did* find grace to overcome the bitter root of jealousy that was crippling his life and ministry.

Before becoming chaplain of the U.S. Senate, Richard C. Halverson, was senior minister at Hollywood Presbyterian Church in Hollywood, California. He was well acquainted with the problem of rivalry among ministers. In his devotional letter *Perspective*, he writes, 'There is a way to peace, but it is very costly. Question is, are we willing to pay the price? If there is to be peace men must renounce things that make for war. Human greed, avarice, prejudice, lust, envy must go! Are you willing to forsake your lust for power, for position? Will you say "no" to the greed that makes you want more than you have? Will you reject the jealousy, which makes it impossible for you to rejoice in another's honor? Will you deny the envy that forces your bitter criticism of the friend who has gotten ahead of you?'[7]

God's Word is more to the point: 'Do nothing from selfishness or empty conceit, but with humility of mind let each of you regard one another as more important than himself; do not merely look out for your own personal interests, but also for the interests of others' (Philippians 2:3-4). Resentment and rivalry among ministers of the gospel is defeated when we allow the life and power of Jesus – the humble Servant of God – to live His life in, and through, us (See third building block of a biblical worldview).

The church at Cali, Columbia was feeling the pressures of drugs and violence. The community that Ruth and Julio Ruibal came to reach as church planters in 1978 was crumbling before their very eyes. Pastor Julio Ruibal called for prayer, but there was rancorous division among other church leaders. At one point Julio withdrew from the pastor's organization, but he saw the need for a unified church, went back, and asked for forgiveness.

Because Julio was outspoken against the drug cartels, his life was in jeopardy. He received a threat and shortly thereafter was shot and killed. At his memorial his wife spoke about her husbands sacrifice and desire for the church to unify. The pastors were so moved that they formed a covenant of unity with each other.

The results were nothing less than astounding. In 1995, the first all-night prayer meeting was held. In nine months, six out of seven drug-lords were arrested. A prayer rally was held in the city's stadium with 60,000 in attendance. Reports indicate that unbelievers at the rally were so overwhelmed by the power of prayer that many were led to receive Christ. The government was so impressed with the arrest-rate among the drug lords that they let the churches use the stadium free of charge.[8] Here is a perfect example of how church unity can help to facilitate both the Great Commission and the Cultural Mandate. A unified church resulted in many hearts getting right with God, plus the culture was affected for good through the timely arrest of several drug king pins.

Racism in the Church is an unspoken source of division among believers. In 1991, I felt led to stir up my gifts as an evangelist and conduct an evangelistic outreach in downtown Washington, D.C. I had been praying about a crusade in the nation's capital since coming to Northern Virginia in 1989. My first move was to share my vision with an inner-city black pastor, whom others claimed had his finger on the 'pulse beat' of the city. During our meeting he was polite and counseled me to avoid moving too quickly without first seeing what God was already doing in the city to bring revival. His suggestions included getting to know the pastors of the city and walking with them for a period of time. If God did want me to preach a crusade in Washington, D.C., He would make it clear in His time. Sounded like a plan.

I began to attend the weekly inner-city prayer meetings, many of which were attended by pastors, city employees, and congressmen who gathered to pray for God's blessings upon the nation's capital. The prayer meetings provided ample opportunities to build relationships with several key black pastors who eagerly shared with me their goals for ministry in the city. I shared with them my vision for an evangelistic outreach, which was consistently met with a high level of interest. One black pastor was kind enough to drive me around and give me a personal tour of the city. Together we searched for possible locations to erect a gospel tent for a future crusade.

Months passed, and one day I said to one of the black pastors, to whom I had grown closest, 'I would like to begin in earnest to plan the crusade.' He agreed and called a meeting of other pastors, all of whom were black. We met in a little restaurant and discussed plans for the crusade over lunch. Although my goal was to preach the crusade, I clearly stated to the men, 'I do not have to be the evangelist. Perhaps God has someone else in mind, including one of you.' But each man responded that his schedule was packed. The mantle fell back on me. Once the meeting concluded, something seemed odd to me. No one asked, 'When is our next meeting?'

The following day, I left a message with one of the pastors. He never returned my call. I drove to the church of another pastor who also had been in attendance at the meeting. He was in but didn't appear eager to talk. I convinced him to give me a few minutes. Before I could say anything, he said, 'You want to discuss the crusade, don't you?' 'Yes', I replied. With a grimaced look, he said, 'John, I don't think you should plan on the men at that meeting being involved. And if they're not involved, I don't think I can.' I responded, 'What do you mean?' As he stood shaking his head and looking down at the ground, he said, 'If they knew what I was about to say, they'd kill me.' I exclaimed, 'What are you talking about?' Then it happened. In absolute anguish, he said, 'John, the problem is that you are white.' You could have knocked me over with a feather. All the prayer meetings, cordial conversations, and relationship building — was it all a farce? The crusade blew up in a flash, because I was 'white'.

When 'racism' appeared in the above subtitle, I'll bet you weren't expecting this story. No, you were expecting a tale about how a minority person was discriminated against. But my experience in Washington, D.C. taught me that racism is a *two-way* street and that the Church is a long way from overcoming it. Before we examine how the Church can overcome racial bigotry, let's take a brief look at the world's answer to the challenge — egalitarianism.

Social Orthodoxy in Theory

Since the French enlightenment, perhaps no doctrine has embodied the liberal humanist worldview with more vigor than *egalitarianism*. One is egalitarian who advocates a *forced* equality in areas such as race, law, politics, and economics. During the 1960s, President Lyndon B. Johnson turned the enlightenment doctrine of egalitarianism into public policy with his call for a 'Great Society'. Undoubtedly, the Civil Rights movement, beginning in the 1960s, did much good in challenging long-held notions of racial disparity. Words like 'justice' and 'reconciliation' have now gained a reputable spot in the marketplace of ideas. Problematically, over the past four decades the usage of these words, within the context of egalitarian doctrine, has resulted in their being divorced from any proper biblical understanding of the terms. The current social theory of race has diminished the *spiritual* meaning of words like 'justice' and 'reconciliation' in favour of a more rigorous defense of civil justice and racial equality. Thus, familiar terms, different meanings. From a racial perspective, this new, liberal humanist worldview is today best represented in the social orthodoxy of the Reverend Jesse Jackson and the Reverend Al Sharpton.

This misguided view of equality is seen early in Scripture. In Genesis 3, Satan projects his own preoccupation for equality with God onto the first couple. 'For God knows that the day you eat from it, the tree of the knowledge of good and evil, your eyes will be opened, and you will be like God, knowing good and evil' (Genesis 3:5). Satan places into Adam and Eve the fear that they may not be equal to God and that He is threatened by their equality. He suggests that this problem can be remedied if the couple will eat of the fruit of the tree of the knowledge of good and evil – a temptation, which becomes the basis for the fall of man.

Soon it becomes clear that equality with God is not enough for Satan. The Bible teaches that Satan's passion for equality is driven by an ungodly pride and overwhelming jealousy, which gives way to a quest for superiority: 'How have you fallen from heaven, O star of the morning, son of the dawn! You have been cut down to the earth you who have weakened the nations. But you said in your heart I will ascend to heaven; I will raise my throne above the stars of God, and I will sit on the mount of assembly in the recesses of the north. I will ascend above the heights of the clouds; I will make myself like the Most High' (Isaiah 14:12-14). At the heart of Satan's quest for equality is his hidden agenda to transcend the One, true God.

The liberal humanist view of equality follows the same path. The contemporary drive for racial justice, in as far as it is indebted to secular humanism, is tyranny by another name. The oppressed soon become the oppressors. We substitute the old tyranny for a new tyranny – the tyranny of racism, the tyranny of sexism, and the tyranny of political correctness. This cycle represents a leading destructive force in the history of nations. How is the Christian message different?

The gospel provides the only source for unity and love between people of different races. Racism is an *emotional* issue – all the more reason we need God's objective viewpoint on the issue (See first building block of a biblical worldview). His Word and Holy Spirit should govern our emotions, and thus our actions, toward people of other races.

Scripture tells us that God does not call His Church to practice racial equality, but unity in Christ (cf. John 17:21). What many call 'racial justice' the Bible calls 'love of the brethren' (1 Thessalonians 4:9). This love is a spiritual fruit of the Body of Christ (cf. Galatians 5:22). The world cannot know or express this fruit until it humbly receives Jesus (cf. John 15:5).

In His story of the Pharisee and the tax-gatherer (Luke 18:9-13), Jesus revealed that the main cause of division between people is a bad spiritual heart: 'The Pharisee stood and was praying thus to himself,

"God I thank thee that I am not like other people" (v.11). Jesus specifically chose a Pharisee to say that the root cause of all disunity, hatred, and bigotry is pharisaical self-righteousness or self-trust (cf. also Luke 6:22; Titus 3:3). Because the Pharisee trusted in his own righteousness for salvation, he couldn't know that his religious 'works' were sufficient to merit God's forgiveness. His spiritual insecurity led him to 'view others with contempt' (v.9). Demeaning the tax-gatherer somehow made him feel better about his own sinful condition. Today many people degrade, debase, and humiliate people of color to prop up their own tattered egos. The cure for self-trust is not 'sensitivity training', but rather is found in the contrite attitude of the tax-gatherer who, in recognizing his sinful estate, thrust himself upon the grace and mercy of Almighty God: 'But the tax-gatherer, standing some distance away, was even unwilling to lift up his eyes to heaven, but was beating his breast, saying, "God be merciful to me, the sinner!"' (v.13). A redeemed child of the King views only his sin with contempt, not other people.

Because God loves all peoples so must we. The word 'racism' is a cultural term not found in Scripture. However, the act of viewing other people-groups with contempt was common among the ancient Hebrews, who were taught that non-Jews were 'God-haters' and stood outside the covenant promises to Israel. During the time of Christ the Jews viewed Gentiles as 'dogs' and 'unclean'.

Acts 10 records a miraculous work of God that led to the inclusion of Gentile believers in the Church. Cornelius was a centurion of the hated Roman army. Although many Jews held him in high regard, Cornelius was still an 'unclean' Gentile. One day an angel of God appeared to Cornelius, whom Scripture describes as 'a devout man, and one who feared God with all his household' and told him to send for Peter who was at Joppa. Meanwhile, God gave Peter a vision of a great sheet coming down from heaven, lowered by four corners to the ground. Inside the sheet were all kinds of animals, creatures, and birds, which were considered unclean foods to a Jew. To Peter's great shock, a voice exclaimed, 'Arise, Peter, kill and eat!' (v.13). 'By no means, Lord, for I have never eaten anything unholy and unclean,' Peter responded (v.14). The voice replied, 'What God has cleaned, no longer consider unholy' (v.15).

The purpose of the vision was to teach Peter that people of all nations were now to be included in the gospel. Therefore, he should no longer call any man unholy or unclean. Upon meeting Cornelius, Peter said, 'I most certainly understand that God is not one to show partiality' (v.34). The home of Cornelius was full of Gentiles. Peter began to preach. Then suddenly the Holy Spirit was poured out upon all the Gentiles who were present. The Jewish delegation accompanying Peter to the home of Cornelius was amazed.

Acts 11 records Peter's defense of his ministry to the Gentiles before the apostles and the brethren at Jerusalem. Peter retold the history of his vision and God's miraculous gift of the Holy Spirit to the Gentiles. The Jerusalem church concurred with Peter that the gospel was for all people, not just the Jews. They said, 'Well then, God has granted to the Gentiles also the repentance that leads to life' (v.18). God does not keep the gospel from people because of gender, skin color, national origin, or educational background. The love of Christ is for all peoples, tribes, nations, and tongues (see fifth building block of a biblical worldview).

The gospel brings a new social order, which disallows racism. God's common justice for society was summarized in Christ's brilliant synopsis of Old Testament law: 'You shall love the Lord your God with all your heart, and with all your soul and with all your mind, this is the greatest and foremost commandment. The second is like it. You shall love your neighbour as yourself' (Matthew 22:37-38). No EEOC checklist or civil rights initiative designed to level the playing field can substitute itself for the two great commandments as the foundation for social justice. Each day we choose whether to love God with all our hearts, minds, souls, and strength, and our neighbour as ourselves. The collective decision we make as a people dictates the racial temperament of society.

Moses laid a compelling choice before the ancient Hebrews: 'I call on heaven and earth to witness against you today, that I have set before you life and death, the blessing and the curse. So choose life in order that you might live, you and your descendants' (Deuteronomy 30:19).

According to the Bible, justice is not the result of a quota. Rather, justice is what one deserves. It is the God-determined result of moral choices people make with respect to obedience or disobedience. When we choose to hate, to practice racial intolerance, we bring the curse of God's law upon our lives. James writes, 'But if you show partiality, you are committing sin and are convicted by the law as transgressors' (James 2:9). But when we choose to obey God and love other races from a heart of mercy, God's great blessing is ours individually and as a nation. What would happen to racism if all people practiced the two great commandments? Racism would stop!

Overcoming racial bigotry is a tremendous task. But unless the Church demonstrates love and unity between believers of all races, how can we expect the world to solve racism? This is no time for secular solutions to spiritual problems. *In a new Christian activism, men and women of faith will rise up and defeat the sin of racism through the reconciliation provided in, by, and through, the shed blood of Christ.* We must, for the witness of the Church is at stake. It is the gospel of Jesus Christ that provides a point of commonality and unites in God a people from every tribe, nation, and tongue. Every church and Christ-centered organization must preach Christ, teach Christ, and live Christ. Christ is the answer. It is to this end that we shall pray and work together to forge a world without prejudice or disparity.

Now let's turn our attention to four areas that fall within the scope of the Cultural Mandate, beginning with the fine arts.

Eleven

TOWARD A REFORMATION OF THE ARTS

During the early 1980s, I was privileged to be a student at the Yale University Institute of Sacred Music. The Institute is an interdisciplinary think-tank that is shared by the Yale Divinity School and the Yale Graduate School of Music. I attended classes in both schools. The principle focus of the Institute is to further study and discourse on the relationship of Christianity to culture. My role at the Institute also permitted me to take courses at the department of Christianity and the Arts, where I studied art history (principally painting and architecture) and many of the underlying religious themes found in numerous art masterpieces. Here are some of the conclusions regarding art I arrived at during that time, all of which have since matured. I begin with a brief commentary on the Church's reaction to current developments in modern art.

The Present Dilemma

Contemporary trends in modern art have certainly become a hot-button issue. From Andres Serrano's blasphemous *Piss Christ*, a large photo of a crucifix immersed in urine, to Chris Ofili's controversial depiction of the Virgin Mary with elephant dung, to Renee Cox's *Yo Mama's Last Supper*, a five-panel photo which depicts Christ as a nude woman, there are ample reasons for Christians to be concerned about the growing irreverence in art. Moreover, both Serrano and Ofili received financial support from the United States Government (National Endowment for the Arts or NEA), a move that incensed cultural conservatives and which motivated them to put pressure on their elected officials to eliminate government funding for the NEA.

While it is tempting to follow other writers who have detailed many examples of sacrilegious art and suggest ways in which the Church can fight to eliminate the NEA, I have chosen to take a different direction. The reason is because the above discussion, although it is important, is not about art. It is a debate over morality. As we shall soon see, ethical and moral considerations function as non-negotiable ingredients in the creation of art. Nevertheless, art must not be limited to these factors.

I dare say that most believers would have little to say about art were it not for the fact that much of it has become scandalous. But the future of art will continue to be in question if Christians remain little more than art critics. Art also calls for our *positive* contribution – something that requires much study and thoughtful reflection. However, the Church of today has failed to offer serious reflection upon the nature of art and its role within the Christian community. The Church is producing no great artists in the line of Rembrandt, Van Gogh, or Rouault (at least none that have risen to prominence). The word 'masterpiece' is missing from the vocabulary of the Church. But what is more disappointing is the reason for this failure. The Church no longer encourages great art. The flourishing, artistic environment and the pressure to produce top-quality compositions that once gave us Michelangelo's ceiling of the Sistine Chapel, or Giotto's priceless fresco, *The Life of St. Francis*, has vanished. And, with rare exception, so has the wealth of gifted artisans that once marked the Church as the leader in the creation of magnificent works of art. *Today the scandal is not the existence of outrageous art. Rather, the greater scandal is that the Church has no great art to offer in its place.*

Nonetheless, this is not a new problem. It began when, after the sixteenth-century reformation of the Church, there came a needed and renewed zeal for the law of God. True, many blessings came to the Church as a result of its newfound commitment to the Law. However, the unfortunate by-product of people's enthusiasm for the second commandment in particular ('Thou shalt not make for thyself an idol, or any likeness of what is in heaven above or on earth beneath or in the waters under the earth'), was an unnecessary, institutional suspicion of *all* art, which has lasted to this day.

I would be wrong to suggest that the Church's anxiety over art is purely the result of a misreading of the second commandment. The influence of Christian pietism in the creation of a Christian 'sub-culture' affords an equally important explanation for the widespread scarcity of great art within the Church. Pietism has become a modern day 'Harold Hill,' who once warned River City of the dangers of a 'pool-hall, libertine men, and scarlet women', but who today warns the world of the dangers of painting, film, poetry, literature, and music.

In 1981, Franky Schaeffer, in his book, *Addicted to Mediocrity: 20ᵗʰ Century Christians and the Arts* commented that the Church had abdicated its role in the creation of great art, and instead followed, rather than led, popular culture with the production of 'Christian doodads, trinkets, tee-shirts, and bumper stickers'.[1] Sadly, some twenty years later, little has changed. Most art that is either appropriated by the Church or is produced by believers continues to be mediocre. Christian clip-art has become a metaphor for contemporary Christian art, which reveals a type of pseudo-intellectualism, or 'sweet Jesus' mentality, that fails to provide a vision of real beauty and therefore of transcendence. What is the answer?

A new Christian activism must seek to birth a reformation of the fine arts within the Church. We must seek to encourage what the twentieth-century, French priest and artist, Marie Alain Couturier, sought to encourage – great art, sacred art. Problematically, the Church's disdain for 'indecent' art and what it believes should be a proper moral and political response to it has become its position on art. If believers are going to demonstrate obedience to the Cultural Mandate, we must balance our fight against lewd art with seeking to advance great art. The following points are intended to help the Church rediscover the nature of great art so that it might begin to produce it once again.

Most of my remarks will centre on painting because within the fine arts it is the easiest to use as a forum for discussing our topic. However, most of the conclusions we arrive at regarding painting can be applied to all other areas within the fine arts with only minor modification.

For art to be great, the artist must have a saving relationship with God. This point represents Christianity's distinctive contribution to the furtherance of great art. As I previously mentioned, there is a 'moral' component to art. More precisely, the act of doing art takes place within a moral context. Art is simply a creative extension of an artist's spiritual values and worldview, which help to define his relationship to God. Every brush stroke, film edit, musical phrase, or architectural design must therefore exhibit the quality of *aesthetic deference* to the Lord of all creativity.

The Dutch theologian, Cornelius Van Til, argued there is no such thing as a 'brute fact' – a part of reality that somehow escapes divine interpretation. Likewise, there is no such thing as 'brute art'. All forms of art, as they articulate a moral position, summon Holy judgment. The ancient prophet Isaiah declared that the acceptability of man's work before God cannot be divorced from the matter of ethics: 'And all our righteousness are as filthy rags' (Isaiah 64:6, NIV). Without a redemptive relationship between the artist and his Creator, the artist's labour, although it may reflect the interests of beauty in a broad sense, will fall short in gaining God's full approval. It is therefore not enough to seek great art in beautiful colors, sounds, proportions, and shapes. Rather, 'right values' must also flow from the artist's hands, as those values flow from his heart.

It was another gifted Dutch theologian, Hans Rookmaaker, who said the main reason for the decline of modern art is the fact that man's creativity is marked by his infectious desire for human autonomy from God's ethical demands.[2] Rookmaaker saw the history of art in terms of man's struggle to define both himself and his world ontologically and epistemologically. Who am I? What is there to know? These questions, according to Rookmaaker, have fueled man's search for meaning, which in turn, have given rise to his conscious creativity in the arts.

Unfortunately, man's historic search for meaning has not always been marked by his quest for the One, true God of the Bible. Instead, the spiritual search of many artists has been characterized by arrogant rebellion against the Lord. The only hope for modern man, and consequently for his art, is to return to God. Where art is broken, it is because man is broken by sin. Art is nothing more than an image of something that exists in God's universe. But man is also an image — the image of God. If man, as the image of God, remains broken and is not restored in Christ, how can a broken image produce a complete and meaningful image of something else?

This begs an important question: 'Does this mean that only Christians are capable of great art?' For example, Pablo Picasso was not a believer, yet he is considered one of the greatest painters of all time. Undoubtedly, Picasso, and other gifted unbelievers like him, demonstrated technical brilliance and aesthetic vision in their compositions. But what is important to remember is that these artists were working from a *deficit*. While from a human perspective, their life-production may be considered 'great', sin had reduced them to mere vestiges of the image of God, meaning that their work never reached its *full* potential. In a *spiritual* sense, their work was *not* sound. Indeed, had Picasso trusted Christ and been restored in the image of the Creator-God, his genius would have been even greater! Another Dutch churchman, Klaas Schilder, in commenting upon the spiritual 'deficit' in unbelieving artists, remarked, 'Our conclusion then is that culture is never more than a mere attempt and that, since it is restricted to remnants only, it is a matter of tragedy. God has indeed left something behind in fallen man. But these are only "small remnants" of his original gifts...they can never produce any work that is sound.'[3]

But Christ is the restorer of man. In Chapter I, we learned that 'God's purpose for the world is to restore everything that was lost at the fall — both in man and in the rest of creation — to its proper role of worshipping and glorifying Him.' In Christ, man receives back those elements of the image of God that were lost through sin, and his life and work are redirected to the glory of God. Only Christ can restore art, because only Christ can restore the artist's heart so that his full potential to create can be fully realized.

Great art is the result of an artist who understands his role in furthering his craft. The artist's role includes a practical level that is concerned with *artistic validity.* He must ask, '*Why* am I doing this?' 'Do I create for the love of art or for the love of money?' 'Do I work tirelessly to churn out productions just to be accepted by the local critics or is my work intended as an offering to God?' If an artist's motivations are not in keeping with the nature of great art, he will not create it.

Additionally, the artist's role includes a purely creative level that focuses on the *goal of artistic expression.* An artist must ask, '*What* am I doing?' 'Do I have a goal for my composition?' The key-point of a biblical worldview states, 'The world and all that it contains is subject to the eternal purpose and plan of God.' Clearly, God has a goal for art – an eternal goal. Art is to serve the forward movement of history toward its climactic end when then all things, including art, will be subjected to Christ (cf. I Corinthians 15:27). How does this work? Art facilitates God's plan when it *glorifies* Him. But how can an artist glorify God through a painting, for example?

What the Artist is Not

To begin with, a painter (and artists generally) must understand his limits. He is not a revelator. The inspiration he receives is unlike that received by holy men of old, who spoke, 'Thus says the Lord.' His is not the job of special revelation, but of *general* revelation. Like the image of God in man and the wonders of tree, hill, and sky, the beauty of art directs our attention to the fundamental truths of the existence of God and of His divine attributes. This is as far as an artist can take us. Although, through his use of brush and palette, a painter can *represent* the meaning of God's special work in Christ, he cannot *impart* its meaning. This work is reserved for the Word of God in co-operation with the Holy Spirit.

Thus, the artist is not a prophet, but he is *almost* a prophet. While the artist shares the prophet's role in confronting us with the fundamental issues of life, the prophet differs in his ability to resolve these issues with unmistakable clarity.

The artist is not a priest, but he is *almost* a priest. Although his canvas is a world full of symbols that represent a spiritual reality beyond themselves, the priest takes us beyond what symbols *can* mean to what they *do* mean.

Poised Between Two Realms

If the above descriptions fall short of describing the artist's goal, what can illustrate his goal more fully? The goal of the artist is to be like the *horizon* – touching both finite world and infinite heaven. Suspended as it were between two realms, the artist's job is to link the material world of paint and canvas (or possibly sheet music, celluloid, or words), with the supernatural world of transcendent values. In Van Gogh's *Night Café*, the painter, and former missionary, uses color as language. He paints what he sees with his soul and uses color to exaggerate his message. By moving from a dark foreground to a light background, we are drawn backwards into the painting. The painting wants to draw us from our world of the common and the ordinary, to a world of transcendent quality, objective meaning, and thus, the God of all meaning.

At the same time, however, an artist must not permit a deliberate goal to shackle pure, unencumbered self-expression. The life of great art is born out of the unhampered spirit within the artist, working with a diligent hand in light of the respect, humility, and modesty he brings to his subject. M.A. Couturier expressed it best: 'A work is truly a work of art only if it comes out of the depths of its author's spirit, and from even further down than that – I would say out of his guts.'[4]

A man once asked me, 'John, do you establish a goal before you preach and know exactly where you are going in a message, or do you follow some loosely prepared notes and allow for the inspiration of the Holy Spirit?' I replied, 'I think through every word before preaching, and then when I begin, I forget it.' Likewise, a painter, for example, must have a goal before taking up the brush. Then he must forget it. He must organize at every level. But once he begins to paint he must put all of it aside and permit his gift to take flight. An artist who leads his work too closely will cause it to be cramped and stifled. The gift must lead, or else the art will suffer. Practically speaking, what must an artist accomplish in order for his composition to glorify God? Let's answer this question as though we were observing a painting.

Steps to a Masterpiece

For a painting to glorify God the composition must, from the outset, direct my sensory interest to the work itself. Beyond this, I should be able to understand that the artist has worked the physical materials in such a way that I sense the joy, serenity, or horror he felt while painting. Additionally, I should discern a Christian 'consciousness' in the composition through the artist's use of color and form. And I should sense his faith reaction to specific social and historical forces leading to the consummation of all things.

But the artist must go further. Not only must he impress me with his journey of faith, but also he must *arouse* my faith. His creation must contain the power of inner suggestion, the power to inspire. An artist's goal must be to provide people a 'point of departure' to a deeper reality that transcends the finite and the mundane. He should provide a vision of God that stirs within us a sense of holy awe and wonder. Through his work he should seek to usher us into the presence of a world of absolute meaning through his use of less than absolute lines, forms, and shapes. And he should strive to inspire all of our senses with a vision of beauty that would otherwise remain inaccessible to us were it not for the presence of his work.

Through Roualt's *The Holy Countenance*, the painter wants to stimulate reflection on Christ. Using luminous colors, simplicity of form, and solemnity of contour, Roualt conceives Christ in pain and suffering due to the effects of sin in the world. Christ came to bear the sins of many and to identify with our suffering. Yet comfort is fleeting. Roualt also wants to confront us in our disbelief. It's as if the painting declares, 'You decide!' Roualt's Christ is, as the artist Cocagnac put it, 'The way of grace between man's misery and the love of God. It was the misery and loneliness of man that was Roualt's personal and Christian starting point.'

To capture a message with this level of impact in a composition, an artist must also be a *visionary*. He must consider his materials and their use only in light of the general effect of the whole. Yet he cannot know whether he is achieving this effect, except for his vision for the work. Additionally, an artist must foresee that his composition will be made of 'little compositions', which may at first appear antagonistic to each other but, which, once put together will serve to clarify the meaning of the whole. The Russian Orthodox painter, Wassily Kadinsky, said, 'The creation of the various forms, which, by standing in different relationships to each other, decide the composition of the whole.'[5] Now let's look at a closely related point that enables an artist to create great art and glorify God in his work.

Great art is that which embodies great content. What accounts for the tragedy in Massaccio's *The Expulsion from Paradise*, the power of Bach's *Mass in B minor,* the grief of Rembrandt's *Decent from the Cross*, or the soul of T.S. Eliot's poetry? It is content. But what is content? Content is more than what we see or hear. It is other than paint, form, line, notes, sound, words, juxtaposition of elements, or artistic convention. It goes deeper. Rather, content is the *total* effect of a work of art, something the individual parts of the work cannot account for. Content is that which transcends the material elements of a work, and which continues to draw us to it, to dwell on it, and to be pulled into it. Content is the 'life' of the work.

All artists know they must achieve content, but virtually no one can produce a map to get there. Rather, content is that which is *sought*. Thus, the contemporary painter, Joel C. Sheesley, looks to the writer of Hebrews to say that art content is 'The substance of things hoped for'.[6] I agree that art content is difficult to achieve. Nevertheless, there are procedural factors one can consider in order to facilitate content in a work. Let's look at just three elements of art content: space, color, and form. We begin with a consideration of space in the art of architectural design.

The God that is There and Not There
Is there more space in the Louisiana Superdome or in a chapel? Now let's be clear. I'm not asking which one has more room, but rather

which one has more 'space'. If the architect has captured content in his design, then the answer is the chapel has more space. The explanation is that the chapel contains the *presence of absence*. Standing in the chapel, you sense something is missing. It is not that there is something that needs to be added to the room in order to complete it, but rather there is something present in the room that is greater than the room. This 'something' is also somewhere else. And it draws you to where it is.

Jesus personified the 'presence of absence'. He was fully God and fully man. He was divine and human. His divinity pointed away to God, while His humanity pointed to us. Theologians call it the 'mystery of the incarnation'. However, we must be careful not to allow our experience of the Christian mystery to become an exercise in abstraction. Christ is 'Emmanuel' – God with us. Our experience of Christ is grounded upon God's self-revelation in history. Otherwise, faith becomes thoughtless and unthinking. It produces faithlessness. In all, it is the mystery of Christ which creates within us a sense of reverence and holy wonder and which draws us to Him. Now let's return to the chapel.

What makes a room a chapel? It is the 'presence of absence' – the mystery. In the foothills of the Vosges Mountains of France is the chapel at Ronchamp, designed by Le Corbusier. Within the chapel, *light* is the key to creating a sense of mystery. The unpretentious use of colored glass makes the space neither too bright nor dull. The building allows in only 'prayerful' light through the use of blues, soft yellows, and whites. The peaceful atmosphere with no distracting elements makes the space come alive. The building is neither didactic nor entertaining, but powerful. It displays this power through simple use of perfect lines and forms. However, the lines and forms are not perfect in a 'stylized' sense, but rather are perfect as perfection is found in nature. Through modest use of materials, we learn that less is more. We are inspired, not manipulated.

In addition to communicating spiritual power, the chapel also conveys architectural 'action'. It is not cut *into* nature, but seems to flow *out of* nature on its way toward heaven. There is also an architectural 'language' to the chapel, an acoustical phenomenon, which allows it to 'speak'. The aesthetic effect of the whole creates a depth dimension that takes us beyond appearances. The 'content' of the chapel is experienced in everything from the artistry of the pews, to the innovative use of a crabshell roof to the eloquence of the rain barrels. The 'presence of absence' can also be achieved in other spheres of art, including music, painting, sculpture, and film. Now let's return to painting and consider art content through the use of color.

Only a Biblical Worldview Accounts for Color's Appeal

The last of the great artists of the Renaissance and the first of the modern era, Eugene Delacroix, observed, 'Everyone knows that yellow, orange, and red suggest ideas of joy and plenty.'[7] We would all agree that color bears the power to suggest. We would also agree that the language of color is universal. 'Red' has the same effect upon a Frenchman as it does upon an American.

There is another universally accepted notion. Bright colors are complimented by sharp forms (e.g. a yellow triangle), and soft colors are well suited by round forms (e.g. a blue circle). This example further illustrates the universal language of color. But it also demonstrates there is a pattern to color in its relationship to other elements in painting. Indeed, if we were to introduce considerations such as texture, contour, harmony, and contrast we would see, depending on how we use color in light of these factors, that color's effect upon men would continue to follow a given pattern. But how do we account for the universal language of color?

The answer is found in God. Specifically, it is discovered in God's unity and simplicity. It is the unity and simplicity of the Godhead – the second building block of a biblical worldview – that supplies the ontological backdrop for our interpretation of color. Yes, there is a subjective element in our interpretation of color. But this fact only further illustrates, that for color to elicit a given, universal response it must be part of a greater fabric – a world of relationships that find their meaning in God. In what way can an artist use color to give glory to God?

He can use the *function* of color to express spiritual truth. It was Kadinsky who recognized that color falls into two great divisions:

warm and cold, light and dark. Therefore, he taught that color has four shades of appeal: warm and light or warm and dark, or cold and light or cold and dark. 'Generally speaking, warmth or cold in a color means an approach respectively to yellow or blue...The movement is a horizontal one, the warm colors approaching the spectator, the cold ones retreating from him.'[8]

Kadinsky also taught that color functions according to an excentric or concentric movement. 'If two circles are drawn and painted respectively yellow and blue, brief concentration will reveal in the yellow a spreading movement out from the center, and a noticeable approach to the spectator. The blue, on the other hand, moves in upon itself, like a snail retreating into its shell, and draws away from the spectator.'[9] Based upon Kadinsky's insights, let's see how God – the Master Artist – uses the function of color to convey spiritual truth.

God and His World of Color

Although God painted the sun using a variety of colors, it would appear excentric yellow (also white if we could gaze directly into it). Thus, the sun's color is in harmony with its function: radiating outward and communicating warmth. This fact points to a spiritual truth. As yellow radiates outward, serving to communicate the sun's radiance and warmth, so also the Son is the 'radiance of His glory' (Hebrews 1:3) who came into the world to communicate the Father's warmth. Also, like the reaching of the sun's rays, I did not reach out to God, but rather He reached out to me.

Then there is the relationship between the *blue* of the sky and the *green* of the earth. Typically, blue is a heavenly color. It creates a feeling of eternal rest. Its concentric movement causes it to pull in and away from the observer. Also, there is the concentric green of the earth. Green is the most restful of all colors. However, green differs from blue in that it does not convey supernatural rest, but rather earthly peace. Furthermore, green is the result of combining yellow with blue. Likewise, the redemption of the earth (green) is the product of the work of the Son (yellow) who, in heaven's economy (blue), came to seek and to save those who are lost. Also, because green is the product of the excentric movement of yellow and the concentric movement of blue, the effect on the eye is therefore neutral, motionless. Similarly, by stilling the storm, Jesus illustrated His power to save and that the earth's response to the salvation of God is to be still.

The Color of Revelation

The Bible is also replete with God's masterful use of color. The four horsemen of the Apocalypse (Revelation 6:1-8) appear in colors of *white, red, black, and ashen.* The first horse is 'white', and he rides out to conquer. White is the most reaching of all colors. Because white is the absence of color, it is full of possibilities. No wonder it is associated in Scripture with holiness, the Holy Spirit, and the glory of God. On the other hand, white is difficult to make warm. Like the earth's poles, it wants to be cold, old, and impenetrable. White can therefore have a negative effect upon our lives. A perfect compliment for one that goes out to conquer.

The second horse is 'red', and brings war to the earth. This is the color of power and intensity. Kadinsky sees red as neither excentric, nor concentric. It is 'motion within itself'.[10] Red conveys the feeling of strength and determination. It is fitting, then, that this horse comes to withdraw the Spirit of God and take peace from the earth that men might slay each other.

The third horse is 'black' and brings famine to the earth. Black is not the color of death, but rather the motionlessness and nothingness that precedes death. Used as a background in painting, black causes other colors to stand forward and become sharp. Likewise, it shall be in the moments before death, in this case brought by world famine, that the important issues of life stand out and become clear.

The fourth horse is 'ashen'. This is the color of death. Ashen is a derivative of gray, which is produced by blending black and white — colors that stand at opposite ends of the color spectrum. Jesus said, 'I am the alpha and the omega, the beginning and the end' (Revelation 21:6). Just as a combination of black and white produces the pale effect of ashen, so also it is Christ alone who has the 'authority' (see Revelation 6:8 and fourth building block of a biblical worldview) to produce this rider's dread effects. Now we move to a consideration of form in painting.

The Shape of Great Art

The study of form in painting is a study of culture and its values. Before the advent of modern art, artists paid much more attention to the use of form than perhaps any other element. For example, Renaissance artists such as Giovanni Bellini, Leonardo da Vinci, and Jan Van Eyck endeavored to create 'absolute form' in their compositions. They did so out of a deep and persistent attitude reflected throughout the middle ages that the intellect can obtain knowledge of God only insofar as corporeal objects are related to God and reveal Him. Remember, most people didn't have Bibles at that time. There was therefore a much greater emphasis placed upon 'natural' theology and the need for the physical world to provide *all* knowledge of God. Michelangelo was perhaps the greatest painter and sculptor who ever lived. He was so consumed with his pursuit for the 'perfect form' that he was driven near mad.

It is with Goya (1746-1828) and Delacroix (1798-1863) that painting takes its first step toward modern art. A less rigid appraisal of form now becomes accepted in favour of using the imagination. 'Idealized' landscapes begin to be painted by Constable, Turner, Corot, and Courbet. However, it is with the advent of 'Cubism', and artists Pablo Picasso (1881-1973) and Georges Braque (1882-1963) that the cultural and theological ideals of Renaissance 'high' art, and their impact on form, begin to quickly unravel. The cubist style rejected the traditional techniques of creating form and instead emphasized the flat, two-dimensional surface of the picture plane. All the time-honored, artistic and cultural theories that assisted artists in their attempt to capture 'spiritual' meaning in material objects were discarded. Instead, cubists sought the creation of a 'new reality', The total breakdown of cultural ideals in art came with the birth of 'Dada.' Marcel Duchamp (1887-1968) was its leading figure. A product of the philosophy of 'nihilism,' Dada was a mostly western European movement that sought to destroy traditional culture and aesthetic forms in favour of surrealism and 'authentic reality'.

My brief sketch of art history is intended to make a point: a crisis in artistic form results from a crisis in cultural norms. But the Christian artist must not reflect the low standards of a culture, but rather he is called to elevate them. How can a Christian use form in art to glorify God and help reverse culture's headlong dive into meaninglessness? Here are three general guidelines.

Art form should be understandable. Considered by many to be the greatest art masterpiece of the twentieth century, Picasso's *Guernica* was painted in memory of the bombing of Guernica, France by the Germans during World War II. The problem is that absolutely no one knows what it means. And Picasso refused to offer an explanation for his composition. This approach to art form is unacceptable for a Christian. Paul writes, 'But thanks be to God, who always leads us in His triumph in Christ, and manifests through us the sweet aroma of the knowledge of Him in every place' (I Corinthians 2:16). God wants the believer to 'manifest' the fragrance of his knowledge of Christ in everything he does, including his art. Art form should not veil one's knowledge of Christ behind a curtain of abstractions and inner-meanings, but rather every part of one's composition should bear the unmistakable aroma of Christ by reflecting the beauty and truth that belongs to Him.

Art form should be redemptive. The Norwegian painter, Edward Munch (1863-1944) is considered the father of Expressionism – a vague term that describes many works of art created during the twentieth century that are charged with emotion. Munch's most recognized composition is *The Scream.* Through the use of intense colors and ghost-like forms, the artist captures what he believes to be man's greatest fear – the fear of living.

Fear is unquestionably a common theme found in Scripture. For example, the Bible says, 'The fear of the Lord is the beginning of knowledge' (Proverbs 1:7). What stands out to me in this well-known verse of Scripture is that holy fear is not a dead-end road, but rather is the beginning of something great – the knowledge of God. Munch, on the other hand, represents a trend in art that not only rejected the possibility of knowing God, but also resigned itself to the abyss of despair. While Christian art is free to affirm the plight of humankind and man's age-old struggle with the meaning of existence, it must also depict the way out of this struggle. It must capture the way of grace and redemption that leads people out of the hollowness and terror of facing the future without hope. The Bible says, 'For God hath not given us the spirit of fear; but of power, and of love, and of a sound mind' (2 Timothy 1:7, KJV).

Art form should balance subjective feeling with objective truth. In direct opposition to the extreme subjectivism of Dada, is the French artist, Piet Mondrain (1872-1944). He is known for being the first painter to reject all subjective feeling in art. His work represented what is called, 'Neo-plasticism'. The goal of art form, according to Mondrain, is to avoid any 'personal' involvement with one's subject. Focusing inward involves participation, and participation with objects introduces human suffering and death. If you permit your emotions to follow nature, Mondrain wrote in 1920, you have to accept 'whatever is capricious and twisted in nature'. Mondrain even refused to attach imaginative titles to his compositions for fear that he might prejudice the 'objective' message of his work. (e.g. *Ocean 5, Composition with Red, Yellow, and Blue*).

Although today's culture may be guilty of wallowing in subjectivism, the Christian artist must be free to enlist his feelings, personal experiences, and sanctified imagination in the creation of a composition. The Christian artist is a unique individual. God has given to him the ability to do something, which no other person can do in his place: be himself. His work must therefore demonstrate that he is 'fearfully and wonderfully made' (Psalm 139:14). An artist must study great art in order to do great art. He may even want to copy other great artist's use of form in order to learn technique. But ultimately what separates one great artist from another is an artist's *personality*.

On the other hand, we must also be *met* by truth in art. This is the objective element. An art masterpiece not only expresses an artist's inner-self and causes the observer to ask, 'What does this mean to me?' but also it confronts people with the 'wholly other'. A composition that lacks a transcendent quality – that fails to challenge people with the immeasurable truth of God – fails the test of truly great art. Schelling said, 'Beauty is the infinite presented in the finite.'[11]

Emile Nolde (1867-1956) was a Christian, German expressionist who devoted himself to capturing Christian themes in mostly woodcuts, drawings, and watercolors. One of the founders of Die Brücke (the Bridge) in 1905 along with Erich Heckel, Ernst Ludwig Kirschner, and Karl Schmidt-Rottluff, Nolde sought to use his compositions to strike a prophetic chord and awaken Germany to a new, free, and passionate age.[1][2] The Nazi's condemned Nolde's work as 'degenerate'. Nolde's most famous print, *The Prophet,* is a case study in how to balance raw subjective emotion with the light of objective truth in art.

My hope is that this chapter has offered guidance to the Church in its effort to produce great works of art that glorify the Creator of all. Perhaps the reader uses a different set of standards to judge and/or create great art. That you agree with my particular set of criteria is not important. However, what is important is that we concur that art, in all its various forms, is in need of a Christian presence that is able to bring the truth of God to bear, and do it with utmost skill and mastery. It is to this end that every Christian artist must pray and work.

Twelve

INTERNATIONAL RELATIONS IN BIBLICAL REVIEW

Immigration

Elian Gonzalez. What do you think when you hear that name? I'll tell you what I think. Corruption. Abuse of power. Incompetence. To refresh your memory, Elian Gonzalez was the 6-year-old Cuban boy whom two fisherman, Donato Dalrymple and Sam Ciancio, rescued from clinging to an inner tube off the Florida coast on 25 November 1999. Elian's mother never made it to Florida's shores having drowned in her brave attempt to give her son a new life in America. But freedom for Elian would be short-lived.

During the pre-dawn hours of 22 April 2000, agents of the U.S. Border Patrol and the Immigration and Naturalization Service, in riot gear and brandishing rifles, seized Elian from the home of his Miami relatives and whisked the crying 6-year-old away. The world will never forget the image, captured by a concealed AP photographer, of the military-clad federal cop with his rifle pointed near Elian's face, screaming to Donato Dalrymple, 'Give me the kid! Give me the f—g kid!'

'They never knocked,' said a trembling Donato Dalrymple after the raid. No Donato, they don't 'knock' anymore. And don't be surprised when they don't knock in the future. Within days, Elian was returned to his father and to the control of one of the most brutal, totalitarian dictators in the history of the world – Fidel Castro.

While it is tempting to discuss the use of automatic weapons to resolve child custody cases, I will bite my tongue. Instead, I want to use the Elian Gonzalez fiasco to introduce a commentary on several U.S. immigration and related international affairs problems, all of which have wide-ranging implications for other nations.

If the Elian Gonzalez case demonstrates anything, it's that the state of U.S. immigration policy is in turmoil. The cause of this chaos is simple. *The U.S. has no coherent and consistent immigration policy.* We are very much like Israel of old, when 'every man did what was right in his own eyes'. Clearly, the door is wide open for cultural conservatives to make an important contribution to the area of immigration reform. Why is U.S. immigration policy in disarray? The lack of a uniform plan is easily traced to America's growing disdain for a biblical view of government.

The position that a biblical worldview should *not* inform a nation's immigration policy, and foreign affairs in general, can be traced back to Harry S. Truman's Secretary of State, Dean Acheson:

The discussion of ethics or morality in our relations with other states is a prolific cause of confusion. The vocabulary of morals and ethics is inadequate to discuss or test foreign policies of states...What passes for ethical standards for governmental policies in foreign affairs is a collection of moralisms, maxims and slogans, which neither help nor guide, but only confuse decisions on such complicated matters as the multilateral nuclear force, a common grain price in Europe and policy in southeast Asia. A good deal of trouble comes from the anthropomorphic urge to regard nations as individuals and apply to our national conduct, for instance, the Golden Rule – even though in practice individuals rarely adopt it. The fact is that nations are not individuals, the cause and effect of their actions are wholly different, and what a government can and should do with the resources which it takes from its citizens must be governed by wholly different considerations from those which properly determine an individual's use of his own.[1]

Actually, it is Acheson's position, shared by many in government, that is a 'prolific cause of confusion'. While not everything Jesus taught in the Sermon on the Mount, for instance, is adequate to guide a nation's foreign policy, this is not to say that ethical and moral considerations play no role in international affairs. The theory that relationships between nations can operate apart from 'moral' considerations is based on the secularist's rejection of the doctrine of sin and his acceptance of the human heart's inherent goodness. The effect of these twin presuppositions upon a broad array of U.S. international relations has been to place pragmatism above principle and diplomacy above defense. But nations that are at odds with the U.S. seldom look to pragmatism and diplomacy to advance their agendas, except for purposes of show. The result is that America has been consistently outwitted on many international fronts with her foreign policy left looking like a pile of spaghetti. However, the key-point of a biblical worldview says, 'the world and all that it contains is subject to the eternal purpose and plan of God'. Even nations are subject to God's eternal plan! World leaders must therefore gain fresh understanding into the depravity of men and nations and look to the Lord of the nations for guidance in all their international dealings.

Speaking of depravity, let's now examine Fidel Castro's historic use of Cuban refugees as political tools.

A Shark off the Coast

While the Mariel Boatlift of 1980 when Fidel Castro allowed 124,776 Cubans to flee communism to freedom in South Florida is remembered as the quintessential event in immigration history, a similar, less-publicized onslaught of Cuban refugees descended on the area in the fall of 1994. When this boatlift was taking place, I was in South Florida assisting my father, who was gravely ill with cancer. One day I stood on the beach looking through my binoculars to what appeared to be several 'dots' on the horizon. The local lifeguard explained that these were rafts, dingies, and other poorly man-made crafts, full of Cubans eager to taste the fruit of American freedom, or free education and welfare, depending upon their motives.

As the exodus appeared to escalate, with 3000 Cubans being fished from the Florida waters in just one day, the *New York Times* reported that the Clinton administration asked the Cuban government to stop the boat people from leaving in return for an offer by the United States to relax its immigration rules and grant residency visas to more than 20,000 Cubans a year. In effect, the United States cut a deal with a brutal tyrant and once *again* allowed him to set the agenda for U.S. immigration policy. But this is exactly what Castro had in mind all along. He knew that by releasing Cubans to South Florida the U.S. government would cry 'uncle' and cave in to his demands. Due in part to the Clinton administration's fear that Castro might release a fresh flotilla of refugees, the president yielded six years later to the dictator's demands to return Elian Gonzalez to Cuba.

A Failed Policy

The U.S. has not always responded so contritely to Castro. We have been tough. How? Economic sanctions. In 1961, the United States imposed the Cuban economic embargo, which severely restricted trade with, travel to, or investment in the island nation of Cuba. The justification for the embargo was based on U.S. national security concerns about Castro's alliance with the former Soviet Union. Recently, the House of Representatives voted to revise this policy by lifting restrictions on travel to Cuba by U.S. citizens. As of this writing, House passage of the amendment faces opposition within the Senate and among the anti-Castro Cuban exile community. However, if the amendment does receive Senate approval and is followed by President Bush's blessing, I'll be one of the first Americans hopping a plane, because Cuba offers some of the best scuba diving anywhere in the world!

While U.S. policy toward Cuba remains in flux, one thing remains sure: the Bible does not support the traditional use of economic sanctions as a means to change the behavior of an evil ruler. Why?

Economic sanctions are a poor substitute for trust in God's power (see fourth building block of a biblical worldview). Proverbs 21:1 says, 'The king's heart is like channels of water in the hand of the Lord; He turns it wherever He wishes.' Note that the Lord, not economic sanctions, turns the heart of the king. It may come as a great shock to policy-makers to discover that there is not one instance in the Bible of God slapping trade and travel restrictions on the ancient Hebrews as a way to correct the poor behavior of a neighbouring king. Of course, pagan nations didn't expect Israelite visitors, and if any showed up they would most likely have been broiled on a stick. However, this only further underscores the implausibility of this option. Today many nations are more receptive to trade and travel than were the Canaanites. But this does not negate the above Scripture. God's power to turn the heart of the king is still available to any nation that calls upon His name.

Largely due to the leadership of President Ronald Reagan, the Soviet Communist system collapsed, resulting in Soviet troops and advisors leaving Cuba to fend for itself. Cuban troops have since withdrawn themselves from Nicaragua and Angola. Nevertheless, in 1992, President George Bush, rather than loosening the embargo, signed the Cuban Democracy Act, which added further restrictions. In 1996, President Bill Clinton signed the Cuban Liberty and Democratic Solidarity or Libertad Act (Helms Burton Law). This law imposed more penalties on foreign companies and private citizens that buy or sell property, which Castro has pilfered from American citizens. A series of stiffening sanctions have now been at work in Cuba for nearly forty years, but Castro has not budged from either his commitment to repressive socialism or his threats to release more boatloads of refugees when it suits him.

The failure to teach Fidel Castro strongly suggests that *economic sanctions do not work.* This is true worldwide. For example, because Iran and Libya fund international terrorism, the United States prohibits investment in Iran and forbids trade with Libya, yet both nations are still fomenting terrorism in numerous parts of the globe. According to a report published by the Institute for International Economics, 'In the modern era the use of economic sanctions has a poor track record. Between 1914 and 1990, various countries imposed economic sanctions in 116 cases. They failed to achieve their stated objectives in 66 percent of those cases and were at best only partially successful in most of the rest.'[2]

Economic sanctions designed to hurt a foreign tyrant only harm the people under his rule. A dictatorship assumes that the dictator has full control over a nation, including its goods and services. This means that an embargo on selling medical supplies and food items to Cuba is only going to hurt the Cuban people, not Fidel Castro. According to another published report, 'The outright ban on the sale of American foodstuffs to Cuba has contributed to serious nutritional deficits, particularly among pregnant women, leading to an increase in low birth-weight babies. In addition, food shortages were linked to a devastating outbreak of neuropathy numbering in the tens of thousands. By one estimate, daily caloric intake dropped 33 percent between 1989 and 1993.'[3] Does anyone think that Castro's caloric intake has decreased since the embargo took effect?

Inflicting harm upon the Cuban people has created a cycle of despair, which has only worsened the refugee crisis. The embargo creates poor living standards. Cubans become unhappy and want to leave. Refugees leave in rickety boats for South Florida. Those who make it add to the already inflated tax burden by utilizing to the fullest the social services that are designed to assist the refugees. Enter angry Floridians. They resent the tax hike, environmental degradation, battles over 'bilingual education', and shifting demographics. American leaders cry 'uncle'. Meanwhile, Fidel is fat and happy back in Cuba puffing on eight-inch 'havanas' and calling the shots on U.S. immigration policy.

Setting a New Course

What is the biblical solution? *A nation must make the Lord its trust* (See third building block of a biblical worldview). When a nation repents of its wickedness and turns to the Lord, it receives God's rich blessing, which places it in a position to deal effectively with tyrants of the world. Moses spoke to the people of Israel, 'Now it shall be, if you will diligently obey the Lord your God, being careful to do all His commandments which I command you today, the Lord your God will set you high above all the nations of the earth' (Deuteronomy 28:1).

Although America is clearly 'above' Cuba in many ways, the island nation continues to be a thorn in America's side. The same could be said of China, Angola, Libya, Pakistan, and a host of other rogue nations. Why is the U.S. having these problems? Joshua revealed what would happen if Israel rejected the covenant and sought after the gods of the surrounding nations. Those nations would become a deadly snare. 'Know with certainty that the Lord your God will not continue to drive these nations out from before you; but they shall be a snare and a trap to you, and a whip on your sides and thorns in your eyes, until you perish from off this good land, which the Lord your God has given you' (Joshua 23:13). America has also rejected God's commandments. Is it any wonder that the U.S. is experiencing the same discipline as ancient Israel?

In his commentary on the book of Deuteronomy, Gary North points out that Israel practiced open borders because immigrants entered Israel on Israel's terms: 'God did not allow public proselytizing or public observance of rival religions. The civil order was established by a covenantal oath to God.'[4] It was also on the strength of Israel's covenantal oath that any external threat posed by a foreign nation was destined to fail. The key to Israel's success over hostile nations did not lie in the capacity to change their behavior, but in changing its own. Similarly, America's ability to safeguard her national interests does not depend upon the weight of economic sanctions, but upon the *spiritual* sanctions we as a people place upon ourselves!

A nation must consider ways to expose people under totalitarian rule to its domestic products with a view toward introducing them to associated ideals of freedom and democracy. While many American policy-makers assume that doing business with nations such as Cuba can only strengthen the Cuban economy and further solidify Castro's approval rating among his people, this is not entirely true. Exposure to the products and ideals of a freedom-loving society often brings with it the values of that society. The more that oppressed people are exposed to democratic values, as those values are based in the Judeo-Christian ethic, the more they will perceive autocratic values in a negative light. The seeds of popular uprising will be planted.

The material benefit of exposing subjugated people to raw goods and services that are in short supply in their home nation can also bring about America's desired result. The key to stopping a flood of refugees and illegal aliens from coming to America, or to any other free and prosperous nation, is to make sure they are happy where they are. But when people are floundering around for basic medical care, food, and disposable goods, you can be assured they will be longing for greener pastures.

The above comments need to be carefully balanced. Deepening trade and investment relations with nations like Cuba, Libya, and China (which should *not* have Most Favoured Nation status), can backfire. This is why the potential of overseas commerce with nations of this caliber must be weighed against their history of human rights abuses, international terrorism, and the effect that doing business can have on native jobs. But never forget that God can still work His will through the most questionable of commercial arrangements.

For example, during Joseph's time the Egyptian Pharaoh was the most corrupt autocrat on earth. But rather than starve out Pharaoh through an economic embargo, God used the evil of the slave market to import Joseph into Egypt where there he assisted Pharaoh in the midst of a seven-year famine. The result was that Pharaoh recognized God and promoted Joseph as a ruler of Egypt. This enabled Joseph to offer famine assistance to his brothers, who earlier had sold him into slavery. Joseph said to his brothers, 'And as for you, you meant evil against me, but God meant it for good in order to bring about this present result, to preserve many people alive' (Genesis 50:20). The sovereign God can even bring good from the vile, international slave market (see key-point of a biblical worldview)!

A nation must understand that true reform in other nations can only occur through the fulfillment of the Great Commission. A pattern of democratic reforms, even the ouster of a nation's leader, can go a long way toward facilitating positive change in an oppressed or outlaw nation. But nothing can replace the gospel as the *real* foundation upon which a nation can experience true liberty and prosperity. Democratic freedom is not possible where spiritual freedom is absent. This explains the failure of the U.S. mission to install democracy on another island, which too has used refugees to its political advantage – Haiti.

Installing Democracy?

'Operation Uphold Democracy', was the U.S. plan that sent a 21,000 strong U.S. military force into Haiti on 19 September 1994, in an effort to remove the *de facto* régime, which took power through a military *coup d'état* on 29 September 1991. The successful overthrow forced leaders of the regime to leave the country, whereby President-in-exile, Father Jean-Bertrand Aristide, was soon reinstalled. Aristide then faced the task of restoring democracy and reconstructing the nation's economy.

Question: How can Aristide 'restore' democracy to Haiti if none had previously existed? Since dictator François (Papa Doc) Duvalier took power in October 1957, Haiti remains one of the Western Hemisphere's poorest countries, exhibiting a non-existent rule of law and few democratic reforms. While many point to political and economic factors to explain these failures, it is the influence of 'voodoo' religion and the stronghold it has over every sphere of Haitian culture that is the real culprit. The communist Aristide, who supports the 'necklacing' of his political opponents, has done little to break Satan's grip upon his people.

The lesson of Haiti is that democracy and idolatry cannot co-exist. God-given rights such as life, liberty, and the pursuit of happiness will only flourish where the gospel has been planted in the heart of a nation. Democracy is not like a carpet that one can 'install'. Rather, democracy is the *fruit of a tree* called Christianity. Unless Haitians understand that ideals of freedom and prosperity ultimately find their source in God, their search for democracy will continue unabated.

While it is not the job of politicians to preach the gospel or oversee church mission boards, there is nothing preventing them from understanding that the ultimate cause for strife within nations such as Cuba and Haiti is the wickedness of the human heart. U.S. Political leaders committed to *real* reform in totalitarian and/or conflict-ridden countries must therefore be prepared to discuss with church and faith-based organizations what can be done to change the spiritual climate of strategic locations around the world. Now let's shift our focus to the U.S./Mexican border.

A Frontier in Chaos

One evening, Robert, 84, sat down to watch TV when suddenly he felt like someone was watching him. He looked up only to find four pairs of eyes staring back at him through his window. Still weak from triple-bypass surgery, Robert, a resident of Douglas, Arizona, tried hard to reach his shotgun resting against an interior door. By the time he returned, the faces had disappeared into the night. Robert's wife, Helen, 78, now seldom ventures into their yard without her 9-mm pistol. 'I'm not racist,' says Helen. 'Why, I have a Mexican daughter-in-law. But we have a major invasion happening in this country.'[5]

The Mexican immigration crisis is spinning out of control. Approximately one million illegal aliens cross from Mexico into the United States each year, and that number is expected to climb.[6] In the twelve months that ended 30 October 2000, U.S. agents captured 389,427 illegal aliens along California's 140-mile border with Mexico.[7] In the first six months of 2000, U.S. agents caught 176,655 illegal immigrants along the 21-mile border of Douglas, Arizona alone![8]

Illegal aliens are the main cause of home invasions and private property damage along the border. 'I've watched the ranches out here turn into garbage dumps,' says Larry Vance, who lives on twenty acres east of Douglas, Arizona. 'I've been burglarized, had a truck stolen and property vandalized. There's no privacy anymore, no peace and quiet. There's thousands of people running through this valley every night.'[9] Mounting frustration is heard from others who complain of cut fences, escaped animals, stolen farm items, and damaged barns and watering troughs. Excess litter also spreads across the border landscape: water bottles, empty canteens, diapers, plastic bags, and clothing – just to list a few items. One rancher interviewed by *Insight Magazine* claimed that three of his steers suffocated from ingesting plastic bags.

Additionally, there is the cost to human lives and dignity. Amid temperatures as high as 122 degrees, both American and Mexican authorities routinely search for Mexicans feared lost and dying in the scorching desert terrain. In 2001, twelve illegal immigrants perished as they tried to traverse barren Arizona desert in 115-degree heat. It was the largest number of illegal immigrants to die at once in the Southwest desert in recent years.[10]

Assault, robbery, and rape are also common dangers faced by immigrants. In April 1999, 'border bandits' attacked two groups of illegal aliens crossing the border near Nogales, Arizona, raping two women. The six men, carrying mini-Uzis and AK-47s made the illegal aliens lie face down before they began kicking victims in the head and ribs, pistol-whipping others, and battering still more with rifle-butts. Members of Mexico's own Federal Judicial Police are suspected as the perpetrators.[11]

The nature of the crisis is also seen in reports of gunfire between members of the Mexican army and U.S. officials. On 14 March 2000, two Mexican army vehicles illegally crossed into the United States, sparking a confrontation with U.S. Border Patrol agents. As one of the vehicles fled back to Mexico, two shots were fired at the Americans. On 17 August 2000, a Border Patrol agent was shot three times in the back while patrolling along the U.S./Mexico border near the New River, but escaped serious injury thanks to his bullet-proof vest. U.S. authorities believe that members of the Mexican army are trying to collect a bounty worth $200,000 that is being offered by a Mexican drug cartel for the assassination of a U.S. law enforcement officer.[12]

Incentives for migrating to the U.S. include the availability of low-skill jobs, higher wages (a third of the Mexican people live on $2.00 a day or less), better standards of living, and expectations of welfare-related benefits. Expatriate communities furnish an attractive support network that fuels the migration northward. Additionally, keeping the flow of immigrants moving is an elaborate and lucrative smuggling network that is estimated to garnish millions of dollars each year. For example, 'coyotes' or smugglers charge as much as $500 a person for a ride to the U.S. border and another $1,500 a person from the border to Albuquerque, New Mexico.

The Biblical Right to Emigrate

Before we look at a possible solution to the Mexican problem, let me ask one question. 'Does the Bible teach that people have a right to emigrate?' Yes. In obedience to the call of God, Abram and his family went out from Ur of the Chaldeans and settled in Haran in upper Mesopotamia (cf. Genesis 11:31). The likely explanation for the move is that the extreme paganism of the Chaldean countryside posed a threat to God's long-range plan of using Abram to raise up a godly seed that would bless many nations. The choice was therefore made for him to emigrate.

Like Abram who found it difficult to obey God in the face of surrounding paganism, people down through the ages have faced the same challenge, but in the form of pagan governments. Biblically, governments are established to defend its citizens from any hostile force that would impede the free exercise of their Creator-endowed rights. To the extent that a government fails to carry out its mandate to punish evildoers and reward the righteous, it is the right of the people to abolish that government and enact a new one. But often this is easier said than done. This is why the Pilgrims followed Abram's pattern and emigrated. When a government is not only idolatrous, but also the 'system' to bring about a new government is given to idolatry, men are responsible to seek liberty for their families by emigrating. The right of people to build a better life under God's law cannot be abridged by the state.

The Great Commission presents a second model – one that reverses God's call upon Abram (cf. Matthew 28:18-20). Rather than call men to cross national boundaries in order to *flee* idolatry, God calls the Church to go *to* the covenant-breaking nations of the world with the gospel. The clear implication of the Great Commission is that the right to emigrate for the purpose of discipling nations supercedes any interests of the state to the contrary.

In the *Church of the Holy Trinity v. U.S.* (1892), the Supreme Court sided with a church in New York City that had contracted with a minister in England to perform services as its rector. At issue in the case was whether or not the church's action violated an Act of Congress, which prohibited the importation of foreign unskilled persons to perform manual services. The Court reasoned that the minister in question was a 'toiler of the brain', not a manual labourer. Justice Brewer wrote in his opinion, 'These, and many other matters, which might be noticed, add a volume of unofficial declarations to the mass of organic utterances that this is a Christian nation.'[13] The effect of the court's decision was to say that the Great Commission takes precedence in U.S. immigration policy.

Contemporary Immigration Reverses the Biblical Pattern

Both biblical models above demonstrate that the free expression of religion should act as the cornerstone of a nation's immigration policy. There are examples in Scripture of people emigrating for economic purposes. Abram moved his flocks and herds into Egypt to escape a severe famine throughout Cannan (cf. Genesis 12:10). Jacob and his family also went to Egypt to escape a famine in Canaan (cf. Genesis 37). However, in these instances, the emigrant took his means of subsistence with him, whereby he became both a spiritual and economic blessing to the new land.

Typically, the pattern in Scripture is that people emigrate in service to the kingdom of God. The Hebrews emigrated from Egypt to the Promised Land (Exodus 12fff). Ezra journeyed from Babylon to Jerusalem 'to teach His statutes and ordinances in Israel' (Ezra 7:1-10). And Nehemiah left Babylon and came to Jerusalem to help rebuild the city wall (Nehemiah 1-2). The link to missions demonstrates that migratory movement among believers has served to aid God's larger purpose for planet earth: to *restore everything that was lost at the fall – both in man and in the rest of creation – to its proper role of worshipping and glorifying Him.*

When emigration is carried out within the context of the spread of God's kingdom it has the material effect of elevating the cultural and economic conditions of nations. However, the Mexican immigration crisis demonstrates the *opposite* effect: most migratory movement from Mexico to the U.S. is conducted within the context of economic motives, resulting in the spread of religious and political pluralism. Permit me to elaborate.

Most Mexican immigrants come to the U.S. seeking economic benefits. This would not be regrettable if the greater percentage of Mexicans became independent after integration and added to the nation's economy. But such is not the case.

The U.S. welfare system encourages immigrant dependency. George Borjas and Lynnette Hinton note that immigrants, including illegal aliens, receive cash and non-cash welfare benefits at higher rates than native Americans. In fact, not only does welfare participation increase among immigrants over time, but also some immigrant groups appear to assimilate into welfare. The net cost of immigrants on the U.S. welfare system is estimated at $16 billion per year, with certain states bearing a disproportionate burden.[14]

Because the mood of the country supports the philosophy of the welfare state, the INS and the U.S. Border Patrol have been given an impossible task. How can these agencies protect the nation's borders from illegal aliens, when at the same time, welfare agencies are holding out a $16 billion carrot?

Economic incentives for illegal immigration create a climate of rampant pluralism. A vicious cycle sets in whenever a nation wittingly or unwittingly permits cash and non-cash benefits to become an inducement for immigration. Gary North notes that when an immigrant is naturalized he then becomes a participant in the modern welfare state with the power to vote more entitlements to himself. Moreover, because an immigrant brings with him the cultural 'gods' of his nation, his vote, as it affects areas of American culture and society, codifies the tenets of pagan gods into law. Democracy becomes a tool for the enforcement of religious and political pluralism.[15]

A note: it is suspected that even *illegal* aliens have voted in large numbers in important elections. In an article for WorldNetDaily.com, Joseph Farah revealed that during the 2000 U.S. presidential race, Bill Clinton sent a personal letter to *unregistered* aliens whose immigration status was still pending. Included in the 'Dear Friend' letter was a voter registration card, compliments of the Democratic Party, along with a personal plea from the president to vote democratic in the upcoming election.[16] Also, Edward Nelson, president of U.S. Border Patrol, charged that the battle over the 2000 presidential election was largely due to 'motor voter' fraud, which allowed the non-citizens and illegal aliens to vote in mass numbers in South Florida.[17]

A Compassionate Answer

What is the solution? There isn't one. Not as long as America continues to be a welfare state that worships the gods of diversity and pluralism. Not even Pat Buchanan's 'wall' running along the U.S. border with Mexico could keep people from that $16 billion carrot. However, there is a biblical solution. *It is found in a combination of the Great Commission and the Cultural Mandate.* The problem in Mexico is not only economic, but also spiritual. In a new Christian activism, U.S.-based churches and missions agencies will do more to evangelize Mexicans (Great Commission), with the goal of discipleship in a biblical worldview of economics and related issues that can change Mexican culture and hopefully stem the tide of illegal aliens (Cultural Mandate).

There are three ways this can happen. *If biblical emigration is in service to the kingdom of God, then more Spanish-speaking American missionaries with backgrounds in economics need to move to Mexico to live and teach.* Organizations like Campus Crusade for Christ International can help facilitate your call to Mexico.

The American church must do more to reach Mexican immigrants with the gospel and a biblical worldview while they are in America. It is estimated that up to one-third of United States immigrants eventually return home. This means there is a wealth of potential indigenous Mexican missionaries in our midst.

In 1998, Mexican immigrants in the U.S. numbered over seven million.[18] Let's assume that the return rate among Mexican immigrants parallels the return rate among all immigrant groups. If 2.3 million (1/3) return home, and of that 2.3 million only 1/2 of 1 percent were to return as Christians with a plan to reach souls and Mexican culture with the gospel, then almost 12,000 Mexicans would be sent to Mexico as Christian missionaries! This is in addition to native-born American missionaries. What would happen to the Mexican immigration crisis within several years of the implementation of this plan? It would be well on its way to being solved.

Mexican evangelical leaders need to pray and work for spiritual revival and cultural reformation in their nation. There is positive movement on this front. Hundreds of Mexican evangelical leaders, including key government leaders, have met with the country's former president, Carlos Salinas de Gortari, for a prayer breakfast at his residence. The event was co-hosted by the Evangelical Confraternity of Mexico and the Alberto Mottesi Evangelistic Association's Project 500 campaign. 'You will always find the doors to this house open,' the president told his guests. His remarks contrasted with decades of official intolerance toward evangelical churches. Mottesi, an Argentine-born evangelist based in suburban Los Angeles, gave a short talk, calling on the country's leaders to practice a biblical worldview by putting Christ first in their national, political, professional, and personal lives. The meeting, said Juan Isais, a veteran missionary with Latin America Mission, 'has given the evangelical church in Mexico a new and reinforced image before the nation's highest authorities, and a legal and social status before the media that from now on will have no reason whatsoever to ignore the activities and beliefs of Mexican evangelical Christianity.'[19]

Conclusion

Today America faces a spiritual threat. America as 'one nation under God' is quickly degenerating into the likes of ancient Athens – a 'city full of idols' (Acts 17:16). However, we would be wrong to pin all the blame for this dilemma upon forces from without. The *real* source of America's spiritual crisis is found within. Our turn as a nation from biblical standards to idols started long before the cultural effects of illegal immigration began to take hold. You have heard it said, 'America is a nation of immigrants.' This is only partly true. America was founded by pilgrim 'settlers' who emigrated to these shores in obedience to the call of God to 'disciple the nations'. Lest we forget our national purpose, which is to glorify the God of heaven, the day will soon come when, to our great embarrassment, the nations will once again be sending missionaries to us.

Thirteen

A CHRISTIAN PERSPECTIVE ON THE ENVIRONMENT

Remembering the Barefoot Mailman

Long before there were sky-high condos, congested roads, and Art Deco hotels, South Florida's 'Gold Coast' was a primitive tropical paradise. From 1513, when Ponce de Leon sailed by, until the mid-1880s, the shore was covered with the same glistening strips of white sandy beaches many sun-worshippers relish today. But reaching the beaches in those early days was no easy matter. Nestled between the east coast and the Everglades to the west, the land between Palm City (Palm Beach) down to Lemon City (Miami) was rough scrabble country fit only for black bears, panthers, and snakes. Thus, very few people ever enjoyed the miles of lapping waves and swaying palms of Florida's virgin coastline. All except one – the postman.

By 1885, the numbers of permanent white settlers in the villages of Palm Beach and Miami had increased enough that the U.S. Postal Service recognized the need to extend mail service to the area. Because there were no interstate highways or railroads, and the inland area was deemed too dangerous for travel, the flat sandy beach was believed to be the best mail route. Consequently, the legendary 'barefoot mailman' was born.

Picking up his mail on Monday morning in Palm Beach, the hardy mail carrier accomplished the first leg of his weeklong journey by sailing down Lake Worth or walking down Palm Beach Island. His goal was to reach the House of Refuge, a place for shipwrecked survivors, at what is now Delray Beach. Tuesday, he walked another twenty-five miles of beach to Hillsborough Inlet, where there he crossed over in a boat he kept hidden in the grassy scrub. He ended the second leg of his trip a few miles later at the House of Refuge in present-day Ft. Lauderdale.

On Wednesday, having already fended off everything from alligators to pirates, the mailman crossed Biscayne Bay into Miami. With only a night's sleep, he began his return journey on Thursday morning, arriving back in the Palm Beach area on Saturday. Sunday was his day of 'rest'.

Although all the barefoot mailmen are worthy of recognition, the most notable is James 'Ed' Hamilton. Upon arriving at Hillsborough Inlet on 9 October 1887, Hamilton found that someone had used his boat and left it on the opposite shore. In an attempt to reach his boat Hamilton braved the waters of the alligator-infested inlet. James E. Hamilton was never seen or heard from again.

The barefoot mailman served the people of South Florida from 1885 to 1893, ending a year after the railroad was completed to Miami.[1]

The story of the barefoot mailman stands at an epochal turning-point in Florida's rich history. On the one hand, he represented America's trailblazing spirit that was willing to sacrifice life and limb in order to conquer a vast wilderness in the spirit of progress. On the other hand, he symbolized the prevailing attitude toward progress during his time that the earth's environmental balance was an inconsequential consideration in light of the benefits promised by the agricultural and industrial revolutions. The 'unhappy' story of South Florida begins some thirty-five years before the barefoot mailman took to its beaches. (Incidentally, I was raised in South Florida, so it is with some level of concern that I share its environmental problems.)

How to Create a Natural Disaster

Although the alligators, wood storks, river-otters, and minks called it home, the uniqueness and importance of South Florida's Everglades (Sea of Grass) was not appreciated by the region's early white settlers. Unbelievably, the first state legislature declared the Everglades to be 'wholly valueless' and petitioned Congress for assistance in draining the 20 million acres of swamp, some 4500 square miles, with a view toward using the mucky soil for crop production. In 1850, Congress obliged. By the 1880s, the same period in which the barefoot mailman was hard at work, construction was underway to build a labyrinth of inland waterways and dykes designed to carry water from the Everglades into the Atlantic Ocean and the Gulf of Mexico.

Linked to this rather ambitious project was a need to address yet another 'obstacle' to the north. Meandering south, the Kissimmee River provides the major source of fresh water for Lake Okeechobee. During periods of increased rainfall, the 470,000-acre lake used to overflow its southern-most banks into the northern region of the Everglades providing native species high concentrations of enriched nutrients. The flow of water then emptied into the Florida Bay and west to the Gulf of Mexico.

The success of the initial drainage projects brought with it a migration of farmers into the path of the potential overflow. With agricultural and urban development needs on the increase, the push to stabilize the region received an added impetus after the hurricane of 1928 caused Lake Okeechobee to massively overflow its banks into developing farm lands, killing over 2,000 people. An answer was sought in the construction of a dyke around Lake Okeechobee and the straightening and channeling of the Kissimmee River.

Water management and flood control efforts intensified as back-to-back hurricanes in the late 40s forced death tolls to new heights. In 1948, Congress authorized $200 million for the purpose of enabling the U.S. Army Corps of Engineers to construct a new massive system of water control improvements under the Central and South Florida Flood Control Project. Approximately 1000 square miles of continuous shallow river has been drained and is now controlled by about 1,500 miles of criss-crossing canals and levees. But at what cost to the environment?

The Kissimmee-Okeechobee-Everglades watershed now bares the unenviable distinction of being the nation's most endangered subtropical wetland system. In short, it's a catastrophe. Once a veritable playland for herons, wood storks, roseate spoonbills, bald eagles, limpkins, black bears, white-tailed deer, round-tailed muscrats, and alligators, the Everglades is now a paradise lost with devastated plant and wildlife species.

Today less than half as much water flows through the Everglades as did just a century ago.[2] Progressive modifications to the hydrology of the ecosystem have caused numerous problems such as pollution of surface and ground water, intrusion of seawater, depletion of soils, reduction of natural habitats, and decline in wildlife.[3] Sixty-eight animal and plant species have been listed as endangered or threatened.[4] These are just a few of the environmental problems facing the Everglades.

The threat to life did not end with the lesser creatures. The 1.7 billion gallons of fresh water that is daily flushed out to sea during the rainy summer months is now posing a major threat to South Florida's water supply. When the Army Corps of Engineers designed the current water control system, population estimates for the region were predicted to be around 2 million by the year 2000. The population of South Florida is currently over 6 million and is expected to double over the next fifty years.[5] Current water sources are already being pushed to the breaking point. Unless something is done, South Florida faces a grave dilemma in the decades to come.

Added to this problem is the challenge of protecting South Florida's water quality from dangerous toxins. Runoff from farm and cattle lands carries unhealthy amounts of insecticides, herbicides, and fungicides into the Everglades. In his book, *The Condor's Shadow: The Loss and Recovery of Wildlife in America*, David S. Wilcove, observes, 'Naturally deficient in certain nutrients, especially phosphorus, the Everglades is vulnerable to agricultural run-off. Farming the muck releases stored phosphorus, nitrogen, and perhaps, other elements. Fertilizers are an additional source of phosphorus and nitrogen (although sugarcane is less heavily fertilized than many other crops), as are the defecating dairy cattle that live around Lake Okeechobee.'[6] What is the proposed solution?

In 1988, the federal government, on behalf of the Everglades National Park and the Loxahahatchee National Wildlife Refuge, sued the state of Florida, alleging that the state had violated state water quality standards by permitting contaminated agricultural run-off to flow into the Everglades. The state was forced to settle and in 1994, a vision for restoring water quality to the Everglades was solidified under the Florida's Everglades Forever Act.

This resulted in the Everglades Construction Project, called the 'largest environmental restoration project in the world'. At an estimated cost of $7.8 billion dollars, approximately 240 miles of levees, canals, gated culverts, and pumping stations are slated for removal over the next twenty years. Federal and state officials also propose re-channeling the Kissimmee River, allowing it to return to its natural winding course. It is hoped this will cause the river to breach several of its levees, returning 40,000 acres of farmland to marsh – an idea that should benefit the ecosystem, but not sugar-growers.

Why have I gone to such lengths detailing the environmental problems facing the Everglades? First, this creates a starting point where everyone can agree. One of the challenges facing any person concerned over the current state and future of the environment is getting to the truth. Numbers of extinct species, habitat destruction rates, global warming trends, and industrial pollution figures all have a funny way of reflecting the political viewpoint of the person or group who is speaking. The Everglades, however, is indisputably one of the few ecosystems that is almost universally viewed as a prime example of the horrendous costs of people's reckless disregard for nature. Second, the Everglades disaster provides a staggering example of how quickly and completely nature can turn from friend to foe when we make economic growth the governing principle in our interaction with the environment.

Today, the plan to restructure and stabilize the Kissimmee-Okeechobee-Everglades watershed represents a massive undertaking. Yet, the problem facing South Florida, while it stands alone as the nation's worst wetlands disaster, is not an isolated environmental concern. From at-risk populations of Florida manatees, to the virtual extinction of the whooping crane in Texas, to the endangered western monarch butterfly in California, the U.S. has a wide variety of genuine ecological concerns. Before I offer guidelines for what I believe should be done to address these concerns as a whole, let's take a brief look at the state of environmental activism today.

How Green Can We Be?

The past several years have witnessed a growing chorus of voices joining the debate over what is best for the environment. Although environmental activists represent a diverse world of scientific, political, social, and religious perspectives, all fall into one of two categories. First, are those who believe that *man is for the earth*. This is the position that places the rights of different habitats, biological communities, and ecological processes above the desires, and often times, the needs, of humans.

A short list of groups representing this view include: The Sierra Club, the National Audubon Society, Defenders of Wildlife, Earth First, National Fish and Wildlife Foundation, The Nature Conservancy, The Wilderness Society, the Political Ecology Group, and the Environmental Research Foundation. Government agencies include the Environmental Defense Fund, the Environmental Protection Agency, Department of Agriculture, U.S. Forest Service, National Park Service, and the Fish and Wildlife Service.

The degree to which humans should defer to nature largely depends upon which one of these environmental advocacy groups is speaking. Positions range from the more moderate, but dominant philosophy of the National Audubon Society with its mandate to 'conserve and restore natural ecosystems, focusing on birds and other wildlife for the benefit of humanity and the earth's biological diversity', to the radical group, Earth First, which believes that people have no right to alter the earth's natural ecological balance, except in cases where the basic survival of humankind is at stake.

Earth First is willing to go to any lengths to achieve its goal of destroying industrialization and returning the earth to its pre-modern past. According to Philip Shabecoff in his book, *A Fierce Green Fire,* 'These radicals...choose...to defend the natural world by direct action, civil disobedience, and the kind of ecosabotage romanticized by the novelist Edward Abbey.'[7] Earth First provides the clearest example of Paul's far-reaching observation: 'Professing to be wise, they became fools, and exchanged the glory of the incorruptible God for an image in the form of corruptible man and of birds and four-footed animals and crawling creatures' (Romans 1:22-23).

An Alternative and Growing Voice

On the opposite end of the environmental spectrum is the second group – those who believe that *the earth is for man.* E. Calvin Beisner comments, 'Man was not made for the earth; the earth was made for man.'[8] And Herb Schlossberg, in his book, *Idols for Destruction,* states, 'First, the dominion mandate means at least that man, not the environment, is primary. Certainly the environment should be protected, but it must be protected for the sake of man, not for the sake of the environment. Anything else is idolatry of nature.'[9] Several organizations representing this perspective include the Interfaith Council for Environmental Stewardship and its Cornwall Declaration, The Heritage Foundation, the Acton Institute, the Environmental Policy Task Force of The National Center for Public Policy Research, the Ethics and Public Policy Center, the Committee for a Constructive Tomorrow, the Greening Earth Society, and many more.

Based in a conservative economic and social philosophy that promotes private property rights, fiscal responsibility, economic development, and individual accountability, these groups reject the top-down, 'command and control' approach to the environment the federal government has pursued in recent years. Instead, they seek, to varying degrees, a non-regulatory, community-based approach to environmental stewardship – one that heralds the advantages of economic development for environmental quality. The vision is called 'conservationism'. According to Angela Antonelli of the Heritage Foundation, 'Conservationists espouse a passionate belief in the wise use of resources and a respect for nature's wonders that is balanced by an understanding of the importance of free-market incentives and property rights in solving environmental problems.'[10]

A Conservative Agenda for the Environment

One might argue that the suggestion that a free-market economy is the best solution for the environment is like saying the best solution to keeping the hen house clean is to allow the rooster to run wild. However, the Acton Institute's Protestant Monograph, *Biblical Perspective on Environmental Stewardship*, offers a reasoned defense of this position: 'These principles indicate that a biblically sound environmental stewardship is fully compatible with private-property rights and a free economy, as long as people are held accountable for their actions...On the one hand, there is a direct and positive correlation between the degree of political and economic freedom and both the level of economic attainment and the rapidity of economic growth in countries around the world. The 20 percent of the world's countries with the greatest economic freedom produce, on average, over ten times as much wealth per capita as the 20 percent with the least economic freedom, and while the freest countries enjoyed an average 2.27 percent annual rate of growth in real gross national product per capita through the 1990s, the least-free countries experienced a decline of 1.32 percent per year. On the other hand, there is also a direct and positive correlation between economic advance and environmental quality.'[11]

How can a free-market democracy oriented toward sustainable economic growth lead to environmental improvement? The idea is that free economies promote competition, which, in turn, encourages less production costs, thus reducing the use of natural resources. As resource use declines, we can expect levels of pollution and other hazards to the environment to decline as well. 'Economists find that free economies outperformed planned and controlled economies not only in the production and distribution of wealth but also in environmental protection. Freer economies use fewer resources and emit less pollution while producing more goods per man-hour than less free economies.'[12]

The document also points out that because property owners have a financial stake in protecting their property, they are naturally the best advocates for an unpolluted and safe environment. 'People naturally want their homes and workplaces, and, by extension, their neighbourhoods, to be clean and healthful, so they seek to minimize pollution...Moreover, a dynamic economy works to reduce pollution by finding the most efficient means of doing so.'[13]

The study continues, 'What we can infer from all these considerations — and what we find confirmed in empirical studies of the real world — is that free economies improve human health, raise living standards and life expectancy, and positively affect environmental conditions, doing all these things better than less free economies do. Further, the wealthier that economies become, the better they foster environmental protection. "If pollution is the brother of affluence", it has been written, then "concern about pollution is affluence's child".[14]

Is there a down side to this plan? Drafters admit that both private and corporate economic development may cause initial levels of pollution and other negative factors to rise; however, because expansion creates affluence, people are able to invest more resources to address the challenge. 'Even if some pollution emissions rise during early economic development, the beneficial effects of increased production to human life far outweigh the harmful effects of the resulting pollution, as demonstrated in declining disease and mortality rates and in rising health and life expectancy, even during that early stage. But soon, increasing wealth enables citizens to invest more resources on environmental protection, and emission rates fall. The result has been termed the 'environmental transition', which mirrors the more widely known 'demographic transition'.[15]

The piece concludes with a practical implementation of its principles of 'exclusivity, liability, and transferability'. It is a private-property system that seeks to balance individual freedom and alteration of the environment with 'full accountability' — as accountability is understood not toward regulatory bureaucracies, but to other members of society. With the two major environmental groups as our backdrop,

I now wish to introduce you to a third perspective on the environment – mine.

This is My Father's World

In keeping with the fact that 'the world and all that it contains is subject to the eternal purpose and plan of God', I suggest that neither is man for the earth, nor is the earth for man. Rather, the earth is for God. The Almighty declares, 'Whatever is under the whole heaven is mine' (Job 41:11). Although the psalmist proclaims, '...the earth He has given to the sons of men', (Psalms 115:16), it is the superior truth that must take precedence: 'The earth is the Lord's and all it contains' (Psalm 24:1).

I agree with the basic goal and strategy of the Protestant Monograph. In fact, shortly we will see another proposal – this one written by Dr. Michael S. Coffman – which is similar in many respects to the Protestant Monograph, and which I believe is also worthy of our support. So why don't I simply recommend one of these plans?

While I firmly believe that a system of private property rights conjoined with a free market economy represents *part* of the solution for protecting the environment, that it is not the entire solution. I believe three important modifications will provide further safeguards for protecting the environment. A new Christian activism will view private property rights as an entitlement that must be constrained by *the role nature plays in God's plan of redemption, one's respect for nature's unity, and one's knowledge of the depravity of the human heart.* Let's begin with nature's important role in redemption.

Applying a Christian Worldview to the Environment

The doctrine of redemption brings us back to one of this book's major points, that God is busy working 'to restore everything that was lost at the fall, both in man and in the rest of creation, to its proper role of worshipping and glorifying Him'. The environment is where we properly take up the discussion of the 'rest of creation'. Unless we understand how the environment relates to the greater issue of redemption, we will never arrive at any plausible solutions regarding what is best for it. How does the environment relate to God's plan of redemption? There are three ways.

The creation serves the Great Commission through the process of natural revelation. Paul writes, 'For since the creation of the world His invisible attributes, His eternal power and divine nature, have been clearly seen, being understood through what has been made, so that they are without excuse' (Romans 1:20).

Paul's point is that deep down everyone knows there is a God. A simple glance at the incredible handiwork of creation and one immediately sees in it the hand of God. Look at the earth and you will see majestic mountain ranges, forests bustling with life, and abundant oceans flowing perfectly in their respective cycles. Then dip beneath the ocean and you will discover an amazing world where the most rich and diverse forms of life exist. In all, our basic, yet incredibly complex earth displays an unmistakable architecture. And where there is architecture on a scale of this magnitude, there must be an architect. The Bible says that men, being created in the image of God, instinctively interpret the world's design as coming from the hand of the Creator – the Master Architect.

Paul also says that natural revelation imparts to all people the knowledge of certain basic attributes of God's nature. Without Bible studies, teaching tapes, or angelic visitations, all mankind understands that God is just and righteous. At some point in everyone's life, they come to the realization, if only for a moment, of impending death and the fact that they will face a God of judgment. And all comprehend that there is a moral distinction between right and wrong, good and evil. This knowledge is attributable to the testimony of nature. Clearly, then, as nature makes man aware of God's just and holy standards, he is 'without excuse'.

We can thus see how the revelation of nature serves God's purposes in evangelism. Because nature makes man aware of the living and true God, and of his sinful condition, there is a 'point of contact' for the evangelist. The presence of an innate knowledge of the Creator in people means there is a spiritual DNA match between our life and the life of God. God is eternal. We are eternal. We shall not find peace, joy, and happiness until we find God. Effective evangelism is therefore that which appeals to the natural knowledge of God, which exists in the heart of the unbeliever.

This brings us to an inescapable conclusion. Whether it is the small franklinia tree, named for Benjamin Franklin in 1785, which was last seen in the wild in 1803, or it is the last passenger pigeon, which died at 1:00 p.m., 1 September 1914, at the Cincinnati Zoological Garden, each part of the creation that becomes extinct leaves us with that much less to point to God. Given the vast array of earth's natural wonders, this may appear to be a minor concern. However, that is not the issue. The role nature plays in facilitating the Great Commission reveals a wonderful reciprocity of creation: creation's sheer magnificence turns the heart toward its Creator, and the heart that has turned to God opens, inevitably, towards creation – toward the awesome integrity of the natural world that is God's gift. There is no part of creation too insignificant that we should take it for granted.

You will recall that this book began with a discussion about the sovereignty of God. What does the sovereignty of God tell us about the environment? It says that *every part of nature is here for a reason.* In other words, there are no random acts or chance occurrences in God's creation. Not a single plant, animal, habitat, watershed, or eco-system is here by accident. All creation serves God's redemptive plan – the Great Commission in particular – in its capacity to create a 'bridge' for effective evangelism. My contention is that if the environment serves the Great Commission, the Church must seek to ensure the health of the environment through the Cultural Mandate.

The creation serves God's redemptive purposes through its worship and glorification of the Lord and His salvation. Even the casual reader of the Bible has been struck by the unusual way in which parts of nature take on human-like qualities in their praise of God and His salvation. Isaiah 55:12 says, 'For you will go out with joy, and be led forth with peace; the mountains and the hills will break forth into shouts of joy before you, and all the trees of the field will clap their hands.' And Psalm 98:8, 'Let the sea roar and all it contains, the world and those who dwell in it. Let the rivers clap their hands; let the mountains sing together for joy.'

It has been argued that the exalted language of trees clapping their hands and mountains breaking forth into song is merely a poetical device intended to point to a spiritual truth that applies to people. For example, in Isaiah 55:12, many contend that linked to the Davidic promise to Israel of her return to the land, is her experience of great joy that is expressed in the vivid picture of nature's rejoicing. This is true and partly explains Jesus' response to some Pharisees, 'I tell you, if these become silent, the stones will cry out!' (Luke 19:40) Jesus' rebuke, couched in metaphor, is aimed at the House of Israel, which had failed to worship Him as God's appointed Messiah. Christ's warning that the rocks will cry out in glad hosannas should His disciples too remain silent, further illustrates the capacity of nature to reveal to men that they are 'without excuse'.

However, we would be wrong to assume that nature's sole function in God's redemptive plan is restricted to that of metaphor. The connection between the blessing and curse in man and the redemption and curse in nature is also to be interpreted *literally*. In Genesis 3:18, because man fell into transgression the ground is cursed. Paul says that just as believers eagerly await the redemption of their bodies, so the 'anxious longing of the creation waits eagerly for the revealing of the sons of God' (Romans 8:19). The rustling branch, the babbling brook, and the whirring wind more than *typify* man's hope. Because all of nature *embodies* such a hope, it too serves its Creator in praise and adulation.

The creation serves and magnifies God's creative and redemptive power by virtue of its inherent qualities. That God declared His creation 'very good' before Adam took his first breath means that nature is good, not because it serves any human purpose, but because God made it. God delights in His creation because it comes from His hand. This is why I am so disturbed by Herb Schlossberg's observation that the environment must be protected for the sake of man and that 'Anything else is idolatry of nature'. I am a certified Divemaster with the Professional Association of Diving Instructors. If I seek to ensure the health of the coral reefs off the coast of South Florida for no other reason than they are marvels of my Father's creativity, am I an idolater? I think not.

I believe that with our conservative disdain for the theory of 'biocentric equality' – that parts of nature have an intrinsic right to exist – that the pendulum has now swung to the opposite extreme to where nature has no right to exist unless we say so. We would do well to remember the ancient Hebrews whose redemptive theology issued into a natural respect for the richness of the land. They lovingly tended the land as the cycles of their celebrations followed the seasons. While their efforts to tame the land were often marvels of ingenuity, they understood well the limits to their mastery – for they knew God as Sovereign of the land. Through such institutions as the Sabbatical year and the Jubilee (cf. Leviticus 25), they acknowledged God's ownership.

It followed that they had to treat the land well – not only to give it rest, but to respect and plant trees, keep water sources clean, create parks near urban areas, regulate sewage disposal, and avoid causing pain to animals. Since the land was God's, not only was it to be protected, but its rich produce was to be shared with the poor (cf. Leviticus 19). In a world where warfare typically included efforts by the victor to drastically degrade the environment of the captive, God instructed Israel to only destroy trees that were not fruit trees: 'For is the tree of the field a man that it should be besieged by you?' (Deuteronomy 20:19)? And if a Hebrew were to come across a bird's nest, he could take the young, but not the mother (Deuteronomy 22:6). The Jewish thinker, Nachmanides, wrote, 'Torah doesn't permit a killing that would uproot a species, even if it permitted the killing [of individuals] in that species.'

Man's relationship to the land during Old Testament times was far from idyllic. The promised abundance had to be teased and more often wrestled from the earth by the sweat of the brow, and the seasons had a way of being fickle. God's 'endless blessing' is in the future when the lion will lie down with the lamb, and humankind will be at peace with all of nature (cf. Isaiah 65:21-25).[16] It is in the context of an ideal vision of man's harmony with the new creation to come, that we seek to know how to carry out the Cultural Mandate as stewards of God's creation.

Back to the Garden Again

Let's read the Cultural Mandate again found in Genesis 1:28: 'And God blessed them; and God said to them, "Be fruitful and multiply, and fill the earth, and subdue it; and rule over the fish of the sea and over the birds of the sky, and over every living thing that moves on the earth."' God's expectations for Adam were relatively few. He was to populate the earth, subdue it, exercise dominion over the animals, care for the garden, and eat of its fruit.

Picking up on the lack of detail in Genesis 1:28, Old Testament scholar, R. Laird Harris, suggests that the Cultural Mandate does not negate or prescribe any one particular approach to the environment. He writes, 'to have "rule over" the earth might as easily refer to free use and development of resources as to our responsibility for their conservation. To "rule over" the animals does not specifically say high dams for power should be rejected so as to avoid bringing an exotic type of little fish to extinction.'[17] Clearly, the Cultural Mandate is not case specific. It does not answer questions like, 'Where should we drill for oil?' However, is there not at least a *general principle* established in the creation account that can offer guidance on where we should drill for oil, or which suggests we think hard before 'bringing an exotic type of little fish to extinction'?

The only restriction (general principle) God placed upon the first couple in their management of the earth was that they not eat of the tree of the knowledge of good and evil (2:17). God's prohibition was not motivated by His fear that man's knowledge of good and evil would make him equal to the Almighty. Rather, the ban was aimed at frustrating any attempt on man's part to pursue intellectual autonomy. Care of God's earth was to be carried out within man's relationship to God and the ethical demands associated with His righteous nature. Certainly this consideration applies to our stewardship responsibilities of the earth today. But how?

You'll recall in Chapter 1 we learned that the second building block of a biblical worldview is the unity and simplicity of God's nature – that God is One. I argued in that chapter that the creation in all its parts reflects this unity. Therefore, my second point which I hope will help strengthen conservatives' approach to the environment is this: *our reflection upon the environment must be governed by a reverent fear of nature's unity – a unity that finds its source in the righteous character of God.*

Addressing the Impact

Although nature consists of a diverse world of birds, reptiles, mammals, vegetation, and habitats, it is also a world of interdependent biological systems. It is estimated that there are up to 100 million plant and animal species on earth, which *together* keep the planet functioning as a habitat suitable for all.[18] Nature's unity – its cohesiveness – also means that impact to, or the extinction of, one species can easily affect several other life forms up or down the environmental chain. The absence of that 'exotic little fish' can become a big problem if that fish happened to be a major food source for a bigger, exotic fish. Environmental scientists call this 'species vulnerability'.

The issues of species vulnerability and rates of species extinction are hotly contested. For example, one estimate indicates that 1 million species will be lost in the next twenty-five years, an extinction rate of one every fifteen minutes.[19] On the other hand, the Protestant Monograph suggests that data supporting high rates of extinctions are significantly exaggerated. The paper quotes two leading experts in the area of species extinction, V.H. Heywood, former director of the scientific team that produced the Flora Europa, the definitive taxonomic compilation of European plants, and S.N. Stuart, executive officer of the Species Survival Commission at the IUCN, who write, 'Known extinction rates [worldwide] are very low. Reasonably good data exist only for mammals and birds, and the current rate of extinction is about one species per year...If other taxa were to exhibit the same liability to extinction as mammals and birds (as some authors suggest, although others would dispute this), then, if the total number of species in the world is, say, 30 million, the annual rate of extinction would be some 2,300 species per year. This is a very significant and disturbing number, but it is much less than most estimates given over the last decade.'[20]

While I concur that rates of species extinction are lower than many estimates suggest, I am not convinced that this decreases the possibility of wide-ranging problems to other species (e.g. species vulnerability). But before I make my case, let's see what else the Protestant Monograph says about species extinction: '...when most people unfamiliar with the ESA [Environmental Species Act] think of a species as being in danger of becoming extinct, they think this means no individual organism of that genetic definition will be left anywhere – or, since the ESA applies to the United States, at least there. (This popular perception certainly lies behind the fear that "species" extinction forever removes elements from the global gene pool.) But in reality, it may only mean that a given population segment of that genetically defined species is endangered; it is entirely possible that plenty of other specimens may thrive in other locations. Many citizens who support expensive policies to prevent extinctions might reconsider if they knew that rather than preventing real extinctions, they were only preventing the removal of a geographically refined segment of an otherwise thriving species.'[21]

The quote correctly states that the decline of a species in one geographical area does not mean that the same species is endangered elsewhere. But it does not follow that the decline of a species will not affect other species living in the *same* geographical area that somehow depend upon its presence.

For example, due to increasing populations in British Columbia, the sea otter was downlisted from 'endangered' to 'threatened' in 1996 by the Committee of the Status of Endangered Wildlife in Canada through the British Columbia Wildlife Act.[22] However, in Alaska there are 150,000-200,000 sea otters and the population is declining dramatically.[23] Are we to assume that a decreasing sea otter population off the coast of Alaska poses no real problem because sea otters are thriving in other parts of the world?

The fact is that negatively impacting or removing a species will affect an ecosystem. The effect will vary depending upon the niche occupied by the species. The sea otter, for example, is a 'keystone' species[24], and its absence from an ecosystem will have a major impact. Jocelyn Kaiser observes, 'Sea otters off the Alaskan coast play a pivotal role in ecosystems: by dining on sea urchins, the animals help preserve kelp forests that feed a range of species from barnacles to bald eagles.'[25]

And David S. Wilcove says, 'The effect of the otters extends well beyond sea urchins and kelp, however. Kelp forests constitute a distinctive and important ecosystem in the North Pacific, providing food and shelter for a wide range of organisms. As kelp decays or is broken apart by waves, it releases organic matter into the marine environment – organic matter that is readily consumed by mussels, anemones, crabs, and other organisms, which are themselves consumed by fish, birds, sea otters, and other top predators.'[26]

Predicting in advance what damage will be done to an ecosystem by removing a species is a risky and uncertain business. Depending upon the 'environmental transition' to offset damage done to nature is akin to playing Russian Roulette. In the Florida Everglades, the environmental transition has made both government agencies and the private sector address a literal plethora of interconnected environmental and human health concerns at a cost of nearly 8 billion dollars of taxpayers' hard-earned money. Does not God expect us to be stewards of our monies, as well as His creation?

The greatest charge that could be laid before those who transformed much of the Everglades into farmland was that they failed to consider the improbable consequences of their actions. Today many think they know the impact industry, deforestation, and urban sprawl are having upon the environment. Conservatives say little; liberals say much. But the fact is no one knows! That's the *real* truth. This is why we must err on the side of caution where nature is concerned. The balance of nature is a far too complex and interrelated system for any man to suggest otherwise. As God said to Job, 'Have you understood the expanse of the earth? Tell me if you know all this' (Job 38:18).

Nevertheless, our need to defer to nature's delicate balance must be tempered by an equally salient point, that *the creation has been subjected to 'futility'.* Paul writes, 'For the anxious longing of the creation waits eagerly for the revealing of the sons of God. For the creation was subjected to futility, not of its own will, but because of Him who subjected it, in hope that the creation itself also will be set free from its slavery to corruption into the freedom of the glory of the children of God. Or we know that the whole creation groans and suffers the pains of childbirth until now' (Romans 8:19-22). While it is fashionable to blame humans for *all* threats to the environment, Scripture suggests that God's curse upon the earth is a major contributing factor toward environmental degradation and species decline.

You may remember in Chapter 6 reference was made to Genesis 3:17-19 where, due to man's rebellion in the Garden, God cursed the ground, making it hard for him to cultivate. The result, Paul says, is that the creation was made subject to 'futility', which is a broad term meaning that the creation is no longer as it was at the start – very good – but is in fact corrupt and declining. E. Calvin Beisner observes, '...the Curse implies that the universe is not now as it was when created (unmixedly good) and that man's sin is not the only thing that has changed it. God's curse has, too. It has made the world hostile to man, naturally unfruitful by comparison with its original fruitfulness, and full of death and decay. Consequently we should not expect, as environmentalists frequently insist, that "nature knows best", or that left to itself, nature knows what to do and it is this "looking after itself" that is nature's mark'.[27]

Today many radical environmentalists suggest that man's very 'presence' is the leading reason that nature is at risk. Fault should certainly be placed at the feet of those who pollute rivers with industrial waste or whose reckless actions cause harm to animals. Nonetheless, to say that man's very presence or his obedience to the Cultural Mandate is to blame for the 'exploitation' of the earth is equivalent to saying that man is responsible for facial wrinkles in old age. Facial wrinkles are going to happen *regardless* of how men live.

Likewise, that nature is on a 'downward slope' means that even if the biocentrists could limit man's interaction with the earth to a bare minimum, nature would still provide enough negative energy to account for much of what is wrong with it. And yes, this means that had the Army Corps of Engineers not dramatically altered the Kissimmee-Okeechobee-Everglades watershed, which I have held up as a prime example of gross land mismanagement, the Everglades would *still* be home to numerous environmental concerns today.

Selling Our National Birthright for a Global Pot of Stew

The third point I wish to inject into conservatives' strategy regarding the environment is a renewed appreciation for the depravity of the human heart. Now before I get to my *real* point, let me focus our attention upon one particular aspect of the depravity of the human heart – the threat the federal government is today posing to American freedom.

In his booklet, *The Decline of Property Rights and Freedom in America*, Dr. Michael S. Coffman, president of Environmental Perspectives, details the original intent of the Founding Fathers, who saw our God-given right to own land as one of the foundational elements to freedom. Coffman also provides an overview of the systematic erosion of the right to private property in America, which has come at the hands of government interference and its usurpation of individual rights. I strongly recommend the reader get a copy of his booklet. The gist of Coffman's thesis is that America is presently witnessing a move toward a 'new feudalism'. Complete centralized control over most of this nation's landscape will have the nefarious effect of elevating the federal government, and perhaps the United Nations, as the ultimate power over the lives of Americans. Personal liberty will be a thing of the past.

In an article for *Mining Voice*, Dr. Coffman notes, 'With the Grand Canyon National Park as his backdrop, President Bill Clinton used the 1906 Antiquities Act to set aside one million acres of land into three national monuments in Arizona, Nevada, and California on January 11 [2000] this year.'[28] This action was not done with the approval or review of Congress. In addition to the federal government's unprecedented lock up of public lands, 'more than 20 million acres of private land could be purchased over the next decade with no congressional oversight'.[29] Using the Clean Water Action Plan, the Environmental Protection Agency and the Department of Agriculture plan to administratively shift 'water protection from point source pollution (a single factory or city) to non-point source pollution over an entire watershed'.[30] Consequently, federal land use jurisdiction will extend to all of the 2,100 watersheds in America, including private property. This use of the Clean Water Action Plan will affect a total of '48 million acres of private property'.[31]

Just three days before leaving the White House, former President Clinton created seven new national monuments and expanded an eighth on 17 January 2001. All totaled, the Clinton administration designated more than 3 million acres as national monuments in 2000 and 2001. U.S. Interior Secretary Gale Norton has indicated that President Bush will not seek to reverse Clinton's land-grabs, but only adjust them so oil drilling, coal mining, and other development can take place.

Moreover, the U.S. government is working to implement the UN's Agenda 21 and the Convention on Biological Diversity (Biodiversity Treaty), which was introduced during the June 1992 Earth Summit held in Rio de Janeiro, Brazil. 'Agenda 21 is a 40-chapter tome focused on reorganizing society around "sustainable" use and development of the planet. Based on socialist principles of equal sharing of all natural resources, Agenda 21 sets a goal to control all human activity to protect the Earth's ecosystems and biological diversity.'[32] Implementation of Agenda 21 and the Biodiversity Treaty in the U.S. is currently being sought through The Wildlands Project, which is designed 'to transform at least half the land area of the continental United States into an immense "eco-park" cleansed of modern industry and private property'.[33] This will be accomplished through the creation of 'reserve networks' across America. These reserve networks will be made up of 'cores', and 'corridors', a mixture of both private and public lands. As a result, 50 percent of the U.S. continent will be restricted or considered off-limits to the public!

The Wildlands Project is essentially the pet project of David Foreman, the principle founder of the eco-terrorist group, Earth First. Foreman summarizes the strategy as an effort to 'tie the North American continent into a single Biodiversity Preserve'.[34] John Davis, editor of *Wild Earth*, is more to the point, when he says the Wildlands Project seeks 'the end of industrialized civilization...Everything civilized must go'.[35] This Orwellian nightmare would close many U.S. industries, block or remove highways and roads, stop all timber harvesting, and what is more, force many hundred of thousands of Americans to relocate.

It is in this context that Coffman urgently calls us to rebuild a system where government exists to protect absolute private property rights limited only by the principle of 'harm and nuisance'. This is a system that places control of the environment at the local level, where it is regulated by a strict system of checks and balances. In 'The Decline of Property Rights and Freedom in America: The Destruction of Our Founder's Intent for the U.S. Constitution', Coffman observes, 'In turn, common law nuisance and harm provisions limit the rights of a property owner to harm their neighbour. Therefore, if an activity or use of property clearly causes harm to a neighbour by causing harm to the environment, the property owner must pay the cost of mitigation or restoration. These activities can be established in regulatory statutes where the regulators are accountable to those within their jurisdiction. However, if a regulation benefits the larger (i.e. a "public good") without a clear and definable harm, reduction of property value must be compensated according to the Fifth Amendment of the U.S. Constitution. Finally, if an activity or use does not cause a definable harm by itself, but does when added to all similar activities or uses preceding it, both the property owner and society should share the cost of diminished property value. Society must bear responsibility because it contributed to the problem as much as the proposed activities or use of the current property owner. Partial compensation according to the Fifth Amendment should be required.'[36]

He concludes, 'In the final analysis, it is private property rights as constrained by common law and significant harm that is the ultimate answer to environmental protection. A continued reliance on heavy-handed laws and regulations will only serve to devastate landowners and deny them the ability and desire to develop creative solutions to our environmental problems. It will also deny them the incentive to creatively provide the natural resources this nation must have to provide the security and standard of living we all enjoy.'[37]

This plan is quite similar to the Protestant Monograph's view of 'exclusivity, liability, and transferability', which I too applaud. However, I am not satisfied to make the law of 'harm and nuisance' or the principle of 'exclusivity, liability, and transferability' the *only* restraint to private property rights. These guidelines only direct our attention to how misuse of the environment may negatively impact other people, but say little about how human actions may harm the lesser creatures and their natural surroundings – that is unless that harm can be shown to affect people. Thus, I want us to be careful how we define, 'harm'.

For if 'harm' is understood only within the context of monetary loss, or personal injury, then any number of actions can harm animals and their surroundings without anyone feeling it in the pocketbook. But if harm is understood within the context of nature's unity (i.e. species vulnerability) – its ability to transfer damage from one species to another up or down the life-chain, resulting in an overabundance of troubles – then we have a different standard for harm. I suggest we must include this additional standard. For us to assume that every potential environmental problem is going to happily intersect with our personal fiefdoms so we will first, notice it, and second, solve it, is expecting too much. There are those additional cases where the 'sparrow' falls and no one notices except God. This fact must therefore be considered equally important in helping us to know what is best for the environment.

Environmental Hazards and Contaminated Motives

Now we come to my real point – *the depravity of all men's hearts.* Remember – not only did the curse affect the ground, making it difficult for man to cultivate, but also the fall has affected man, rendering him unable to care for the earth with a pure heart. While it is true that salvation restores man to his proper role of fulfilling the Cultural Mandate, Christians still are *not* exempt from this fact (cf. Romans 7). The ancient prophet Jeremiah lamented the woeful condition of the human heart: 'The heart is deceitful above all else and is desperately sick; who can understand it' (Jeremiah 17:9). While I appreciate the position espoused by both the Protestant Monograph and Michael S. Coffman, that people will naturally care for land in which they have a vested, financial interest, sadly this is not *always* true. While some will be faithful stewards of their Master's possession, others will squander it (cf. Matthew 25:1-30).

I want to believe that Americans are ready for Congress to reverse the federal government's egregious usurpation of property rights and are eager to act responsibly toward the land where they live and thrive. This *must* be our goal. But the Bible says that while people were created to live in freedom as responsible agents before Almighty God, sin easily causes them to be prideful and careless.

We are not a nation that uses its freedom wisely, but rather we are a people that is quick to turn its 'freedom into an opportunity for the flesh' (Galatians 5:13). We are a nation of affluence and means, yet we do not see our greatness as an opportunity to serve God, but rather boast that we are 'rich and become wealthy, and have need of nothing'(Revelation 3:17). The fact is most Americans are not, as Michael S. Coffman suggests, primed to dream up 'creative solutions' to our environmental problems. Rather we 'lust and do not have' and are 'are envious and cannot obtain' (James 4:2). This is our focus. And this is the root of our problem. Unless we as a nation are sure we will not convert our freedom into autonomy from God, we need not fool ourselves into thinking we are prepared to govern a wilderness. If anything, we shall wander in it.

The philosopher Santayana warned, 'If we do not remember the past, we are destined to repeat it.' Unless our aspiration for the environment is constrained by our humble awareness of the ever-present potential of the human heart to deceive and of our need to depend upon the Holy Spirit, we are bound to repeat the blunders of the past. In short, we must *remember the barefoot mailman*. We must recall that although he represented a pioneering spirit that facilitated the British industrial and agricultural revolutions in America, his was also an age in which pursuit after wealth blinded many to the effect that economic expansion could have in unraveling the balance of nature. Let us grow; let us harness nature, but let us do so out of respect for nature's role in God's redemption, in deference to the awesome unity of nature, and in the awareness that our best of intentions to help the environment will always be blemished by sin.

Fourteen

THE CHURCH AND POLITICS: OBJECTIONS ANSWERED

An analysis of what the Church should be doing to restore planet earth for Christ would not be complete without a discussion of the all-important area of politics. In Chapter 6, I presented several areas where I believe that Christian, political activism is in error. Despite my remarks, there is an important area of agreement: believers must be actively involved in politics.

Politics, however, is no stranger to the evangelical church. When I went to write on this subject, I thought, 'What is the unique need?' It soon occurred to me that although most Christians who labour in politics know *what* they are doing, few know, from a biblical perspective, *why* they are doing it. Just ask any believer who works in politics, either professionally, or as a ministry, 'Why politics?' and he or she will most likely respond, 'I'm working to restore America's Christian heritage.' Certainly this is a noble goal. But what if America had no Christian heritage? What if the Founders had been heathens? Could you defend an active Church in politics solely on the basis of God's call to His Church to restore 'all things' to His glory? *The great need among believers with respect to politics is not for more political involvement, but for more biblical understanding of why we do what we do.*

This book has already provided much biblical support for the idea that Christ's purpose is to restore the earth – all of which can be used to support the Christian's role in politics. It is therefore not my purpose here to review past material. Instead, I want to use the Bible to speak to several objections to the idea of Christian, political activism in the hope of shoring up our commitment to this needful area.

Blinded by Disappointment

In Chapter 8, we examined a portion of Paul Weyrich's *Washington Post* letter where he calls on cultural conservatives to abandon all attempts to win the culture-war. *Blinded by Might,* by Cal Thomas and Ed Dobson, is the book equivalent to Weyrich's letter. Cal Thomas, a nationally syndicated columnist and journalist, and Ed Dobson, an evangelical pastor in Michigan, both worked closely with Jerry Falwell and the Moral Majority in the early 80s. At some point, however, Thomas and Dobson became disillusioned with the Religious Right. They have now joined Paul Weyrich in calling Christians to end any effort to reform the culture, but instead to limit our work to prayers, evangelism, and personal discipleship. In Chapters 4 and 8 of *Blinded by Might,* Ed Dobson offers a number of objections to an active church in politics. In fact, he did such a fine job articulating his protests, I have chosen to follow much of his outline in my remarks. Note: If you have not read *Blinded by Might* and feel you lack the context for this discussion, don't worry. With minor variance, Dobson's objections are not original, but in fact have been around for many years. The reader should have no trouble recognizing them.

I. The Law Cannot Produce Moral Transformation

Ed Dobson remarks, 'Morality is never activated from the top down. It is achieved from the bottom up – one person at a time, one family at a time, one street at a time, one community at a time – until the entire culture is changed – not by laws, but heart by heart. This work of individual transformation is slow and takes a long time. The net effect cannot be easily measured or observed. It is easier to pass a law. But laws do not change people. Trickle down morality does not work.'[1]

Cal Thomas and Ed Dobson call for a 'bubble up' not a 'trickle down' morality to take hold in America. 'Bubble up' morality refers to the effect that changed lives can have in transforming a nation for good. If believers just model Christ to the world and allow their godly influence to be felt in every area of life, then many of America's problems would be solved. 'Trickle down' morality, on the other hand, represents the tired legislative approach of the Religious Right that believes it can change people's behavior through the passage of laws. Both Thomas and Dobson believe that this latter approach has gotten us nowhere and has only corrupted the evangelical church.

Answer: Conservative Christian activists are often criticized because many work to see legislation passed locally and in Congress that promotes 'morality'. You've heard it said, 'You can't legislate morality!' But morality is legislated everyday. It's called the law. Red lights at intersections and no smoking signs in elevators reflect laws designed to modify our behavior. It seems that legislation is only a problem when conservative Christians are behind it. Why? Many believe that if a bill in question lacks popular support people will simply disregard it. Ed Dobson observes, 'The most effective laws *follow* moral consensus — they do not bring about moral consensus.'[2] Oh really?

Did Moses wait for a 'moral consensus' to form among the Hebrews before he delivered the Ten Commandments? No, the Law was delivered to Israel at a time when the people were up to their eyeballs in sin. It seems that Moses took longer to return from his meeting with God than the people were willing to wait. Upon Moses' return he found God's people worshipping a 'golden calf'. Moses responded by shattering the tablets of stone containing the Ten Commandments at the base of the mount. Did God abandon His law because there was no 'moral consensus'? Absolutely not. God ordered Moses to re-cut two stone tablets as a replacement and the Law was instituted.

The Law and Evangelism
The position that law cannot produce moral transformation forgets a major purpose of law is to lead people to Christ. For example, Paul,

referring to the moral law or the Ten Commandments, writes, 'Therefore the Law has become our tutor to lead us to Christ, that we may be justified by faith' (Galatians 3:24). How is the Law a 'tutor'?

First, it reveals the perfect holiness of God. The Law of God is perfect because it flows from the nature of a holy God.

Second, the Law reveals our utter sinfulness and need for a Savior. Because all have sinned and fall short of God's perfect standards, the Law drives us to our knees and shows us our desperate need for Christ. This means that although by itself the Law is incapable of producing moral transformation, it is more than able to lead us to the One who can! In stark contrast to Dobson's position, *moral consensus does not produce the Law. The Law produces moral consensus!*

Today American society is fraught with multitudinous needs. From a purely political/legislative perspective, what is the answer? *The answer is found in a combination of the Cultural Mandate and the Great Commission.* Because the Law is a 'tutor' leading people to Christ, legislation reflecting the moral law of God can only facilitate evangelism, which, in turn, will help lead our nation back to God. In other words, the more concerned Christians obey the Cultural Mandate by supporting laws that reveal the heart of God, the more the Great Commission is assisted, as non-Christians, who are exposed to these laws, see their sin and need for God's forgiveness. Righteous laws and spirit-filled evangelism are not mutually exclusive. God's agenda includes both 'trickle down' and 'bubble up'!

2. All political power comes from God.

Ed Dobson writes, 'When God told Joshua he was neither on the side of Joshua nor on the side of his enemies, he was declaring the truth that God transcends all nations and political parties. He is God. In fact, all political authority is derived from God...God is equally involved in all the nations of the world.'[3]

Dobson is referring to what theology calls God's 'universal kingship'. Properly understood, God's universal rule, or kingship, is linked to his providential control over all people, things, and events in the world as a means toward serving His eternal purposes (cf. Daniel 4:25; Isaiah 10:5-6). The theory here is that if God is King over all the nations, and all political authority comes from God, then God doesn't play any favourites. There are no special nations or political parties who have God on their side. Everyone is equal. Moreover, there is no 'official position' God takes on political issues that believers can rally around. If all political power comes from God, then in some strange sense every government is right, therefore Christians should quit complaining and submit.

Answer: There are two ways we can get ourselves into a real theological mess. The first is by teaching a *particular truth without restriction*. The second is by teaching a *universal truth without distinction*. An example of the first sort comes from the 19th century when it became fashionable to speak about the 'universal fatherhood of God'. More liberally minded folk, who balked at the idea of being 'born-again' and thus becoming part of the family of God through the spiritual act of adoption, stretched the Bible's teaching on the fatherhood of God to include believers and non-believers alike. According to this view, everyone is saved, because everyone has God as his or her Father.

But what else the Bible teaches is that unless a person's heart is changed by the power of the Holy Spirit and is brought into the kingdom of God through regeneration, then God remains their Judge, not their Father (cf. Matthew 7:21). Thus, the fatherhood of God, once seen with the all-important, restrictive 'but', becomes a particular truth for only those who have experienced the new birth.

An example of the latter type of error (universal truth without distinction) is seen in Dobson's position that 'all political power comes from God'. There is a sense in which Dobson is correct. In fact, Paul supports God's universal authority: 'For there is no authority except from God, and those which exist are established by God' (Romans 13:1). But what if we applied this truth without making any distinctions? We would wind up where Ed Dobson is in his position that 'God is equally involved in all the nation's of the world'.[4] This simply is untrue.

Where Dobson's argument runs aground is in failing to distinguish God's *universal* kingship from his *covenantal* kingship. The Old Testament reveals that the nation of Israel enjoyed a special relationship with God. This relationship was carried out through covenant. A covenant is simply an arrangement between contracting parties. Anyone with a mortgage knows what a covenant is. The difference between earthly covenants and the type Israel enjoyed is that God was its author. It was a spiritual covenant that contained God's stipulations and promises and Israel's commitment to obey. God's foremost promise was, 'I will be a God unto thee, and to thy seed after thee' (Genesis 17:7 KJV). This promise carried both temporal blessings and the expectation of eternal salvation.

Dobson agrees that 'God had a special relationship with the Hebrew people.'[5] But then he waffles a bit when he says, 'It would appear from these promises that God is for the Jewish people and against everyone else... But Abram was soon to learn that God was the God of all the nations.'[6]

But God *was* for the Jewish people and against everyone else. Shortly before his death, Joshua preached, 'I am old, advanced in years. And you have seen all that the Lord your God has done to all these nations because of you, for the Lord your God is He who has been fighting for you. See, I have apportioned to you these nations which remain as an inheritance for your tribes, with all the nations which I have cut off, from the Jordan even to the Great Sea toward the setting of the sun. And the Lord your God, He shall thrust them out from before you and drive them from before you; and you shall possess their land, just as the Lord your God promised you' (Joshua 23:2-5).

These words clearly divide God's providential working in the affairs of the 'nations' from His covenantal purposes for the Hebrew people. Even God's universal rule did not mean that the 'nations' were on the same footing with God as were the Hebrews. While God's universal rule reminded His people of His administration over all things for their good, God's universal kingship reminded the nations they stood outside God's promises to Israel. Moreover, Genesis 17:5 ('For I will make you the father of a multitude of nations'), refers to the universal blessing of the gospel, not to the fact that the 'political authority' of the nations has God as its common source.

With God's promise of eternal rewards to Israel came a distinctive call to wage war with the surrounding nations. Although Israel's campaigns point to the Christian's responsibility to pursue holiness through destroying sin, God's partisan political agenda with Israel must not be lost. Yes, the political power of the nations owed its source to God, but that didn't stop God from seeking to destroy it. Only Israel's political machine would receive heaven's grease. There would be no 'smoke-filled' rooms, no bipartisan compromises. The nations were to be 'possessed' (cf. Deuteronomy 4:47). Thus, God's position with Joshua was not that He did not take sides, but that He had His own side, and He wanted Joshua on it. Joshua's enlistment into the Lord's army resulted in an unprecedented victory at Jericho (cf. Joshua 6).

Between God's universal kingship and His covenantal or spiritual kingship, it is the latter that took precedence in the Old Testament and continues to do so today. The 19th century scholar, Louis Berkoff, observed, 'The Kingship of Christ over the universe is subservient to His spiritual kingship. It is incumbent on Christ, as the anointed King, to establish the spiritual kingdom of God, to govern it, and to protect it against all hostile forces...Therefore God invested Him with authority over it, so that He is able to control all powers and forces and movements in the world, and can thus secure a safe footing for His people in the world, and protect His own against all the powers of darkness.'[7] And elsewhere: 'By the *regnum potentiae* we mean the dominion of the God-man, Jesus Christ, over the universe, His providential and judicial administration of all things in the interest of the Church.'[8]

Here Berkoff reflects Paul's teaching: 'And He put all things in subjection under His feet, and gave Him as head over all things to the church' (Ephesians 1:22, See also fifth building block of a biblical worldview). It is to the advantage of the Church that Christ now reigns above all rule, authority, power, and dominion. However, Ed Dobson suggests the opposite, that politically conservative Christians should defer to God's universal working in other world powers. To think differently is to operate on a 'limited perspective'.[9]

It is true that God's master plan for the earth includes using all the political powers of the world. However, God's use of pagan nations in the Old Testament was always *subservient* to His purposes for the

Hebrews. God raised up the Babylonians, not as an alternative to the Hebrews, but as a consequence of Israel's repeated failure to thoroughly destroy the nation's idolatry (cf. Joshua 7; Judges 18). According to Paul, 'all things' have been subjected to the feet of Christ in principle (Ephesians 1:22). It is thus the responsibility of the Church to establish this fact in practice. Failure to challenge all political idolatry shall too result in our chastening.

3. Government has a God-ordained role to play in society.

Ed Dobson observes, 'What should Christians expect from the government of the United States? We should expect the government to maintain an ordered society so that we can live out our faith and pay attention to the greater purposes of God in calling people to faith in Jesus Christ.'[10]

Answer: No Christian activist has ever said government has no God-ordained role to play in society. Just the opposite is the case.

Central to activism's message is a call for government to return to its God-ordained role. Ed Dobson believes that the Religious Right has erred in thinking that government should reflect its religious values. But the real problem in our day is that government is more and more reflecting the values of the devil.

While it is not the role of government to fashion prayers or preach the gospel, neither is it the role of government to lead a campaign of 'religious cleansing' in America. And that's what we're seeing. Ed Dobson comments, 'It [government] was instituted to restrain evil and promote good so that the values of God could be reflected in the lives of the people who claim to follow God.'[11] Fine. But elsewhere he says, 'Therefore, the ultimate issue is not whether you are pro-life or pro-abortion; the ultimate issue is whether you know Jesus personally. The ultimate issue is not whether you are pro-gay or anti-gay; the ultimate issue is whether you know Jesus.'[12] But that's like saying, 'The ultimate issue is not whether you have your hand on a hot stove. The ultimate issue is whether you know Jesus.' Frankly, I prefer to know Jesus, and *not* place my hand on a hot stove. In America we can know Jesus and battle legal abortion and the radical homosexual-agenda without contradiction.

Dobson is right that the role of government is to 'restrain evil and promote good'. But how do we define good and evil? Using the Bible. Then why is he unhappy when the Church works to ensure that the government restrain abortion and homosexuality and protect the unborn? I've heard it said, 'The Church should focus on evangelism and discipleship and leave politics to the professionals.' But the Church doesn't fight abortion or a host of other issues because it insists that government reflect its values. It fights because the values that are currently being reflected in today's government have become hostile, not only to God's values, but also to the Church's task of evangelism and discipleship.

We must not forget it's rather difficult to baptize or christen a baby who's been sucked down the abortionist's tube. How are we going to disciple that baby? To disciple that baby means first fighting for its life, using political influence. If government fulfilled its God-ordained role then we could do as Dobson suggests – spend *all* our time engaged in evangelism and discipleship. But until it does, we are faced with the task of reminding government why it exists.

In 1 Samuel 13, Saul forfeits his place as king by taking upon himself the priestly role of offering sacrifices. But notice it was not one of Saul's political rivals who later confronts the king with his abuse of power, it was the priest Samuel. This shows that although God ordains all the state's authority, there are 'limits' to its power. When a ruler goes beyond his or her God-ordained function, it becomes the necessary duty of the Church to put the matter right.

Although our Christian responsibility in politics comes from the Bible, rooted in the Declaration of Independence is the very same idea that religion and civil government should fulfill separate roles in society, while remaining servants of the Creator. Where civil authority *oversteps* its bounds it becomes the duty of a free people to correct such abuses. Where government becomes destructive of our God-given rights, 'it is the Right of the People to alter or to abolish it, and to institute new Government'. This language mirrors the basic idea that the political face of Christ's universal kingship remains subservient to his covenantal kingship and the interests of true religion (See 1st Answer).

4. Christians have a God-ordained responsibility to government.

Ed Dobson argues, 'Submitting to government authority involves recognizing that authority is from God and then willingly and completely subjecting ourselves to that authority.'[13] Regarding our taxes, he writes, 'Some groups in the United States advocate refusing to pay taxes because some of those revenues would support governmental programs that they disagree with in principle. But the Bible offers no such option. We are to pay taxes whether or not the government is friendly toward Christians.'[14]

Except for rare occasions where civil disobedience is biblically justified, Ed Dobson says that we must completely subject ourselves to the government. Complete subjection? He says that regardless of what out tax money is to be used for, Christians have no option but to pay it. No options?

Answer: Paul says in Romans 13:1-4, 'Let every person be in subjection to the governing authorities. For there is no authority except from God, and those which exist are established by God. Therefore he who resists authority has opposed the ordinance of God; and they who have opposed will receive condemnation upon themselves. For rulers are not a cause of fear for good behaviour, but for evil. Do you want to have no fear of authority? Do what is good, and you will have praise from the same; for it is a minister of God to you for good. But if you do what is evil be afraid; for it does not bear the sword for nothing; for it is a minister of God, an avenger who brings wrath upon the one who practices evil.'

Paul's teaching on Christian submission to civil government, like all biblical subjects, must be seen in light of the whole of the Bible's teaching. No one text, not even Romans 13, can serve as the complete revelation of the believer's relationship to the state. The Bible consistently teaches that not only are believers to be in submission to civil government, but also those who govern are to be in submission to God (cf. Psalm 2; Daniel 4:34-35). No government can say it rose to power on its own (cf. John 19:11). God has established governing authorities to reward those who do good and to be an 'avenger' upon those who do evil. Biblically there is no double standard for good and evil. All nations must honor God's law or be brought to an end. (Daniel 2:31-35).

The Bible is clear that the magistrate is not free to create and enforce his own arbitrary set of laws to serve his own ignoble ends (cf. Isaiah 5:20). To do so would be a license for tyranny, something Jesus opposed (cf. Luke 22:25-26). As a 'minister of God', the civil government is charged with upholding God's justice, not man's quest for totalitarian control over others. Nations that throw off God's law face severe punishment. The blessings and curses that relate to the Law given to Israel apply equally to all nations of the world (cf. Psalm 82:7).

Clearly, there are many kings and dictators in history who failed to uphold God's justice, but instead perpetrated their own brand of evil (e.g. Hitler, Mao, Stalin, and Pontius Pilate). But in the larger context of the Bible, we see that Paul is not giving *carte blanche* to all governmental actions. Rather, he is pointing to God's *intended design* for government. He is mainly concerned with submission to the *principle* of authority – the function that God has appointed the magistrate to fulfill. Gary DeMar, writes, 'Paul is describing what a ruler's proper function is. The apostle is not making a moral judgment about any particular ruler or political party. Rather, his words describe what civil governments ought to be and ought to do.'[15]

Those opposed to any type of resistance to the government point out, 'When Paul urged Christians in Romans 13 to submit to governing authorities, Nero was Emperor of Rome, and he was far worse than anything today.'

Paul wrote the letter to the Romans in AD 57 during the early part of Nero's reign. Bible scholar Dr. Greg Herrick writes, 'There appears to be no indication that at this time he [Nero] was a tyrant and brutal ruler. The Jews had been expelled in AD 49, but that was under Claudius and things appeared to be different in AD 57. There was a problem with "tax protests" under Nero in AD 58, but this does not appear to be relevant at the time of the writing of Romans. Therefore, we may assume that political conditions were fairly stable and that the Christian church which was undoubtedly born in the synagogues at Rome enjoyed the status of *religio licita* as they were largely seen to be within Judaism's fold.'[16] The context of Romans 13 reveals that there is no basis to conclude that Paul was encouraging Christians to submit to political oppression. His main concern, as I previously mentioned, was submission to the principle of authority as it comes from God.

Never Smack a Bee-Hive

The Apostle Peter, although he agrees in principle with Paul, has a different concern regarding submission to civil authority. He writes, 'Submit yourselves for the Lord's sake to every human institution whether to a king as the one in authority, or to governors as sent by him for the punishment of evildoers and the praise of those who do right. For such is the will of God that by doing right you may silence the ignorance of foolish men. Act as free men, and do not use your freedom as a covering for evil, but use it as bondslaves of God. Honor all men; love the brotherhood, fear God, honor the king' (I Peter 2:13-17).

Peter is writing in approximately AD 64 when Nero's ruthless campaign against Christians was about to begin. Peter calls Christians to submit to the governing authorities, but like Paul he does not have in mind blind, uncritical obedience to the state. Whereas Paul was concerned about submission to the principle of authority, Peter is looking for a way to protect the Church in the face of coming persecution. Dr. Greg Herrick notes, 'He appears to take Christian tradition on church-state relations and apply it to the Christians so that the state will not entertain the accusations and decide to persecute the Church. That is, the Christians are to silence the slander by doing good and in this way the state will not be provoked to disciplinary measures (cf. 2:15).'[17]

Submission At All Cost?

There are many people who agree that the power and scope of government should be limited. But they would hasten to add that even when government does not recognize its legitimate role, believers must submit nonetheless. But is this true? Yes, we are to submit to unjust laws as long *as there is no possibility of change.* This is what our dear brothers and sisters in China and Libya are *forced* to do.

However, Dobson suggests that persecuted Christians in foreign lands couldn't care less that their governments operate according to biblical principles. 'The Christians in Uzbekistan do not expect their government to reflect their values. The believers in Egypt and elsewhere do not expect their government to reflect their values. The only people who expect their government to reflect their religious values are countries where religion and politics are synonymous.'[18]

First, I believe that persecuted believers would change public policy where they minister in a 'New York second' if they had the chance. Second, that persecuted Christians in other countries may not 'expect' their governments to reflect their values is immaterial. Jesus taught in the parable of the talents that there are those who have less opportunity than do others. Because Christians in oppressed nations have less opportunity to bring about social change than do American Christians is no justification for our lack of effort. As Jesus said in yet another parable, 'From everyone who has been given much, much will be demanded; and from the one who has been entrusted with much, much more will be asked' (Luke 12:48 KJV).

Some Practical Steps

In America, there are ample opportunities to resist unjust laws while remaining true to the Scriptures:

We can engage in vocal opposition. Notice that when Jesus stood before Pilate He made it clear that Pilate's ultimate authority came from God. But He also pointed out that just because Pilate was exercising his God-given authority, this did not excuse his actions. Jesus was quick to say that although those who had delivered Him up had committed the 'greater sin', Pilate's actions constituted a sinful abuse of power nonetheless. 'You would have no authority over Me, unless it had been given you from above; for this reason he who delivered Me up to you has the greater sin' (John 19:11).

Christians can band together to form organized opposition. The midwives refused to obey the king of Egypt in killing the male children of the Israelite women (see Exodus 1:15-22). But where God's people failed to resist governmental tyranny and oppression, the results were devastating. Few of Israel's kings possessed a greater capacity for evil than Manasseh. He erected altars to Baal, practiced witchcraft, and placed the carved images of heathen gods directly in Solomon's temple. Can you believe that not one single priest raised a voice against the king? The result was that Manasseh shed so much innocent blood that it filled Jerusalem from one end to the other (cf. 2 Kings 21:1-16)!

Christians can offer Godly alternatives. Daniel refused to eat the rich foods King Nebuchadnezzar chose for him and his three Hebrew friends to eat. Instead he offered a plan that would allow them to eat a restricted diet of vegetables and water for a period of ten days. The king was so impressed with the results, he placed the young men directly into his personal service (cf. Daniel 1:8-21). Christian engagement in the political process is one way we work to promote Godly alternatives to unrighteous laws.

Render or Surrender Unto Ceasar?

Then there is the tax issue. This is a very important subject, mainly because the power to tax lies at the heart of a government's ability to oppress. Former Supreme Court Justice John Marshall wrote, 'The power to tax involves the power to destroy.'[19] Many agree yet would hasten to add that even though we may be oppressed by too large a tax burden, God insists we pay it regardless of how high the tax, or what the money is to be used for. Is this true?

Yes, we need to pay our taxes if we wish to avoid the 'slammer'. But this doesn't mean God has given the state broad taxing power. Biblically, a government is permitted to tax, but only within the bounds of its legitimate functions. Jesus said to render unto Caesar what is 'due' him. But today we live in an age of open-ended taxation. Indeed, it is estimated that the current tax rate in America is approximately 1000 percent higher than during the time of the Boston Tea Party![20] How did we get ourselves into this mess?

Reversing the Tax-Spiral

The history of the tax is an interesting study. It began when the nation of Israel rejected God as their king and demanded a human facsimile. 'Now appoint us a king for us to judge us like all the nations' (1 Samuel 8:5). They got a king all right – in the person of Saul. The ability to operate the new government required money that was provided through a new system of taxation. But God was displeased. The people's demand for an earthly king constituted their rejection of God as their king. 'And the Lord said to Samuel, "Listen to the voice of the people, in regard to all that they say to you, for they have not rejected you, but they have rejected Me from being king over them"' (v.8). This was perhaps the costliest part of Israel's decision. Rather than look to God as their deliverer, Israel now sought salvation in a political messiah.

Since then, the tax has represented a downward spiraling trend. Not only are believers required to pay taxes, but we are also required to pay God's tithe. 'Will a man rob God? Yet you are robbing Me! But you say, "How have we robbed Thee?" In tithes and offerings. You are cursed with a curse, for you are robbing Me, the whole nation of you!' (Malachi 3:8-9)

Here is how the downward spiral begins. There is only so much money in our bank accounts – right? By the time the average American pays for the cost of living (which incidentally is driven by usury and greed), and then pays taxes to Uncle Sam, he or she often doesn't have the money left over to pay 10 percent in tithe. Now obviously there are those who after taxes, do have the money to pay their tithe, but for whatever reason, choose not to pay it. But I'm not talking about them. I'm referring to those people who, after taxes, have found themselves either unable to pay the total amount of their tithe or are in a position where, if they did pay, it would cause great hardship.

Here's the bigger problem. God doesn't care what our excuse is for not paying our tithes. We are still responsible to pay them, and when we don't we are robbing God. God's discipline, which can affect any number of areas in our lives, soon follows. Once we begin to feel the back of God's disciplining hand, what is our habit? Our recent history as a society has been to turn to the state for assistance. This, in turn, means a greater tax burden to pay for the aid, which leads to paying less tithe, which leads to more discipline, which leads to more cries to the government, and so forth.

How do we reverse the process? The tax system operates according to supply and demand. Let's kill the demand by repenting of our lack of trust in God as our king. Stop looking to the government for help in all of life's challenges. Over time, this will decrease the supply side of the equation, and we will begin to see less government services, which will lead to fewer taxes. As the tithe is restored, the Church can then use that money to replace governmental programs with diaconal ministries. Once again, the world will discover God's compassion, not Caesar's. Now I know what you're thinking. 'That's so simplistic! Everyone would have to do this for your plan to work!' You're right. We call it revival. So why don't we have one?

Final Thought

Of all the spheres within American culture, politics is the common denominator. The Church cannot be working to restore 'all things' to the glory of God, while, at the same time, maintaining it is too 'holy' to involve itself in politics. The holiness of the Church is *all the more reason* that believers must persevere in this place that is so prone to corruption and sleaze. If Cal Thomas and Ed Dobson are correct that many in the Christian political cause were blinded by the same lust for power and might that marks the world, then that is to our discredit. But it doesn't need to be this way. Because believers are ambassadors of the kingdom of light, we are the only ones who can enter politics non-aligned with any political faction that seeks earthly power. We are the only ones who can bring *real* change. This is no time to retreat.

Fifteen

CLOSING CHALLENGE

In his autobiography, *Just as I Am*, Billy Graham tells about a conversation he had with John F. Kennedy shortly after his election: 'On the way back to the Kennedy house, the president-elect stopped the car and turned to me. "Do you believe in the Second Coming of Jesus Christ?" he asked.

"I most certainly do", I replied.

The president asked, "Well, does my church believe it?"

"They have it in their creeds", I responded.

"They don't preach it", he said. "They don't tell us much about it. I'd like to know what you think."

I explained what the Bible said about Christ coming the first time, dying on the Cross, rising from the dead, and then promising that he would come back again. "Only then", I said, "are we going to have permanent world peace".

"Very interesting", he said, looking away. "We'll have to talk more about that someday." And he drove on.'

Several years later, the two met again, at the 1963 National Prayer Breakfast. 'I had the flu', Graham remembers. 'After I gave my short talk, and he gave his, we walked out of the hotel to his car together, as was always our custom.

'At the curb, he turned to me. "Billy, could you ride back to the White House with me? I'd like to see you for a minute".

"Mr. President, I've got a fever", I protested. "Not only am I weak, but I don't want to give you this thing. Couldn't we wait and talk some other time?" It was a cold, snowy day, and I was freezing as I stood there without my overcoat.

"Of course", he said graciously.

But the two would never meet again. Later that year, Kennedy was shot dead.

Graham comments, 'His hesitation at the car door, and his request, haunt me still. What was on his mind? It was an irrecoverable moment'.

What did John F. Kennedy want from Billy Graham? Was he ready to receive Christ? We'll never know. As Dr. Graham said, it was an 'irrecoverable moment.'[1]

Have you ever found yourself confronted by a situation similar to the one Billy Graham faced? Many times I've thought, 'If I could just go back in time, I would say this or that.' Everyone has an 'irrecoverable moment' in his or her life. Perhaps you would give anything to have a few extra minutes with your late father so you could share the gospel with him, or just to tell him, 'I love you.' Or maybe you imagine hopping in a time machine and going back five years to do something you left undone.

Unfortunately, there are no time machines, just time. And it always marches forward. The day is coming when time to demonstrate obedience to the Cultural Mandate and the Great Commission will run out. Someday we shall all stand before Christ at the judgment seat to give an account for our obedience to His call. Are you being 'salt' and 'light' in a world that Christ died to save? Or have money, security, and professionalism become your focus?

The sad truth is that many people will face 'irrecoverable moments' as they stand before Christ. The things they should have said and done will stream across their minds like ticker tape. This is why it's so important to take full advantage of today's opportunities to live and minister for Christ while there is still time. Paul writes, 'Therefore be careful how you walk, not as unwise men, but as wise, making the most of your time, because the days are evil. So then do not be foolish, but understand what the will of the Lord is' (Ephesians 5:15-17).

I want to offer two points, which are intended to challenge and motivate you to make the most of every opportunity to help restore planet earth to the praise of our great God and King while there is yet time.

Christ calls us to use our God-given gifts and abilities in His service with the understanding that ministry often involves risk. One of the greatest impediments to people serving in ministry is fear of the unknown. This is true with respect to both the Cultural Mandate and the Great Commission. Jesus spoke to this fear in the parable of the talents (cf. Matthew 25:14-30). Here a businessman is about to go on a journey. Before he leaves, he entrusts money to his servants with the expectation they will each develop what he has given them. To one he gives five talents (a talent is a unit of coinage), to another, two talents, and to yet another, one talent.

Upon his return, the businessman discovers that two of his workers invested his money wisely, doubling it. To these servants, the master says, 'Well done, good and faithful slave; you were faithful with a few things, I will put you in charge of many things, enter into the joy of your master' (v.21).

But the third servant hid his one talent in the ground for fear that he might lose it. What if he squandered his only talent through investment? To ensure the talent would be there upon his master's return, the servant placed it in safekeeping. An act that was meant to protect his master's property turned out to be a great sin that cost this man the kingdom of God.

His boss exclaims, 'You wicked, lazy slave, you knew that I reap where I did not sow, and gather where I scattered no seed. Then you ought to have put my money in the bank, and on my arrival I would have received my money back with interest...cast out the worthless slave into the outer darkness; in that place there shall be weeping and gnashing of teeth' (v.26, 27, 30).

Too many of us are like the 'lazy slave'. We like to play it safe. Most of us fear taking risks. We recoil at the thought of doing something speculative or being on the 'cutting edge'. That is unless someone can offer some guarantees that there's a soft landing to catch us lest we fall off the edge and crash. It was this fear of risk-taking that led the faithless servant not to invest his master's money.

The 'talent' refers to more than money. Perhaps God has placed a spiritual gift, ability, or material resource in your stewardship, which He wants you to use in His service. Like the faithless servant, many believers are afraid to invest their 'talent' for the glory of God. Some fear rejection. While others worry that their step of faith will hurt their pocketbook.

But ministry is risky. It stretches you beyond your comfort zone. It forces you out of your upwardly mobile, predictable lifestyle into the uncertainties of doing the impossible. It provides a context where all your insecurities bubble to the surface and where, in your reluctant transparency, you are forced to trust God. Being a faithful steward means more than protecting the status quo. It also requires us to be flexible, spontaneous, and willing to face new challenges. As a 'fool for Christ' you may be mocked, scorned, ridiculed, and vilified. Why? Because you dared to step forward. You dared to risk. But it's worth it if someday we hear Him say, 'Well done, good and faithful servant.'

There is another reason many believers hide their 'talents'. We live at a time when eschatology has made its way into the mainstream of American culture. Thanks to authors Dr. Tim LaHaye and Jerry Jenkins, the distressing idea of being 'left behind' when Christ returns has had a profound impact on countless individuals. It's not my purpose to debate different theological viewpoints on the 'rapture'. I only wish to say that the positive effect of the LaHaye/Jenkins series of books on people must be tempered with this caution: typically, whenever the Church has emphasized the Lord's return, large numbers of believers tend toward isolationism.

Ask the average evangelical believer, 'What does it mean to be prepared for the return of Christ?' and he or she will likely respond, 'Living a life of holiness.' Holy living is certainly important. After all, Christ shall return, not as a lowly baby in a manger, but as a judge with a winnowing fork in His hand to separate the wheat from the tares. Nevertheless, we must be careful to avoid a 'bunker mentality'. Believers whose major focus is piety and separation from the world tend to see the world as 'evil' and themselves as a 'holy remnant' with so much vigor that, not only do they live apart from the world, but also from the world's needs. According to the parable of the talents, being prepared for Christ's return means more than not doing bad deeds. It also means being found doing good deeds. We are to invest all the resources God has placed at our disposal toward building His kingdom in this world. Christ will not only judge our sins of commission, but also our sins of omission – the things we should have done, but didn't.

Are you investing your gifts and talents in service to the kingdom? Can you lead a small group Bible study in your community? Why don't you get involved with your church's evangelism program? Perhaps you need to start one? Are you fed up with local politics? Maybe God is calling you to run for political office? Public education is also in need of reform, journalism needs a Christian influence, medical research is begging for someone to bring a biblical worldview, and the Internet represents a cutting edge area of culture where ethics is clearly lagging behind the technology. Somewhere, someplace, you can make a difference.

Christ calls us to use our God-given gifts and abilities in His service with the promise of eternal rewards. Meredith Wilson, composer of the delightful musical The Music Man, entitled his autobiography *And There I Stood With My Piccolo*, from a story told him by an old Moravian flute player: 'A very important king hired a whole orchestra to play for him one night during his supper, just because he felt lonesome. This orchestra played great and the king was so delighted that before going to bed he said, "Boys, your playing gave me whips and jingles, and just for that you can all go to my countinghouse and fill your instruments with gold pieces."

'I can still hear that happy clatter as sack after sack of golden delights streamed into the tuba and slithered down the neck of the bassoon and spilled out over the bells of the French horns. And there I stood with my piccolo!'

When the heavenly King honors our efforts for Him at the final judgment, I want to be standing there with more than a piccolo. I want to serve my Lord faithfully on earth because I know the Lord will reward everyone according to what he has done.[2]

Wilson's story illustrates that at the final judgment each person's record will be revealed and Christ will reward the righteous according to what they have done. Paul writes, 'For we must all appear before the judgment seat of Christ, that each one may be recompensed for his deeds in the body, according to what he has done, whether good or bad' (2 Corinthians 5:10). Just as all farmers do not reap the same size crop, so all believers will not reap the same rewards in heaven. Paul remarks, 'Now he who plants and he who waters are one; but each will receive his own reward according to his own labour' (I Corinthians 3:8).

There are two major schools of thought on the subject of eternal rewards. One teaches that believers will receive rewards in heaven based on their performance as Christians. The second school proposes that the reward of believers is identical to the fullness of salvation in heaven. Although there are Scripture verses that can be used to support both schools of thought, my study leads me to agree with the first school. In addition to being rewarded all the blessings of salvation, believers will, to varying degrees, be rewarded according to their righteous deeds.

Some people disagree. They point out that service to Christ should not be motivated by the expectation of heavenly rewards. Rather, we should serve Christ out of gratitude and love. Any theology that focuses upon what we can get from God, instead of what God has done for us, is misguided. Also, they would add that salvation is wholly by grace, not by works, a fact that negates the possibility of rewards for works, which we have done. Do we dare to compare our puny good works to the perfect life, death, burial, and resurrection of the matchless Christ? Additionally, they contend that Christ is the only reward anyone should ever desire in heaven. Anything else pales in comparison.

While I wholeheartedly agree that one's motivation for serving Christ should be out of gratitude, the fact is that Jesus Himself presented rewards as a motivation for obedient service (cf. Matthew 24:14-30; Luke 12:41-48). Additionally, it is no more inconsistent to say that God rewards righteousness, although salvation is a gift, than it is to say 'work out your salvation with fear and trembling, for it is God who is at work in you, both to will and to work for His good pleasure' (Philippians 2:12-13). Finally, Christ would be all the reward

I would need in heaven as well. Throughout this book, I have repeatedly stated that our principle motivation in serving Christ should be that He receives all the glory. But what if it glorifies Him to reward me according to my obedience? Then I will be pleased to receive it.

Are you living your life in expectation of your eternal rewards? Paul writes, 'While we look not at the things which are seen, but at the things which are not seen; for the things which are seen are temporal, but the things which are not seen are eternal' (2 Corinthians 4:18). The things of the world: the house, the car, your sports equipment, all have a way of depreciating. They don't last; neither do our earthly bodies. They shall all turn to dust. A person would be foolish to order his life around the short-lived things of this world.

Jesus said, 'Do not lay up for yourselves treasures upon earth, where moth and rust destroy, and where thieves break in and steal. But lay up for yourselves treasures in heaven, where neither moth nor rust destroys, and where thieves do not break in or steal' (Matthew 6:19-20). The body of David Livingstone was buried in England where he was born, but his heart was buried in the Africa he loved. At the foot of a tall tree in a small African village the natives dug a hole and placed in it the heart of this man who they loved and respected. If your heart were to be buried in the place you loved most during life, where would it be? In your pocketbook? In an appropriate space down at the office? Where is your heart?

God is calling you to store up wealth in things that are eternal. Only your righteous acts shall accompany you to heaven, nothing else. When you stand before your heavenly Father, will you explain to Him that pursuing your career and making money was more important than helping to fulfill the Great Commission? Will you tell Him you would have obeyed His Cultural Mandate, but working to have 'things' and making a good impression at the country club preoccupied your time? You only have one life to live. The choices you make in this life will determine your rewards in eternity.

How can you lay up treasure in heaven? Whenever you see the hungry and feed him, the naked and clothe him, the sick and distressed and administer to their needs you are laying up treasure in heaven. Whenever you are sharing the good news of Jesus Christ with a world lost in sin, you are storing up treasure in heaven. Each time you love the unlovely, forgive the unforgivable, and show grace to the undeserving you are depositing treasure in heaven. Whenever you are 'salt' in a culture of disbelief, although the world may speak evil against you, treasure is being laid up in heaven in your name. What thief can enter in and steal this treasure? It lies in heaven, beyond his reach.

Book Summary

Throughout this book we have learned that God is working to restore all creation. Since the fall of man, God has been reclaiming from Satan what rightfully belongs to Him. The obvious implication for Christian service is that God's mission must be the Church's mission. God's call is clear. Believers are more than churchgoers whose focus is carving out our niche in this world. Our focus is Christ. Our mission is to reach the world with His message.

But what the Bible tells us is that unless we have in some way affected everything that makes up the world with His message, then sadly, we have failed in our mission. Souls are not enough. Institutions are not enough. The arts and sciences are but a fraction of the challenge. The Christian position is that everything that is in the world is here for the glory of God. To Him it must be presented. For many people, giving their lives in service to the kingdom of God will involve an element of risk. Make no mistake. There is a cost to discipleship. On the other hand, we can take comfort in the fact that obedience to God's call will result in eternal rewards that ultimately serve to glorify Jesus Christ.

I hope this book has been illuminating, encouraging, and challenging. I close with these words from Paul, 'Now to Him who is able to do exceeding abundantly beyond all that we ask or think, according to the power that works within us, to Him be the glory in the church and in Christ Jesus to all generations forever and ever. Amen' (Ephesians 3:20-21).

POSTSCRIPT

Since the unprecedented terrorist attacks of 11 September 2001, the free-loving world has been at war with terrorism. Following the attacks, I thought, 'Here I'm writing a book about God's plan to *restore* His creation. How do I interpret these senseless acts of cruelty?' In a startling way, God assured me from His Word that His plan is still on track.

Perhaps the reader is familiar with the devotional, *Daily Walk*. The Scripture passage for 11 September 2001 was taken from Amos 9:

> I saw the Lord standing beside the altar, saying, 'Smash the tops of the pillars and shake the Temple until the pillars crumble and the roof crashes down upon the people below. Though they run, they will not escape; they all will be killed...Then, at that time I will rebuild the City of David, which is now lying in ruins, and return it to its former glory' (vss.1, 11, TLB).

The parallel between the prophet's warning to ancient Israel and the events of September 11 is bone chilling. Judgment would begin at the Temple, the center of the nation's life, the place where an idolatrous people sought spiritual and material blessing. God's warning was to smash the tops of the building, causing it to crumble to the ground where scores of people would be buried beneath tons of rubble. Although rescuers would work tirelessly ('though they dig down to Sheol' v.2), no one would escape the judgment of the wicked.

Amos' words, while bad news to the wicked, were good news to the righteous. The prophet's assurance that God's discipline 'will not be permanent' (v.8), conveyed hope. The unfolding events would work to bring about a renewed earth of peace and prosperity. Friends, be assured that America, and the world, stand at the brink of revival, proving once again that *the world and all that it contains is subject to the eternal purpose and plan of God!*

Endnotes for Earth Restored

Chapter I

[1] A.W. Pink, *The Sovereignty of God* (http://www.pbministries.org/books/pink/Sovereignty/sov_01.htm).

[2] John Calvin, *Psalms*, 4(2): pp.104-5.

[3] Bill Bright, *God: Discover His Character* (Orlando, FL: New Life Publications, 1999), 35.

[4] *Westminster Confession of Faith.*, 4th ed. (Glasgow, Scotland: Free Presbyterian Publications, 1985), 25.

[5] R.C. Sproul, *Almighty Over All* (Grand Rapids: Baker Books, 1999), 117.

[6] Ibid., 117

[7] Ibid., 114

Chapter 2

[1] N.T. Wright, *Colossians and Ephesians*, Reprinted. (Grand Rapids: Wm. B. Eerdmans Publishing Company, 1989), 77.

[2] Ibid., 76-77.

[3] Steve McVey, *Grace Walk* (Eugene, OR: Harvest House, 1995), 17.

Chapter 3

[1] Cal Thomas, *Blinded by Might* (Grand Rapids: Zondervan Publishing House, 1999), 96.

[2] Summarized from John Stott, *Decisive Issues Facing Christians Today*, 7th ed. (Grand Rapids: Fleming H. Revell, 1998), 16. Note: Stott's point does not obscure God's special purposes for the ancient Hebrews, a matter that is taken up in fuller detail in Chapter 14 of this book.

[3] Barna Research Online, 'President Clinton's Character is a Non-Issue to Born Again Christians,' 1 August 1999. Electronically retrieved from (http://www.barna.org/cgi-bin/PagePressRelease.asp?PressReleaseID=36; Internet).

[4] George Grant, *The Micah Mandate* (Chicago: Moody Press, 1995), 92.

[5] (http://www.geocities.com/Broadway/Balcony/4772/program2.html; Internet).

[6] Number of deaths is the combined total from two reports of the National School Safety and Security Services, 'School Related Violent Deaths and Shootings' 1999-2000 (http://www.schoolsecurity.org/trends/

school_violence99-00.html; Internet), and 'School Related Violent Deaths, Shootings, Bomb Incidents & Crises' 2000-2001 (http://www.schoolsecurity.org/trends/school_violence00-01.html; Internet).

[7] C. Gregg Singer, *A Theological Interpretation of American History*, 2nd ed. (Philipsburg, New Jersey: Presbyterian and Reformed Publishing Co., 1981), 108.

Chapter 4

[1] D. James Kennedy, *Led by the Carpenter* (Nashville: Thomas Nelson Publishers, 1999), 178-179.

[2] Bill Bright, *Witnessing Without Fear* (Orlando, FL: New *Life* Publications, 1993), 18.

[3] Ibid., 38.

[4] Meredith Kline, *Kingdom Prologue*, Volume I (a self-published work, 1986), 55.

[5] John Stott, *Decisive Issues Facing Christians Today*, 7th ed. (Grand Rapids: Fleming H. Revell, 1998), 119.

Chapter5

[1] The Pastor's Story File (Platteville, CO: Saratoga Press), August 1995.

[2] D. Martin Lloyd-Jones, *God's Way of Reconciliation: Studies in Ephesians 2* (Grand Rapids: Baker Books, 1985), 18.

[3] James Montgomery Boice, *Romans: God and History: Romans 9-11* (Grand Rapids: Baker Books, 1993), 1240.

[4] Leon Morris, *The Epistle to the Romans* (Grand Rapids: Wm. B. Eerdmans Publishing Company, 1988), p. 390, quoted in James Montgomery Boice, *Romans: God and History: Romans 9-11* (Grand Rapids: Baker Books, 1993), 1241.

Chapter 6

[1] Jerry Falwell, *Falwell: An Autobiography* (Lynchburg: Liberty House Publishers, 1997), 383.

[2] Cal Thomas and Ed Dobson, *Blinded by Might* (Grand Rapids: Zondervan Publishing House, 1999), 24.

[3] FreeRepublic.com (http://www.freerepublic.com/forum/a372f8e68190b.htm; Internet).

[4] CLRP Press (16 July 1999). (http://www.clrp.org/pr_99_0716vapba.html; Internet).

[5] Ibid.

[6] Political Quotes, 8 November 2000 (http://www.jmacsnippets.com/Quotes_Political.htm; Internet).

[7] Cal Thomas, *Blinded by Might* (Grand Rapids: Zondervan Publishing House, 1999), 90.

Chapter 7

[1] Abraham Kuyper, *Anti-Revolutionaire Staatkunde,* Volume I (Kok, Kampen, Netherlands: 1917), 265ff, quoted in Frederick Nymeyer, 'A Great Netherlander Who Had One Answer To The Problem of Liberty Destroying Liberty, Namely, Sphere Sovereignty.' *Progressive Calvinism* (February, 1956), I.

Chapter 8

[1] Paul Weyrich, 'Separate and Free,' *The Washington Post,* 7 March 1999.

[2] Ibid.

[3] *The Merriam-Webster Dictionary.* (http://www.m-w.com/cgi-bin/dictionary; Internet).

[4] Weyrich, 'Separate and Free,' *The Washington Post.*

[5] Peter J. Leithhart, 'What is the Kingdom of God?' *Contra Mundum,* Number 5, Fall 1992.

[6] *Illustration for Biblical Preaching,* 291.

[7] R.T. France, *Mathew* (Grand Rapids: Wm. B. Eerdmans Publishing Company, 1990), 134.

[8] The Jesus Film Project (http://www.jesusfilm.org; Internet)

[9] Wycliffe Bible Translators (http://www.wycliffe.org; Internet)

[10] *Religion Today News Summary,* 9 August 2000.

Chapter 9

[1] Jim Cymbala made this statement during a radio interview break.

[2] Martyn Lloyd-Jones, *Joy Unspeakable,* 4th ed. (Wheaton: Harold Shaw Publishers, 1988), 119.

[3] Some Favourite Quotations (http://www.ldolphin.org/quotes.shtml; Internet).

Chapter 10

[1] Francis Frangipane, 'Becoming the Answer to Christ's Prayer' (http://www.inchristsimage.org/ArticleDetailsNoBook_40.asp; Internet).

Endnotes

2 *The John Ankerburg Show*, 25 June 2000.

3 Ibid.

4 .John R.W. Stott, *God's New Society: The Message of Ephesians* (Downer's Grove: IVPress), 151.

5 According to Hans Rollmann, for *Restoration Quarterly,* Vol. 39 Number 3, this statement is not original with Augustine, but rather is the product of an irenic Lutheran theologian and pastor living in Augsburg during the early seventeenth century by the name of Peter Meiderlin.

6 The Pastor's Story File (Platteville, CO: Saratoga Press), November 1993.

7 Richard C. Halverson, 'Perspective,' 23 April 2001.

8 *Transformations: A Documentary,* produced by Global Net Productions, (The Sentinel Group, 1999).

Chapter 11

1 From publisher's comments on back cover of Franky Schaeffer, *Addicted to Mediocrity: 20ʰ Century Christians and the Arts* (Crossway Books, 1981).

2 Summary of Hans Rookmaaker, *Modern Art and the Death of Culture* (London: Inter-Varsity Press, 1970).

3 Klaas Schilder, *Christ and Culture* (Winnepeg, Manitoba: Premier Printing, 1977), 59.

4 Class notes, 'Religious Consciousness in Modern Art', Yale University, 1982.

5 Ibid.

6 Full text of article by Joel C. Sheesley, 'The Substance of Things Hoped For', is found at (http://www.iamny.org/articles/articletxt.html; Internet).

7 Cited in Paul Signac, *D Eugene Delacroix au Neo-Impressionisme* (Paris: Floury, 1899).

8 Wassily Kadinsky, *Concerning the Spiritual in Art* (New York: Dover Publications, Inc., 1977), 36.

9 Ibid., 36, 37.

10 Ibid., Figure II, between pp. 36 and 37.

11 Cited in Don Hudson, 'On Earth As It Is In Heaven: Is Art Necessary for the Christian?' (http://www.leaderu.com/marshill/mhr02/don1.html; Internet).

12 Spaightwood Galleries. (http://spaightwoodgalleries.com/Pages/Nolde.html; Internet).

Chapter 12

[1] Dean Acheson, 'Ethics in International Relations Today' *Amherst Alumni News* (Winter, 1965), 2–3.

[2] Gary Clyde Hufbauer, Jeffrey J. Schott, and Kimberly Ann Elliott, *Economic Sanctions Reconsidered: History and Current Policy,* second edition. (Washington, D.C.: Institute for International Economics, 1990), 92-93.

[3] 'Denial of Food and Medicine: The Impact Of The U.S. Embargo On The Health And Nutrition In Cuba' (Washington, D.C.: American Association for World Health, March 1997), 2.

[4] Gary North, *Inheritance and Dominion: An Economic Commentary on Deuteronomy*, Chapter 16, 'Genocide and Inheritance.' (http://freebooks.entrewave.com/freebooks/docs/html/gnde/Chapter16.htm; Internet).

[5] Tim McGirk Douglas, 'Border Clash', *Time Magazine*, August 2000.

[6] Samuel P. Huntington 'Reconsidering Immigration: Is Mexico a Special Case?' (Washington, D.C.: Center for Immigration Studies, November 2000), (http:// www cis.org/articles/2000/back1100;Internet).

[7] Ben Fox, *Associated Press.* (http://home earthlink.net/~surferslim/update2.html; Internet).

[8] Glynn Custred, *The America Spectator,* October 2000.

[9] Quoted in Sean Paige, 'Raiding Arizona', *Insight On The News Online* (http://home.earthlink.net/~surferslim/update2.html, Internet)

[10] Daniel J. Wakin, '12 Illegal Immigrants Die in Arizona Desert', *New York Times On The Web*, 24 May 2001.

[11] Tim Steller, 'Border Bandits Assault Illegal Alien Groups; 2 Women Are Raped', *The Arizona Daily Star,* 20 April 1999.

[12] Rene Romo, 'U.S. Border Patrol Agent Shot Near Columbus, N.M., Body Armor Likely Saved Life', *Albuquerque Journal,* 20 April 1999.

[13] Justice Brewer in *Church of the Holy Trinity v. United States,* 143 U.S. 226 (1892).

[14] Andrew M. Yuengert, 'Catholic Social Teaching on the Economics of Immigration', *The Journal of Markets and Morality* (Spring 2000), quoting George J. Borjas and Lynnette Hinton, 'Immigration and the Welfare State: Immigrant Participation in Means-Tested Entitlement Programs', *National Bureau of Economic Research Working Paper*, no. 5372 (December 1995).

[15] Summary of Gary North's analysis of illegal immigration's impact on religious pluralism, *Inheritance and Dominion: an Economic Commentary on Deuteronomy* (Tyler, TX: Institute for Christian Economics, 1999), Chapter 16.

[16] For fuller description, see Joseph Farah, 'Voter Fraud, Again!' *WorldNetDaily,* 6 November 2000.

[17] Edward Nelson, PRNewswire, 9 November 2000.

[18] Samuel P. Huntington 'Reconsidering Immigration: Is Mexico a Special Case?'

[19] National and International Religion Report, Vol. 7, No. 1

Chapter 13

[1] David J. Castello, 'The Barefoot Mailman', *The Boynton Beach Times,* 10 October 1997.

[2] Susan D. Jewell 'Restoring South Florida's Future', U.S. Geological Survey. (http://sofia.usgs.gov/sfrsf/plw/sffuture.html; Internet).

[3] Ibid.

[4] Ibid.

[5] Ibid.

[6] David S. Wilcove, *The Condor's Shadow: The Loss and Recovery of Wildlife in America* (New York: W.H. Freeman and Company, 1999), 178.

[7] Philip Shabecoff, *A Fierce Green Fire* (New York: Hill and Wang, 1993), 123.

[8] E. Calvin Beisner, 'A Christian Agenda for Environmental Protection.' (http://forerunner.com/forerunner/X0142_Environmental_Protec.html; Internet).

[9] Herb Schlossberg, *Idols for Destruction* (Nashville: Thomas Nelson, 1983), 171.

[10] Angela Antonelli, 'The Environment, Promoting Community-Based Stewardship', *Issues 2000: The Candidate's Briefing Book,* The Heritage Foundation.

[11] Acton Institute, 'Biblical Perspective on Environmental Stewardship.' (http://www.acton.org/ppolicy/environment/theology/m_protest.html; Internet).

[12] Ibid.

[13] Ibid.

[14] Ibid.

[15] Ibid.

[16] Although he has given permission to use his article without reference, I wish to acknowledge Rabbi Daniel Swartz 'Jews, Jewish Texts, and Nature: a Brief History' in this section on Jewish attitudes toward nature. (http://www.coejl.org/learn/je_swartz.shtml; Internet).

[17] R. Laird Harris, 'The Incompatibility of Biblical Incentives with the Driving

Forces of World Economic Systems', an address at Baylor University, 1988, 3.

[18] Eugene H. Buck and M. Lynne Corn, 'Endangered Species: Continuing Controversy' *CRS Issue Brief for Congress,* The National Counsel for Science and the Environment, 5 April 2001. (http://www.cnie.org/nle/biodv-1.html; Internet).

[19] 'The Extinction of Species' (http://www.geocities.com/RainForest/Canopy/5486/species.html; Internet).

[20] Acton Institute, 'Biblical Perspective on Environmental Stewardship.'

[21] Ibid.

[22] Vancouver Aquarium Marine Science Center (http://www.vanaqua.org/visitors/faq/AQUAFACT/seaotter.htm#anchor221318; Internet).

[23] Ibid.

[24] A 'keystone' species is one that plays such a pivotal role within an ecosystem that many other species become dependent upon its presence.

[25] Jocelyn Kaiser, 'Sea Otter Declines Blamed on Hungry Killers', *Science,* 16 October 1998, 90.

[26] Wilcove, *The Condor's Shadow: The Loss and Recovery of Wildlife in America,* 151.

[27] E. Calvin Beisner, 'Shining a Light in a Dark Place' (http://www.acton.org/publicat/randl/97mar_apr/beisner.html; Internet).

[28] Michael S. Coffman, 'Globalizing Mining in America: Is It Environmental Concern That's Driving Mining Out Of The United States Or Rather Politics On The Grandest Scale?' *Mining Voice,* March/April 2000.

[29] Ibid.

[30] Ibid.

[31] Ibid.

[32] Ibid.

[33] Ibid.

[34] Ibid.

[35] Ibid.

[36] Michael S. Coffman, *The Decline of Property Rights and Freedom in America: The Destruction of Our Founder's Intent for the U.S. Constitution* (Bangor, ME: Environmental Perspectives, Inc., 1996), 38.

[37] Ibid, 17.

Chapter 14

[1] Ed Dobson, *Blinded by Might* (Grand Rapids: Zondervan Publishing House, 1999), 70.

[2] Ibid., 70.

[3] Ibid., 102.

[4] Ibid., 104.

[5] Ibid., 103.

[6] Ibid., 103.

[7] Louis Berkof, *Systematic Theology,* 4th ed. (Grand Rapids: Wm. B. Eerdman's Publishing Co., 1979), 410-411.

[8] Ibid., 410.

[9] Dobson, *Blinded by Might,* 103.

[10] Ibid., 107.

[11] Ibid., 109.

[12] Ibid., 108.

[13] Ibid., 111.

[14] Ibid., 113.

[15] Gary DeMar, *God and Government,* vol. I (Atlanta: American Vision, 1989), 73.

[16] Greg Herrick, 'Paul and Civil Obedience in Romans 13:1-7.' (http://www.bible.org/docs/nt/books/rom/rom13.htm; Internet).

[17] Greg Herrick, 'Romans 13:1-7 and I Peter 2:13-17: A Brief Comparison.' (http://www.bible.org/docs/nt/books/rom/rom13.htm#P345_126695; Internet).

[18] Dobson, *Blinded by Might,* 168.

[19] Chief Justice John Marshall in *McCulloch v. Maryland* 17 U.S. 316 (1819).

[20] *Hannity and Colmes* (Fox Television) 10 February 2000.

Chapter 15

[1] Billy Graham, *Just As I Am : The Autobiography of Billy Graham* (San Francisco: Harper Collins, 1997), 395, 399.

[2] *Preaching* Vol. 9, Number 6.

Christian Focus Publications publishes biblically-accurate books for adults and children. The books in the adult range are published in three imprints.

Christian Heritage contains classic writings from the past.

Christian Focus contains popular works including biographies, commentaries, doctrine, and Christian living.

Mentor focuses on books written at a level suitable for Bible College and seminary students, pastors, and others; the imprint includes commentaries, doctrinal studies, examination of current issues, and church history.

For a free catalogue of all our titles, please write to

Christian Focus Publications, Ltd.
Geanies House, Fearn, Tain,
Ross-shire, IV20 1TW, Great Britain

For details of our titles visit us on our web site

http://www.christianfocus.com